The Complete Book of Grant Writing

Learn to write grants like a professional

NANCY BURKE SMITH & E. GABRIEL WORKS

SOURCEBOOKS, INC.®
NAPERVILLE, ILLINOIS

This publication is designed to provide accurate and authoritative information in regard to the subject matter covered. It is sold with the understanding that the publisher is not engaged in rendering legal, accounting, or other professional service. If legal advice or other expert assistance is required, the services of a competent professional person should be sought.—From a Declaration of Principles Jointly Adopted by a Committee of the American Bar Association and a Committee of Publishers and Associations

Published by Sourcebooks, Inc.
P.O. Box 4410, Naperville, Illinois 60567–4410
(630) 961–3900
Fax: (630) 961–2168
www.sourcebooks.com

Library of Congress Cataloging-in-Publication Data

Smith, Nancy Burke.
   The complete book of grant writing: learn to write grants like a professional / Nancy Burke Smith,
E. Gabriel Works.
       p. cm.
   ISBN-13: 978-1-4022-0667-2
   ISBN-10: 1-4022-0667-4
   1. Proposal writing for grants. I. BurkeSmith, Nancy and Works, E. Gabriel. II. Title.

HG177.S63 2006
658.15'224—dc22

                                    2006012969

Printed and bound in the United States of America
SB 10 9 8 7 6 5 4 3 2

DEDICATION

This book is dedicated to:
Isabelle Merz, for her years of love and support. You are my best friend.
Dirk Koning, a giant of a friend.

CONTENTS

INTRODUCTION

This book may be the first of its kind—a collaborative effort between an experienced grantwriter and an experienced grantmaker developed to provide views, tips, and information from both sides of the grantseeking experience.

From it, you will learn the difference between what we call reactive and proactive grantseeking; in the former case, responding to requests for proposals; in the latter, actively searching for matches between potential funders and nonprofit applicants. You'll learn who makes grants and how, where to find funding opportunities, and how to design and complete the grantwriting process through both of these approaches.

We show you the five core components of grant proposals: an abstract, statement of problem, project description, evaluation plan, and budget narrative, and you'll learn the intricacies of developing each one. In addition, we point out a dozen or more other sections you may encounter in your grantseeking and provide samples and tips for developing your response.

Because we believe that all good writing is grounded in a deep understanding of one's audience, we share with you the funder's view throughout the book: what makes grants compelling to funders? What are their red flags and non-negotiable issues? How do they make decisions, and how do you develop professional relationships with funders?

We have included more than twenty samples demonstrating every form of writing a grantwriter may be asked to compose: grant proposals, preproposals, concept papers, letters of inquiry, interagency agreements, support letters, media releases, and progress reports. We have two entire chapters dedicated to annotated sample proposals, one illustrating different types of grant requests and a second showcasing writing for different types of nonprofit organizations.

Finally, we share important lessons on what to do when you are funded and what you can do when you are not.

We have closed with a chapter on grantwriting as a career. We leave it to you to choose your path: write grants as a concerned volunteer, as a consultant, as an executive director, as a fundraiser, or as a project manager. However you use what you've learned, you will be writing grants like a professional.

CHAPTER 1
Grantmakers and Grantseekers

What is a Grant?

In general, a grant is funding provided by a charitable-giving foundation, public charity, or a government agency to a nonprofit organization that enables the nonprofit organization to perform specified activities for the common good. Grants may also be made by corporate giving programs or nonprofit intermediaries, which pass through funding from another source.

What is a Grant Proposal?

A grant proposal is a narrative description of the work that a nonprofit organization plans to undertake to fulfill both its own and the grantmaker's goals. The proposal includes, at minimum, a description of the problem to be addressed, a detailed plan for addressing the problem, what it will cost, and what results the grantmaker can expect from the proposed project or initiative.

After the proposal is accepted by the grantmaker and a grant award is made, the grant proposal forms the basis for a legally binding contract between grantmaker and grant recipient. By signing the contract, the recipient (grantee) agrees to perform mutually agreed-on plans of work and to report its progress toward fulfilling the terms of the grant and achieving the goals set forth in its grant proposal.

Who Qualifies for Grants?

Most grants are made to nonprofit 501(c)(3) organizations: designated public charities made exempt from federal income tax under IRS code 501(c)(3). Nonprofit 501(c)(3) organizations include such institutions as schools, hospitals/clinics, religious organizations, homeless shelters and services, social service agencies, arts/cultural organizations, universities, and many others. To maintain its 501(c)(3) status, a public charity must pass a public support test showing that it receives its financial support from a broad segment of the general public. Therefore, a nonprofit organization should not seek most of its funding from one source. If it does so successfully it could forfeit, or "tip," from its nonprofit status, making it ineligible for any other charitable gifts.

Private foundations are restricted by law to fund *only* public charities and some government agencies, such as police and fire departments, unless they follow a lengthy and complicated process called "expenditure responsibility." Community foundations and government agencies may fund a non-501(c)(3) if the grant is for a charitable purpose such as relief of poverty, advancement of education or religion, promotion of health, government or municipal use, or another purpose that would be beneficial to the community.

Grants to individuals are rare except in the case of scholarships and instances such as commissions for artworks, translations, or scientific research. (There are many resources on the specialized topic of grants to individuals; they are not covered in this book.)

Who Writes Grants?

Most often, grant proposals are written by the director or other staff member of the applying nonprofit organization. Individuals who work in development or fund-raising often are called on to have grantwriting skills. There are also professional grantwriters who write grants for a fee, which is paid by the nonprofit organization.

The job of a grantwriter may or may not be limited to the actual writing of a grant proposal. The level of involvement varies based on the individual grantwriter's level of skill and knowledge, the position the grantwriter has within the applicant organization, and the type of approach used in grantseeking.

What Do Grants Fund?

Grantseeking is a form of fund-raising in which money is requested for a defined purpose and a specified time period. Most grants fund programs or projects developed by the nonprofit organization to respond to a specific problem or need. Other relatively common types of grants include:

- Capital: A grant for a building, equipment, renovation, or construction
- General Operating: An unrestricted grant for the everyday operations of the applicant organization

---

A Decade of Change

In the last ten years, grantwriting has grown both easier and more difficult. Several innovations have streamlined the grant search and application process.

· The federal government has launched a notification service that makes requests for proposals from all federal departments available to any person who signs up for the service.

· The federal government and many foundations have established electronic submission forms and processes. You can submit a proposal (and often a report of progress) without shipping or hand delivering.

· Search engines help grantseekers find funding sources with the use of just a few key words.

· Grantwriters once had to send letters or call to learn more about funders or to request guidelines and annual reports; today, most grantmakers post this information on their websites where it is easily accessible.

What's more difficult? Philanthropy in general has become far more sophisticated than it once was. Today, grant proposals must focus strongly on outcomes and evaluation. Progress reports require data to support detailed explanations about what the grantee has accomplished with grant funds. At one time, any decent writer could write a grant proposal; today, successful grantseeking requires more than writing skills alone. Now, a good grantwriter must also be a good strategic planner, an analytical reader, a master of basic accounting principles, and a perpetual student of the field.

The federal budget for the next five years decreases grant money available to fund programs of interest to nonprofit organizations. To make up for these reductions, private giving from all sources, including foundations and public charities, will have to grow at a rate two or three times that of recent years. Whether that compensatory growth is likely or not, the facts point to increasing competition among grantseekers—and an increasing need for highly skilled grantwriters.

- Technical Assistance: A grant made to strengthen the nonprofit organization's staff development, infrastructure, or other function that needs improvement
- Endowment: A grant that is to be invested in perpetuity so that the nonprofit can draw earnings from the fund to support its defined purpose
- Challenge: A grant made to stimulate giving from other sources; the donor releases funds only after the grantee has met the challenge (usually a specific amount of money to be raised) outlined in the grant agreement
- Matching: Funds that correspond to those of other donors; e.g., funds will match two to one those of other donors within a specified time frame
- Demonstration: A grant made to develop an innovative project or program that, if successful, will serve as a model for others' replication
- Start Up: A grant to cover the costs of starting a new project or organization; start up grants are also called "seed grants"
- Exploratory/Planning: A grant that enables an organization to flesh out a good idea, develop a stronger project and project implementation plan, or test a theory or plan of action

Two Approaches to Grantseeking

There are two primary approaches to grantseeking: reactive and proactive. Reactive grants are those developed in response to a request for proposals (RFP). Reactive grant proposals are much like bids for a job and require grantwriters with strong analytical reading and good writing skills. Proactive grants are those that involve identifying appropriate funding sources to support a specific nonprofit organization, program, or problem-solving initiative. Approaching grantseeking proactively requires a well-planned strategy and an overall knowledge of potential donor sources and their interests and motivations for funding.

CHAPTER 2
Reactive Grantseeking

What Is Reactive Grantseeking?

Reactive grant proposals reflect the common bidding practice used throughout the business and government sectors. When a large manufacturing company, for example, looks for a parts supplier, it often develops a request for bids (RFP) outlining what it is looking for in terms of product, delivery, quality, and reliability. Supply companies then bid on the project by responding in writing with a proposal for how they will manufacture and deliver the part, what it will cost to do so, and what their qualifications are for both providing the part and doing it better than anyone else. Similarly, when a city government decides to construct a public project, it too seeks bids or proposals, first from engineers and later from construction companies.

In the case of what we call reactive grants, a grantmaker chooses an issue or problem, determines the way in which it wishes to address the issue, then releases an RFP to solicit proposals for carrying out the work. Reactive grantseeking, then, centers on identifying RFP opportunities and writing a proposal in response to the invitation from the funder—"reacting to the RFP."

Who Makes Grants via RFP?

Government RFPs
Within its departments, the federal government determines priorities for domestic programs it wants to launch. The departments publish these programs in the Federal Register or Catalog of Federal Domestic Assistance (CFDA) in anticipation of allocated funding in the annual budget. Barring unforeseen budget constraints, the projects are allocated funding and a formal RFP is released by the federal department.

State governments also have priority projects that are funded through a competitive RFP process. The funding level and the number of programs funded varies with the budget allocation for the program and the availability of funds over and above those needed to operate the state budget. State RFPs may or may not be published, but are often available on websites of the state departments or are mailed to potential applicants identified by the department.

Foundation RFPs

On occasion, some foundations, most often those with a national or international focus, may release an RFP when they launch a special program to notify eligible organizations of the opportunity. Few foundations use the RFP process exclusively; many do not use it at all. When they do, they often implement a two-step process. Interested applicants first write a preproposal, which the foundation uses to narrow the field of funding candidates. Based on the preproposal, the foundation then invites selected organizations to submit a final proposal on which the grant determinations are made.

Regranting RFPs

RFPs are also often issued for a process called regranting. Regranting results when a foundation, public charity, or smaller unit of government receives a larger grant on the condition that a portion of the grant be offered through an RFP process to other (usually locally based) nonprofit organizations.

For instance, a community foundation might receive special funds earmarked for a specific effort and issue an RFP to local organizations that they believe might be interested in developing and proposing a relevant project. This occurred when, in some states, the funds from the tobacco settlement judgment were distributed to community foundations to regrant to local organizations that offered educational or smoking cessation programs.

Nonprofit organizations are sometimes called on to regrant funds and to serve as intermediaries between the grantor and the organizations that receive portions of the larger grant. Recently, for instance, the federal government has emphasized creating more opportunities for faith-based and community organizations (FBCOs) to receive grants. The problem, however, is that most small FBCOs do not have the capacity to administer federal grants and report on their outcomes. The structure for solving this problem calls for larger nonprofit organizations to apply for a federal grant as a fiscal agent. If they receive the federal grant, a designated percentage is set aside for regranting, and the intermediary nonprofit issues RFPs to local FBCOs. It then administers grant funds and coordinates all reporting regarding outcomes and grant fund spending to the federal government.

Block grants, such as the Community Development Block Grant (CDBG) or the Local Law Enforcement Block Grant (LLEBG) are other examples of regranting programs. These grants are made by the federal government to states or cities to enable local improvement initiatives. Although the future of block grants is in question on the federal level, to date they have served as a means for local governments to be intermediaries between federal grant programs and local organizations that meet priorities for community development. Smaller communities applied directly to the federal or state government for CDBG or LLEBG funding each year, while larger cities received an annual allocation to regrant to local nonprofit organizations.

Winning Reactive Grant Proposals

The first rule of writing—whether you are writing a report, a grant proposal, or even a letter—is know your audience. The second rule of writing builds on the first: concentrate not on what you need or want to say, but on what the audience needs to know. In this last case, grantwriters are pretty lucky. The RFP will state clearly what the audience wants to know and in what order they want to learn about it.

As a grantwriter, then, it is your primary responsibility to learn all you can about who will be reading and judging your proposals.

When RFPs are released by the federal or state government, proposals are read by peers of those who submit. For instance, department of education proposals are read by educators; department of justice proposals by law enforcement personnel. Individuals from around the U.S.—often former grantees from the same program—are recruited to read and score proposals.

Proposals submitted to foundations are generally read by staff and/or trustees, and, in the case of community foundations, some selected community members who are part of a prescreening committee. Intermediary nonprofits often convene a group of interested and objective community members to review proposals for regrant funds.

As a writer, you need to put yourself in the place of the reader and analyze your proposal from his or her perspective. If you are writing to an educator, you must use vocabulary and concepts familiar to that reader—and use them knowledgeably. If you are writing to a group of local trustees, foundation staff, or community people, they often know as well as you do (and sometimes better) the depth of community problems, the capacity of local organizations to address the problem, and what's been tried before. The grantwriter must never talk down to this audience. You must know the history of similar efforts in the community, be familiar with the various appropriate collaborative organizations, and, if possible, be aware of the different biases among the readers.

Requests for Proposals (RFPs)

Where can I find Them?

Government RFPs

Federal and state governments publish grant programs and RFPs on their websites. Departments within the state government may notify their constituents about funding opportunities and direct them to the department's web page to learn more.

Every year the federal government publishes the Federal Register, (also called the Catalog of Federal Domestic Assistance or CFDA), which contains all potential grant offers for that year. Today, RFPs are also released on the federal government's website: www.grants.gov. Anyone can sign up to receive notifications from any or all of the federal departments or can visit the website at any time to do a search for a specific type of grant.

If you sign up for automatic notification, an announcement from grants.gov is sent directly to your email box and may look like this (the number of RFPs listed varies):

Sample: Grants.gov Email Notice

The following grant opportunity postings were made on the Grants.gov Find Opportunities ("FedGrants") service:

DOJ Headquarters
Office of Justice Programs
NIJ FY06 Communications Technology Grant
http://www.fedgrants.gov/Applicants/DOJ/HQ/OJP/2006-NIJ-1132/listing.html

DOJ Headquarters
Office of Justice Programs
NIJ FY06 Information-led Policing Research, Technology Development and Testing and Evaluation Grant
http://www.fedgrants.gov/Applicants/DOJ/HQ/OJP/2006-NIJ-1142/listing.html

HHS National Institutes of Health
Diet-Induced Changes in Inflammation as Determinants of Colon Cancer Grant
http://www.fedgrants.gov/Applicants/HHS/NIH/NIH/PA-05-125/listing.html

CNCS Office of Grants Management
Washington, DC
2006 Learn and Serve America Community-Based Grant Program
Modification1
http://www.fedgrants.gov/Applicants/CNCS/OGM/OGM/CNCS-GRANTS-102405-002/listing.html

Please do not respond to this message. This is a post-only mailing. To unsubscribe from this notification service, go to the following URL and then follow the instructions for unsubscribing:
http://www.fedgrants.gov/unsubscribe.html

When you want to learn more about the RFP, you simply click on the URL link for that grant to take you to the full announcement and the application package. Though there are other details such as due dates and CFDA numbers, here are some highlights of what you would find if you selected the last entry, the Learn and Serve America Community-Based Grant Program. The subsequent web page information shown on page 9 provides a summary of information about the grant opportunity. If you find your organization is eligible and that you have a program that fits the purpose of the RFP, you would use the link at the bottom of the information page to take you to the full grant announcement.

Sample: Grants.gov Summary

Expected Number of Awards: 16

Estimated Total Program Funding: $4,500,000.00

Award Ceiling: $500,000.00

Award Floor: $350,000.00

Cost Sharing or Matching Requirement: Yes

Eligible Applicants
- Private institutions of higher education
- State governments
- Public and State controlled institutions of higher education
- Native American tribal governments (Federally recognized)
- Native American tribal organizations (other than Federally recognized tribal governments)
- Nonprofits having a 501(c)(3) status with the IRS, other than institutions of higher education
- Nonprofits that do not have a 501(c)(3) status with the IRS, other than institutions of higher education
Additional Information on Eligibility:
- State Government--must be State Commissions for Community Service
- All other entities--must act as Grant Making Entities (GMEs): GMEs are defined as public or private non-profit organizations in existence at least one year at the time of application, experienced with service-learning, and proposing to make subgrants in two or more states.

Description
The purpose of this grant competition is to promote the development and sustainability of high-quality community-based service-learning programs in youth-serving community organizations across the nation. Funds will be used by intermediary organizations to create curriculum materials; support training and technical assistance activities; make subgrants to local organizations that will implement service-learning programs for youth ages five to seventeen; and strengthen, expand, and anchor a network of youth-serving community-based organizations that implement service-learning programs.

> In this case, the federal government does not wish to entertain proposals for small grants and has determined that it would take $350,000, minimum, to operate a successful program at the scope they envision.

> You will need to link to the full announcement to learn more about the cost sharing or match requirements. Some nonprofit organizations do not have access to cash-match funding but can provide in-kind contributions. Some may have to forego the grant opportunity based on the level and type of cost sharing or match requirements.

> If the organization planning a response is not listed here, it is not eligible. For instance, a local K-12 school district would not be eligible for this competition.

> An award to a GME would have a portion available for regranting.

> The federal government is looking for one larger organization in the community to be the umbrella for a network of service-learning programs and to be the intermediary grantmaker (regrantor).

Foundation and Intermediary RFPs

When foundations and intermediary grantors issue an RFP, they generally send the announcement to organizations they have identified as being eligible. For instance, an intermediary to FBCOs might send the RFP to several churches in an area, a large foundation might send an RFP to mayors of specific cities, and a community foundation might send one to all organizations that have done similar work in the past. They will also frequently post the notice on their website to make it available to those who were not notified directly and to provide additional information for those who were. If you do not directly receive an RFP, but you hear of it in another way, go ahead and explore the grantmaker's website to determine your organization's eligibility.

Another source of information on foundation RFPs is the Foundation Center (www.fdncenter.org), which provides regular notifications of foundation RFPs through a Listserv. If you sign up, every few weeks you will receive an email bulletin of new grant initiatives, foundation RFPs, or notifications of open calls for programs.

Sample: Foundation Center Email Notice

The headline briefly states the foundation name and program purpose.

The deadline for submissions is provided.

A link for additional information is provided.

This grant opportunity is geographically focused in the city where the corporation is headquartered. Geographic limitations apply in the case of many corporate and family foundations and of all community foundations. See proactive grantseeking for more information about foundations.

The grant award maximum or range of funds is provided.

The purpose of grants funds is explained in the body of the message.

"Corporate" Foundation Offers School Fitness and Nutrition Program in Minneapolis-St. Paul

Deadline: December 15, 2006

A philanthropic program of Minneapolis-headquartered Corporation, Inc. (http://www.corporation.com/), the Corporate Foundation's Fitness and Nutrition program supports exemplary school fitness and nutrition programs and encourages new and innovative ways to promote physical activity and good nutrition before, during, and after school. FAN grants are only available in Minnesota's seven-county metro area.

Funds are intended to add to, not replace, school funds already set aside for fitness and nutrition initiatives. Maximum grant awards are $5,000, and priority will be given to schools that serve socio-economically disadvantaged students. Schools and parent organizations affiliated with schools are encouraged to apply.

Grants supporting existing fitness or nutrition programs in school are intended to help public and private K-12 schools reach the "next level" as they prepare or implement an existing plan to serve their students better. For example, a middle school that has removed sugared sodas from its beverage machines may want to hire a nutritionist to recommend improvements to the school's lunch and snack program.

Grants for new and innovative ways to promote physical fitness and nutrition programs will also be made to schools demonstrating measurable efforts to improve the health of their students. Examples include activity fee scholarships for disadvantaged youth and nutritional assessments of school cafeterias.

Visit the Corporate Foundation Web site for specific program information, an application form, and/or to review general guidelines that apply to all foundation programs.

The email first presents a table of contents of the grants announced in that issue, then provides details and a web page link to the programs. A sample entry is shown above.

Reading and Analyzing RFPs

There are several key items to look for in an RFP before your organization develops a proposal. These things include:

- Eligibility Criteria: Your organization must be eligible to apply. Eligibility criteria can include a number of factors about the organization and/or its target population including geographic area, number of people in the community living below poverty level, the annual budget of the applicant, and many more. If you are unsure what constitutes an eligible applicant, call and check. For instance, an announcement might say that local education associations (LEAs), meaning school districts and intermediate school districts (ISDs), and public and private entities are eligible. Be sure that the applicant or

The Foundation Center

The Foundation Center's mission is to strengthen the nonprofit sector by advancing knowledge about U.S. philanthropy. As such, it is an important reference source for grantwriters. The organization collects and provides access to information on U.S. foundations and the grantseeking process through its website, print and electronic publications, library/learning centers, and a national network of Cooperating Collections. It also provides a message board where grantwriters and fund-raisers can ask and answer specific questions about their work (www.fdncenter.org).

target population meets the absolute priority for funding; for example, how does the grantmaker define public and private entities? Those that do not fit the eligibility requirements will be disqualified.

- Project Purpose: Make sure that the purpose outlined in the RFP is something that the nonprofit organization has already planned to work on. In other words, don't just go after a grant opportunity because it's there and your organization qualifies. It may seem counterintuitive, but if it's not something that matches the mission or objectives of the organization, the eventual costs (both monetary and human), will outweigh any initial benefits to the organization's cash flow.

- Deadline: Be sure that there is enough time to design or tweak an existing program model and describe it in detail. You will need at least two weeks to put together a strong application and gather all the necessary supporting materials. This is another strong reason for being sure that the RFP describes something you already have planned—there is never enough time between the release of an RFP and its application due date to design something entirely from scratch.

- Number of Grants: If there are going to be only three or four grant awards made nationally, you'll be facing stiff competition. Be sure that your program is both responsive to local needs and well planned before you submit.

- Funding Limits: Do a draft budget of the costs of implementing your project plan to be sure that you can deliver the project for less than the amount of the grant or that you know where other funds will be found. Be sure to review spending requirements; for instance, some grants mandate that 5 or 10 percent be allocated to an evaluation, or they may make travel to a national conference a mandatory line item. Also, if there is a percentage of the grant award that will be regranted, be sure that the applicant organization can administer the fund with the remainder of the award.

> One of the primary skills a good grantwriter brings to the proposal writing process is the ability to read the RFP clearly and analytically. This skill is closely tied to the grantwriter's knowledge and understanding of audience. Inexperienced writers want to tell everything they know rather than responding to questions, in order, and in detail. The grantwriter analyzes the RFP and identifies what the audience wants to know, then writes relevant responses.

- Match Requirements: Often RFPs will contain a match requirement, stating something like, "grantees must provide a 10 percent match in year one, a 25 percent match in year two, and a 50 percent match in year three." Your organization must, then, have a realistic plan for raising the funds needed to leverage a federal grant. You jeopardize more than the current grant and may even incur rare but possible legal action if you fail to meet match requirements in a grant.

To recap, use the RFP announcement as a first step to analyze whether your nonprofit qualifies to apply and whether directors and staff of the organization understand what the grant program is about and if they (a) believe that it is something they have been wanting to do anyway, and (b) can agree to the terms as outlined in the RFP (e.g., that it is their mission and within their capacity to serve as an intermediary grantmaker, network coordinator, and curriculum and technical assistance provider). You must also draft a budget with the organization to ensure that all the expenses they need to implement the project (a) are allowable, and (b) can be accomplished within the grant funding limits.

If the program announcement fits your organization's priorities, download the application package for the grant announcement. You will receive forms and additional instructions including page limits and more detail about what to include in the narrative, as described in the sample.

Sample: Grant Proposal Narrative Instructions

The grantor has provided instructions for submitting your proposal electronically through the government "eGrants" system. In this case, you may submit a paper application instead as long as you meet the deadline for the eGrants submission and your narrative conforms to the stated length limits.

This is an excellent example of why grantseekers need to read between the lines. Though it is not stated in the eligibility requirements, the fact that this report of past organizational accomplishments is required means that the government is looking for experienced high-capacity organizations, possibly those that have served as intermediaries for other grant funds.

These page or character limits are absolute. EGrants will cut off narrative that exceeds the limits. Their staff will discard paper applications that exceed the page limits.

A *consortia* is two or more organizations that have formed a collaborative to apply for the grant with each having specific responsibilities to perform functions of the project.

Specific points of the three-year plan are listed in 1-9 below.

Again, reading between the lines, you understand that the grantor is looking for organizations that are experienced intermediaries.

If the grantee intends to solicit proposals from subgrantees, the applicant would describe that process here.

If institutions change, the initiative may sustain itself.

Regrantors should also coach subgrantees on programs and reporting if needed.

PART 2. Application Narrative Sections

Sections 1-8 are text boxes in eGrants. Click on the heading of each one to enter text, or cut and paste your text into the box.

1. Executive Summary—One double-spaced page, 12 point font, or 2,000 characters.
    Briefly summarize your proposed program. Include the projected number of participants, subgrantees (if applicable), service goals, and main activities.

2. Summary of Accomplishments—One double-spaced page, 12 point font, or 2,000 characters.
    Briefly summarize the accomplishments from prior Learn and Serve and/or other Corporation program funds you have received.

3-8. Proposal Narrative—The maximum combined length of sections 3-8 is 41,000 characters (including spaces) in eGrants, or approximately 20 double-spaced pages with 12 point font.
IMPORTANT: When responding to the below questions, be sure to refer to the guidance provided in the Notice of Funds Availability (NOFA) related to the program for which you are applying. The length of responses to each of the narrative sections is up to the individual applicant.

3. Three-Year Plan—All applicants must submit a three-year plan that outlines major milestones, key tasks, and corresponding dates for the development and management of your proposed program.
    Note: Consortia applicants must demonstrate that they have the experience and capacity to publicize a grant competition and identify, award, monitor and support high-quality subgrantees engaged in meaningful service-learning activities. Consortia applicants should explicitly address the following points in their three year plan and/or in the additional narrative responses below.

    1. Overall subgranting and portfolio management strategy and how it will support the goals of this grant competition and the priorities of your organization;

    2. Subgranting selection and awards process, including the purpose(s) for each of your subgrant types (planning, sustaining, leadership, etc.) and rationale for the level of funding for each type;

    3. Fiscal/programmatic monitoring and oversight of subgrantees;

    4. Strategies for supporting policy development and institutionalization of service-learning at state and local levels;

    5. Training and technical assistance (TA) to support subgrantees and others within your network. Include how TA will be provided, by whom and when;

    6. Data collection and evaluation strategies, including support for subgrantees to use required data collection systems and instruments;

7. Partnership development and maintenance at grantee and subgrantee levels that strengthen your network's ability to use service-learning;

8. Sustainability efforts, including funding diversification and policy development; and,

9. Expansion of service-learning to new institutions/organizations and schools.

4. Needs and Activities

Needs: Describe the specific community needs your program will address and how these needs were identified.

Strategy: Describe your strategy for meeting those needs and your rationale for that strategy.

Description of Activities: Describe your proposed Service-Learning activities and how they support your strategy.

> Use data to describe the need and cite sources for information.

> Your strategy should derive from and respond to the identified need.

5. Strengthening Communities to Support Service Learning (Consortia grantees may reference responses provided in Section 3 above.)

Community Partnerships: Describe the community partnerships you intend to develop, including well-defined roles for private schools, and/or faith- and/or community-based organizations where appropriate.

Sustainability: Describe how your program will work to institutionalize Service-Learning at the grantee and, if appropriate, subgrantee levels.

Adult Volunteers: Describe how you will generate additional adult volunteers to support or help coordinate your efforts. Estimate the number of volunteers you expect to recruit.

> Where will service learning take place and why?

> *Institutionalizing* means to make service learning a part of the organization's mission and means of operating.

6. Developing Participants

School and Community-Based Participants are defined as youth aged 5-17 engaged in service through the program.

Higher Education Participants are defined as students, faculty, administration or staff of the institution, or residents of the community who are engaged in service through the program.

Support: Describe your plans for involving participants in the program planning as well as training, supervising, developing, and recognizing participant efforts.

Citizenship: Describe your plan to ensure participants in your program develop civic responsibility; attaining new levels of citizenship knowledge, skills and attitudes, and developing life-long habits of service.

Disadvantaged Youth: Describe strategies for engaging and/or serving disadvantaged youth in your program model.

Diversity: Describe how your program will provide opportunities for participants and volunteers to serve together with people of different backgrounds (such as ethnicity, race, religion, socioeconomic status, age and physical ability).

Number of Participants: Estimate the number of participants you expect to engage in the first year of your program.

> Also describe the role adults (e.g., mentors) will have in the project plan.

> Emphasize diversity in your need statement and describe how planned diversity can enrich all participants' experiences.

7. Organizational Capacity

a. Ability to provide sound program and fiscal oversight;

b. Experience administering a federal grant;

c. Qualifications and roles of key staff people responsible for the program;

> Applicants should have some experience managing grant funds and implementing large initiatives.

In other words, describe how the organization will work during the grant period to make sure that government, nonprofit organizations, local foundations, businesses, and citizens see the value of the work and become willing to help the applicant sustain the program after the grant period.

d. Programmatic track record of accomplishment as an organization;

8. Budget/Cost Effectiveness
Explain how your program builds community support for your program at the local, state and national levels.
Describe the other sources of support used by your program and your plans and ability to expand this support
Describe plans for supporting Learn and Serve national identity and publicizing your program.

The Grantwriter's Role in Responding to RFPs

Because the grantwriter is the person on the team with the responsibility to thoroughly read and understand the requirements and priorities contained in an RFP and translate the project accordingly, he or she should also participate in the project design, even if the grantwriter is not on the staff of the organization.

The grantwriter is a bridge between the requirements of the grantor and the needs and desires of the potential grantee. In the above example, the grantwriter and organization leaders need to discuss the match requirements, the need for the applicant organization to have a strong and positive background as an intermediary, and much more. Together, they may have to identify potential subgrantees so that the writer can describe them accurately and vividly.

It is also the grantwriter's job to gather data that indicate a need for the project or that can help describe a problem the organization is attempting to address. If the grantwriter cannot make the case with data, the team should again discuss the merits of proposing the project.

Following Directions

RFPs are really directions for developing a grant proposal. You, as the grantwriter, must follow those directions exactly. It may be as simple as following the outline provided and presenting the information in the order requested in that outline, or the directions may be quite detailed, prescribing the font and size type you must use, page limits, margin sizes, line spacing, type of paper to use, use of bindings or staples, and much more. This is particularly critical when it comes to government grants. There are people sitting in government offices who measure your margins with a micrometer and look through papers to make sure that not even one line is single-spaced when the RFP says to double space. Your grant proposal will go straight to their circular file if you have failed to follow the directions.

Being disqualified for a technical error is heartbreaking, but there is a reason beyond that for following the directions. Government grant reviewers are given score sheets and a stack of proposals to review. If they have to work to find whether you've responded adequately to a section of the proposal, they will reduce your score. If they can't find the section because you've put it in the wrong place, they will assume that you missed it. On the very rare occasion that a section of a proposal is not applicable to your organization, you must still enter the headline and write "not applicable," or risk having the reviewers reduce your score because they assume that you chose not to respond.

Preproposal Requirements

Letters of Intent

Letters of intent are used for reactive grantseeking. They are sent by potential grantseekers to notify the grantmaker that they intend to submit an application. They are different from letters of inquiry (LOIs) described in chapter 3. The government agency or foundation requesting a letter of intent is usually trying to determine how many grant proposals it is likely to receive so it can recruit sufficient numbers of readers or allocate enough staff members to review the proposals. A letter of intent is not used to help determine whether or not you are eligible to apply or to determine the potential success of your proposal.

Sometimes letters of intent are mandatory. In these cases, unless your letter of intent arrives by the required deadline and your agency's name is added to a list of proposers, your later application will not be read. If you haven't decided yet whether you will apply for a grant, send a letter of intent anyway. Sending one does not obligate you to apply.

Letters of intent can and should be very brief. Be sure to include the name of the agency that will be applying, as in the following sample:

> ABC nonprofit, Anytown, USA, intends to apply for the Learn and Serve grant, federal register #4861586, due on November 3, 2008.

Many funders provide a form that you can complete and fax back, such as the sample that follows:

Responsive Programs

A responsive program responds to two things: the mission and strategic objectives of the nonprofit organization applicant and the program defined and funded through the RFP. A good and ethical grantwriter will not get involved in projects that "chase dollars"; that is, those grants that are not clear matches between the needs of the beneficiary population, the mission and objectives of the nonprofit applicant, and the requirements of the grantor.

Sample: Letter of Intent

NOTICE OF INTENT TO APPLY
FOR 2008-2010
EVEN START FAMILY LITERACY
PROGRAM GRANT

Submit this form no later than January 1, 2007 to assist State Department of Education staff in determining the number of reviewers that will be necessary.

Submission of this notice is not a prerequisite for application of grant funds, nor does it obligate the organization to submit an application.

Please mail or fax this form to:
State Department of Education
Office of School Excellence
Early Childhood and Parenting Programs
P.O. Box 123
State Capital, USA
FAX: (123) 555-1234

Organization: _____

Contact Person: _____

Phone: _____

Fax: _____

E-mail: _____

County(ies) to be Served:_____

Preproposals

When a foundation issues an RFP, it often requires a two-step process for application: a preproposal designed to reduce the number of applicants and a final proposal (by invitation to those selected from the preproposals) from which the foundation will select its grantees. In the following example, a large foundation that funds projects throughout the U.S. sent RFPs to the mayors and civic leaders of identified mid-size cities in the U.S. The cities that were interested in applying to participate in a project to identify and train nontraditional leaders completed a narrative preproposal regarding their history, current state of leadership, the reasons they wanted to be a part of the project, and their tentative plans for identifying emerging leaders. The foundation then selected approximately half of the preproposals and invited those applicant cities to submit a final proposal for funding. A sample preproposal is shown on page 17.

Sample: Preproposal

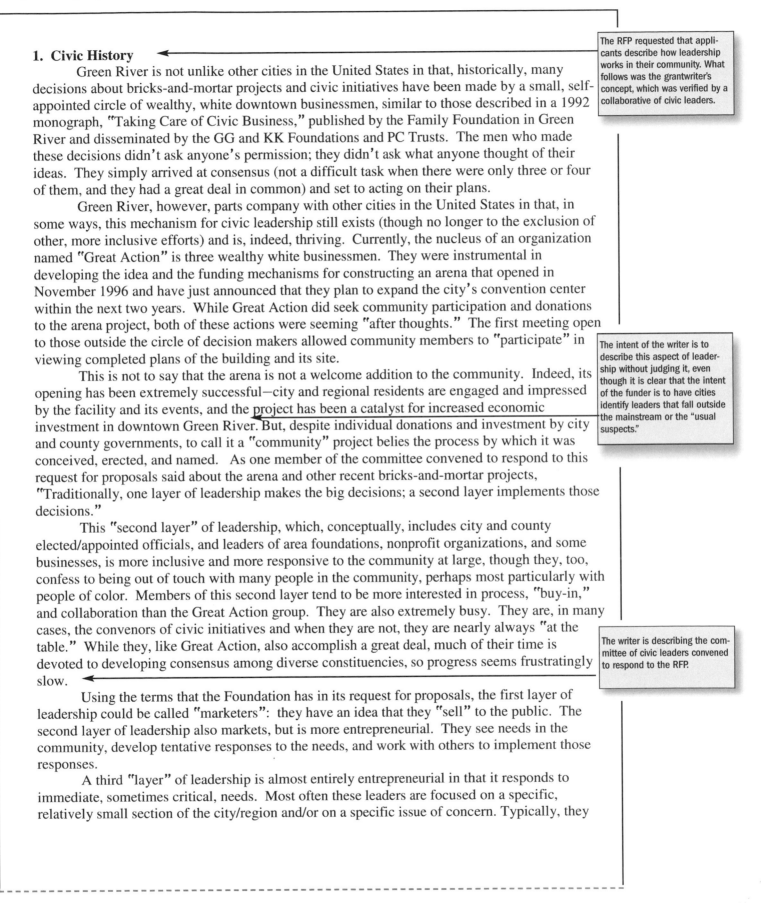

1. Civic History

> The RFP requested that applicants describe how leadership works in their community. What follows was the grantwriter's concept, which was verified by a collaborative of civic leaders.

Green River is not unlike other cities in the United States in that, historically, many decisions about bricks-and-mortar projects and civic initiatives have been made by a small, self-appointed circle of wealthy, white downtown businessmen, similar to those described in a 1992 monograph, "Taking Care of Civic Business," published by the Family Foundation in Green River and disseminated by the GG and KK Foundations and PC Trusts. The men who made these decisions didn't ask anyone's permission; they didn't ask what anyone thought of their ideas. They simply arrived at consensus (not a difficult task when there were only three or four of them, and they had a great deal in common) and set to acting on their plans.

Green River, however, parts company with other cities in the United States in that, in some ways, this mechanism for civic leadership still exists (though no longer to the exclusion of other, more inclusive efforts) and is, indeed, thriving. Currently, the nucleus of an organization named "Great Action" is three wealthy white businessmen. They were instrumental in developing the idea and the funding mechanisms for constructing an arena that opened in November 1996 and have just announced that they plan to expand the city's convention center within the next two years. While Great Action did seek community participation and donations to the arena project, both of these actions were seeming "after thoughts." The first meeting open to those outside the circle of decision makers allowed community members to "participate" in viewing completed plans of the building and its site.

> The intent of the writer is to describe this aspect of leadership without judging it, even though it is clear that the intent of the funder is to have cities identify leaders that fall outside the mainstream or the "usual suspects."

This is not to say that the arena is not a welcome addition to the community. Indeed, its opening has been extremely successful—city and regional residents are engaged and impressed by the facility and its events, and the project has been a catalyst for increased economic investment in downtown Green River. But, despite individual donations and investment by city and county governments, to call it a "community" project belies the process by which it was conceived, erected, and named. As one member of the committee convened to respond to this request for proposals said about the arena and other recent bricks-and-mortar projects, "Traditionally, one layer of leadership makes the big decisions; a second layer implements those decisions."

This "second layer" of leadership, which, conceptually, includes city and county elected/appointed officials, and leaders of area foundations, nonprofit organizations, and some businesses, is more inclusive and more responsive to the community at large, though they, too, confess to being out of touch with many people in the community, perhaps most particularly with people of color. Members of this second layer tend to be more interested in process, "buy-in," and collaboration than the Great Action group. They are also extremely busy. They are, in many cases, the convenors of civic initiatives and when they are not, they are nearly always "at the table." While they, like Great Action, also accomplish a great deal, much of their time is devoted to developing consensus among diverse constituencies, so progress seems frustratingly slow.

> The writer is describing the committee of civic leaders convened to respond to the RFP.

Using the terms that the Foundation has in its request for proposals, the first layer of leadership could be called "marketers": they have an idea that they "sell" to the public. The second layer of leadership also markets, but is more entrepreneurial. They see needs in the community, develop tentative responses to the needs, and work with others to implement those responses.

A third "layer" of leadership is almost entirely entrepreneurial in that it responds to immediate, sometimes critical, needs. Most often these leaders are focused on a specific, relatively small section of the city/region and/or on a specific issue of concern. Typically, they are leaders of churches, board members/executive directors of area nonprofit organizations, advocates, neighborhood organizers, or members of issue-based task forces. In general, they are either directly affected by the decisions made in their groups or are very close to others who will be affected by the decisions and activities the group undertakes.

The importance of inclusive and diverse participation varies across these three levels of leadership and among the various groups that comprise the levels. Great Action, for instance, makes no apologies for being exclusive—as long as they are successful in accomplishing their goals. The second group works extremely hard at composing decision-making bodies that are inclusive and diverse—to the extent that their progress is sometimes stalled or stilled while they build consensus. The third group develops naturally in that membership is most often based on interest rather than invitation. If the subject or area is of interest to people of color, the third-layer leaders will convene a diverse group, though not from an intent to do so. When leadership emerges within these third-layer groups, it appears to be based on the individual's ability and willingness to act, rather than on his or her gender or ethnicity. At the risk of over-generalizing, it can be said that the first layer exercises power, the second shares power, and the third empowers.

There are other, more "hidden" leaders who don't fall into neat categories; for instance, a woman in Crest Neighborhood who is trying to save a neighborhood branch library. For economic reasons, she can't attend meetings of the county or the main library, but she has mobilized others around the issue, and they have designated a spokesperson who ensures that, if those behind the effort cannot be visible, the issue will be.

Demographics for Green River are attached to this proposal. But numbers don't tell the whole story about the city. Economically and socially, this city should not have had race riots in the late 1960s—but we did. During a focus group of "second-" and "third-tier" leaders, convened to respond to the foundation's request for proposals, the writers discovered that we don't communicate across tiers; we don't communicate within the layers; and we don't communicate well with constituencies of any leadership group. In particular, we don't communicate well at all between races/ethnic groups.

The writers also learned that too many in this community are alienated, unheard, and disenfranchised—so many, in fact, that leaders in the minority community are predicting a backlash in the coming decade unless we begin to discuss openly plans for the city and region, and to learn from residents what exactly would improve their lives before leadership attempts another "quality of life" initiative.

2. Past Public-Private Initiatives

Green River has had dozens of laudable public-private initiatives and nearly as many failed efforts. Those discussed in this section and the next were chosen as representative of different types of initiatives.

As already discussed, the recent construction of the Big Arena (named for one of the founders of Big Corporation and a principle donor) is a socially and economically successful public-private initiative, as was another bricks-and-mortar project, the Big Museum.

Although it lacked strong minority involvement and was virtually dismissed by traditional leadership at the time, one initiative, "Voices and Visions," which convened volunteers from every walk of life to discuss their individual and collective visions for downtown Green River, has since been termed a success. People envisioned a cultural center in the core of the region, and various initiatives are putting the pieces of that center in place today.

Side annotations:

In describing "third-layer leaders" and hidden leaders, the grantwriter is describing those who are likely to participate in the leadership development initiative offered by the funder.

The RFP requires a separate page of demographic information including the racial/ethnic, gender, and age composition of the community, its major businesses, and the median income of residents.

The writer's intent is not to criticize the way that leadership works; it is, rather, to show that the leaders have identified a need to do a better job of identifying and bringing in emerging leaders from different constituencies and backgrounds.

This section should give an indication to the funder of how the city applicant has performed in the past—what has been successful and what has failed and, if possible, proposed reasons why things have failed or succeeded.

They dreamed of core city residences for every income and more pedestrian activity, and today several older buildings are being converted to residential lofts and city planners have recently approved a plan to reopen the main downtown street to limited vehicular traffic without sacrificing wide pedestrian ways. In addition, Local State University is expanding its downtown campus in response to a vision for an educational center that draws residents of all ages to the city.

Several urban redevelopment initiatives have been successful, including a contract between the city and the Business Draw Program, which markets Green River to businesses and industries looking for new sites. On a smaller scale, an economically depressed area worked with the city to forgive taxes on dilapidated historic storefronts, which the neighborhood organization has restored, one at a time, and leased to residents to bring back a once-thriving commercial strip on the city's southeast side.

Another successful public-private initiative is Green Valley Metropolitan Council, which promotes regional ownership and voice in infrastructure issues such as safety, transportation, and waste management. Although relatively new, Metro Council holds promise for becoming the organization that will encourage and achieve cooperation among the thirty units of government in Green County.

Failures have included an effort to create a shopping mall in downtown. Though as many as twenty retailers leased space in a 5,000 square-foot building at one time, traffic, especially after traditional business hours downtown, never met that of stores in suburban malls. The downtown anchor store closed after six years; the mall itself closed several months later and remains empty today.

> The instructions asked for a review of civic initiatives including a brief analysis of those that failed.

Another effort that failed was the Citizens League of Green River. This grassroots initiative convened volunteer citizens on task forces to learn about and make recommendations about local social and civic issues. The League was criticized because it did not implement the recommendations made by the task forces, and the organization lasted less than five years before it ran out of funding. In spite of its brevity, it could lay claim to having provided a training ground for emerging leaders in the issue areas it studied.

The South Bank was an attempt by a few African American residents to open a bank run only by African Americans and serving only African Americans. Although none of the principals was an experienced banker, they resisted assistance from established banks, fearing that white people would take over or take away their project. The project failed after only two years.

> The better the applicants can pinpoint reasons for failures, the better able they may be to take a different course next time.

3. Current Leadership Efforts

There is currently only one, well-known formal leadership training initiative in the community: Leadership Green River, which is housed at the Green River Chamber of Commerce. The program admits approximately thirty-five applicants per year based on their personal leadership efforts and promise and their vision for and commitment to Green River and the larger region. The program tuition is $1,900, but some applicants are able to raise the money from their employers or other sponsors. Trainers use an integrated approach to community issues and provide new leaders with a view of systems and their functions. The first layer leaders described above think that Leadership Green River is unnecessary, a mere resume builder.

> Since the grant will be made eventually to train emerging civic leaders, the applicant must explain what leadership training efforts are already in place and why emerging leaders are not a part of those efforts.

There also exist several informal opportunities for leadership, such as the Family Foundation's Civic Leadership Discussion Group, a diverse group of known civic leaders who have met monthly for approximately one year to discuss improving race relations.

Churches too are working in the area of improving race relations. Green River Center for Ecumenicism (GRACE) established the Racial Justice Institute, which assists area congregations in addressing racism, in diversifying their congregations, and in working collaboratively. The Emmanual Empowerment Corporation is the product of several ministers (black and white, all males) who traded pulpits one Sunday, shared stories with their congregations about how others lived, and established a formal means to improve economic equity by connecting those who want to work with those who have jobs.

Perspective 21!, convened by the Green River Community Foundation, offered approximately thirty applicants a chance to discuss child abuse and the local child protection system. The Foundation has since worked internally to implement the task force's recommendations.

Act As One is an outgrowth of discussions held with David Rusk, author of "Cities without Suburbs." The steering committee, composed of approximately ten Green River leaders, plans to have all the community foundations in the region hold a joint conference on social, infrastructural, and economic issues, in the hope that a regional approach to some of these issues may prove successful.

The Police Review Board was first suggested and rejected by city commissioners. It later arose as a demand, primarily from the minority community and has just been put in place. The ten members of the Board are charged with hearing both sides of disputes between citizens and police officers when officers are accused of inappropriate behavior.

The National Issues Forum convenes dozens of ongoing discussion groups for people interested in in-depth discourse on issues that affect the nation and the region. Each Green River neighborhood organization appears to have its own project, including but not limited to the commercial district restoration and the library projects described above; a successful neighborhood revitalization project, Cheery Hills, which pressures absentee landlords to sell their properties to people willing to live in the neighborhood and participate in clean-up efforts; and an effort by Bell Park to bring a healthcare clinic to within walking distance of elderly neighbors.

> Though the grantwriter appears critical of those on the applicant team—who are all established civic leaders—it is absolutely necessary to show the funder that there is room for improvement and that the training for emerging leaders is necessary in this community.

The initiatives listed above are ostensibly open to all. But that's not the reality. In truth, established leaders nurture involvement among selected friends, convene other known leaders on new initiatives, and keep decision making pretty much within their own circles (or "layers"). Currently, there is no mechanism or process in the city, the county, or the region to facilitate or host open discourse among the layers of leadership or between leadership and residents. There is no door into leadership circles for people who are not already inside.

4. Leadership for the Next Century

"Think regionally, act locally" might be a good slogan for leadership in the coming decades. While Metro Council can assist governmental units that wish to save their taxpayers money by collaborating on infrastructure improvements, many of the units of government in Green County and in the west-state region seem to pretend that they are islands unto themselves. Leadership must make clear that what happens in the core city affects those who live in the suburbs and rural regions, and conversely, what those in the outlying areas do and don't do affects life for those who reside in the city. City taxpayers, though the least wealthy in the

> The RFP requested that applicants describe what leadership skills and abilities they believed would be necessary in the coming years.

region, are the ones who pay for the new services and buildings in downtown. Suburbanites take advantage of all the city has to offer and then return to their homes without contributing much to the standard of living for those in the city beyond the general price of admission to one event. Leaders in the twenty-first century will need to be less parochial, more inclusive—simply more concerned about the quality of life for every person in the region.

Our leaders will need to be educated, so they, in turn, can educate others, particularly about local issues. Green River has one primary newspaper, which prides itself in challenging the leadership structure. Recently, however, some of the criticisms, particularly of efforts to improve the downtown area, have become mean spirited and are serving to divide residents of the city.

Leaders in the coming decade will need to value diversity—of age, ethnicity, race, gender, and opinion. They'll need to listen—to hear what people need and be prepared to respond with actions and initiatives that will meet those needs. They will need to have a strong network of others who can act both quickly and deliberately, which will require that they have already worked through the lengthy, sometimes painful and frustrating process of achieving general consensus among their peers and constituents. ◄

> This is linked back to the need identified earlier among second tier leaders for time-consuming consensus building activities.

Our leaders will need vision. They will require a better understanding of poverty and, more, of people who are poor. They will lead out of a calling to serve, rather than an ego-driven need to be known.

5. Participation

If selected, the writers of this proposal would contact individuals from each of the layers of leadership described in the first section of this proposal. In fact, while developing this preproposal, the steering committee convened a diverse focus group of leaders from neighborhood organizations, nonprofit organizations, advocacy groups, and small businesses to discuss leadership and decision making in our community. Every one of the more than thirty people in attendance expressed an interest in a more inclusive leadership training effort. One said that, currently, gaining entrance and acceptance to traditional circles of leadership was based on being liked or having money, rather than on the skills or commitment the individual could bring to the effort. Many said that the only voice they felt they had in local decision making was through their ballots.

They and the writers of this proposal would include leaders from area churches, ethnic centers, foundations, Camp Fire or other youth service organizations (including participating youth), schools, National Issues Forum discussion groups, and neighborhood centers, along with more traditional leaders such as graduates of Leadership Green River, governmental leaders/employees, leading business owners, and, hopefully, a member of Great Action. ◄

> In the preproposal, the writer is identifying some of the individuals who might participate in the emerging leaders' training initiative.

6. Appropriateness

Green River needs an infrastructure that connects leaders of diverse backgrounds, interests, financial resources, and skills, that links efforts to enhance communication, avoid unnecessary duplication, and preserve limited resources. While our community often has the resources and energy to address issues, it usually does so by individual organizations. Projects run parallel to each other; nonprofit organizations with similar missions, like businesses with similar products, often compete rather than join forces.

The opportunity to submit this preproposal has been valuable for the steering committee and focus group participants. We've talked about how decisions get made and what the perceptions are of those not in the traditional circle of leadership. We talked candidly about what it feels like to be unheard and unheeded, and what that means to the future success of all civic efforts. The preproposal has enabled us to focus on what is right and what is wrong with leadership in our community—where we do a pretty good job of meeting needs and where we simply react to the nearest controversy or crisis.

Our community lacks a forum where people with ideas can get them off the ground and where others can respond on behalf of their constituencies about the relative merits or drawbacks of plans. The steering committee developed a model for such a forum, which is illustrated in the attachment.

It is critical that established leaders in Green River begin to listen to diverse voices and opinions. The focus group was a good start on convening various layers of leadership and emphasizing minority opinions. However, if follow-up on the idea forum or another type of more diverse leadership effort is left to local organizations, its funding agent would become its owner. The owner would make decisions about who would be invited, and nothing would change. The steering committee hopes that, with Foundation's support, a new leadership structure would be owned by the community and accessible by people who have not traditionally taken part in the initiatives described in this proposal. If selected, Green River would like to develop the type of leadership that consists of a whole made up of parts, rather than parts making a whole—in other words, leaders who work as a team rather than a collection of individuals each doing his or her part on behalf of the group.

> This gets to the heart of the matter. If the national program would enable the city to develop such a forum, this city has identified a need and willingness to participate.

Learning More

Grantseeker Workshops

There are both grantwriter and grantseeker workshops. Grant*writer* workshops teach you the generic fundamentals of writing grants, much of which you can learn by using this book and practicing your craft in real-life situations. Grant*seeker* workshops are provided by the grantmaker and are designed to provide an overview of the grant opportunity, tips on writing a competitive application, and responses to questions posed by attendees.

Some grantseeker workshops are mandatory. That is, the funder will state in the RFP that in order to be eligible to apply, a representative from the nonprofit organization must attend the workshop. When you go, be absolutely sure that you sign in so the grantor knows that your application is eligible. Attendance at a workshop does not mean that you must apply; in fact, most mandatory workshops are required because the funder wants the nonprofits to be absolutely clear about the program and the eligibility criteria before they go to the effort of developing a proposal.

Government workshops are now becoming a thing of the past. Today, you can ask questions via email or through the website offering the proposal. Also, some agencies are offering call-in times so you can participate in a conference call with other grantseekers. The federal government will occasionally hold grantseeker workshops when it releases a new, relatively large grant program. The workshops are generally provided in three or four key regions of the country to afford the greatest number of people the opportunity to attend while reducing costs to the extent possible. State governments most often hold workshops in the capitol city and in one or more of the larger urban centers in the state. Intermediaries will, of course, hold workshops for local applicants in a local center. Foundations rarely have workshops in conjunction with the release of an RFP. If you have questions about the RFP, you should call the program or grants officer listed as the contact person.

What Will You Learn?

Here's a guarantee: you will learn something new at every grantseeker workshop you attend, whether it is specific to the grant opportunity under discussion or just a general tip on how to write better proposals.

Workshops are the best place to ask questions and to hear answers to other people's questions—issues that may not have occurred to you. Bring a list of questions formed while reading the RFP so you can make sure you get all the answers you need to write a strong proposal. For instance, if you were attending a workshop about the Learn and Serve America grant you looked at earlier in this chapter, you might want to be sure to clarify that the $500,000 award ceiling is for one year of the three-year grant, since that is only implied in the RFP.

Generally, workshop topics will cover:

- An explanation of the enabling legislation (for government grants)
- A thorough description of eligibility requirements for applicants
- A discussion of specifics of the grant requirements, including, in many cases, what funds qualify as match dollars, the role of in-kind contributions, and similar budgetary concerns
- A brief "how to" on writing the specific proposal; clarification of what the grantor is looking for and what its reviewers prefer not to see included
- A question and answer period

Another thing you'll take away from grantseeker workshops is a general understanding of which other agencies are applying for the grant; in other words, your potential competition. There may arise opportunities for collaboration when agencies have similar missions and geographic focus. Collaboration or partnership between two like agencies is far preferable to submitting competing grant applications for the same work with the same population.

> **When You Don't Want to Attend the Workshop**
>
> Some grantseeker workshops are deadly boring, and if they are not mandatory, you will be tempted to skip them, especially as you build experience and expertise in reading and responding to RFPs.
>
> Carefully weigh the pros and cons. You have a guarantee that you'll learn something new at every workshop. But if it is information you can get another way, is it worth investing hours in another workshop? Do you already know who else is applying and have you worked out collaboration or agreements with other applicants if relevant? Have you been to a workshop sponsored by this agency before? If not, it's probably a good idea to go.

Contacts and Questions

Contacting a federal government staff person used to be "mission impossible" even when the RFP provided telephone numbers. Today, however, it is much easier to get answers to your questions through a telephone call or email to a federal or state government staff person. Look in the RFP for a list of contacts and information for how to reach them. When you are responding to a government-sponsored RFP, you are not developing relationships with the funder. These contact individuals are there only to respond to questions. Be sure to check the website (www.grants.gov) for any FAQs (frequently asked questions) before posing yours and taking up the contact's time.

State Single Point of Contact, DUNS Number

State Single Point of Contact (SSPC) and DUNS number are two items you will only encounter in federal grants. They may flummox you or your organization unless you know what they are and how to address them.

The SSPC is a person in your state or multi-state region who has been assigned by the government to coordinate applications coming from all organizations within your state in reply to specific RFPs. If an application must also be sent to the SSPC, it will say so in the RFP and provide a list of the SSPCs in every state. If the RFP does not contain SPOC contact information, it is not flagged for state/region coordination.

You should send one copy to this person on the day you send your proposal, not because the SSPC is as strict about deadlines, but so you don't forget that this is a requirement. If you send it just to be safe and it wasn't mandated, you are likely to receive a note saying that the SSPC is not reviewing that grant. This does not mean that the government agency is not reviewing your grant, just that you made a minor error in sending the proposal to the SSPC.

The DUNS number is required on the cover sheet (standard form 424.a) for all federal grants. The Dun and Bradstreet D-U-N-S number is a nine-digit identification number used by the federal government to keep track of financial reports of different businesses and organizations. If your organization does not have a DUNS number, apply for one either by telephone or on-line (smallbusiness.dnb.com), and receive it quickly (usually within 24 hours).

CHAPTER 3
Proactive Grantseeking

What Is Proactive Grantseeking?

Proactive grantseeking involves finding potential funding sources for a nonprofit organization's programs and initiatives. It requires that the grantseeker understand philanthropy as practiced by charitable giving foundations, is able to research specific foundation giving patterns, and can make practical and realistic connections between the mission and goals of the nonprofit organization and those of prospective funders.

Collectively, at the turn of the twenty-first century, foundations held approximately $486 billion in assets and made more than $29 billion in grants annually. Direct corporate giving adds approximately $10 billion more to charitable giving totals. However, foundation and corporate grantmaking together account for only about 17 percent of all charitable giving in the U.S. Individuals and bequests provided the rest of the estimated $203 billion given in 2000.

A comprehensive fund-raising strategy for any nonprofit organization, therefore, should include building a base of individual donors as well as using both proactive and reactive grantseeking.

> ***TIP***
>
> Proactive grantseeking requires a well developed knowledge of foundations, foundation programs and personnel, and ways to approach the funders. If you have never written a grant before, practice your skills using the reactive approach. Find an RFP that looks interesting and respond on behalf of the appropriate nonprofit organization.

Who Makes These Grants?

Most foundations make grants through a competitive application process. According to the Foundation Center, at the close of 2004, there were nearly 78,000 foundations in the U.S.—of these, 66,500 were active grantmaking foundations. Ninety-three percent of all foundations are classified as small with less than $10 million in assets. Only approximately forty foundations in the nation have assets of more than $1 billion. Further complicating the landscape are the variety of foundation types, giving methods, and grant requirements, requiring that a grantseeker work to understand where the foundations are and what each does.

How Foundations Do Business

The business of foundations, and consequently, the approach you take in contacting them for grants, varies by type, asset size, governance structure, and focus (program areas). Many foundations publish grantmaking guidelines. These documents describe program areas or what the foundation is specifically interested in funding. Occasionally you will see that a foundation only makes grants to preselected organizations. In these cases, the foundation does not accept unsolicited applications for funding.

Proactive grantseeking involves finding or requesting guidelines and analyzing them to determine whether the foundation would be interested in reviewing a proposal from your organization.

Foundation Type

There are two broad categories of foundations: private foundations and grantmaking public charities.

The largest group of foundation funders are private foundations, defined by the Foundation Center as nongovernmental, nonprofit grantmaking organizations with endowed funds, managed by their own trustees or directors. Private foundations make grants to carry out their charitable purposes of maintaining or aiding social, educational, religious, or other charitable activities serving the common good.

By law, private foundations must donate 5 percent of their total assets annually through grantmaking. Assets grow larger or smaller annually through investments. When their investments earn more than 5 percent return, the foundation grows and its grantmaking increases; when they earn less, the foundation asset base (called "corpus") decreases, which reduces the amount of funds available for grantmaking in subsequent years.

Private Foundations

Independent foundations are a broad category of foundations that are governed by a board that is independent of other entities. Independent foundations comprise almost 89 percent of foundations and account for roughly three-quarters of foundation giving. Both the country's largest and smallest foundations fall into this category.

There are two subcategories within independent foundations: family foundations and new health foundations. *Family foundations* are distinguished from other independent foundations by the makeup of the board. Family foundation trustees are primarily related to the donor, whereas independent foundation trustees are selected for their reputation and experience in the foundation's program or interest areas. Most independent foundations began as family foundations and evolve over a period of years.

The vast majority of family foundations have relatively small assets and use few or no professional staff. Some family foundations look deceptively small, as they may maintain a small permanent endowment and pass-through more substantial funds from family members for grantmaking.

New *health foundations* are the second and growing subcategory of independent foundations. These foundations are formed when nonprofit hospitals or other health organizations convert to for-profit status. Because nonprofits receive donations and tax exemptions, their assets must be permanently dedicated to charitable purposes. During the conversion process, the value of these assets is often placed in a newly formed foundation.

Corporate foundations are private foundations endowed by a corporation in perpetuity. Many corporate foundations do not maintain substantial endowments and instead fund grant budgets through annual gifts from their corporate donors that rise and fall with company profits. Often, founders and higher-level executives of the corporation serve on the board and have a significant role in grantmaking decisions. There are approximately 2,500 corporate foundations in the U.S.

Corporate giving programs are grantmaking programs established and administered by for-profit corporations. They are not separately endowed as corporate foundations are; therefore, the amount of annual giving from a corporate giving program varies with the profits earned by the company. Corporate giving programs may include cash or product gifts or a combination of the two.

Operating foundations are a confusing subset of private foundations in that the endowment is used to fund the foundation's own operations (i.e., its research or other programs). Few operating foundations make grants outside their operations. There are approximately 2,800 operating foundations in the U.S.

Grantmaking Public Charities

These 501(c)(3) tax-exempt organizations have a charitable purpose and derive their funds from multiple donors. While these organizations qualify to receive donations, they are classified as grantmaking public charities because they also make grants for charitable purposes. In contrast to independent and corporate foundations, public charities have no payout requirement.

Two kinds of grantmaking public charities are community foundations and public foundations. *Community foundations* make grants for charitable purposes in a specific community or region. The assets of a community foundation are derived from many donors and are held in a series of funds, each with different grantmaking requirements. A community foundation also raises money to increase the corpus of the foundation. There are approximately seven hundred community foundations in the U.S. Community foundation giving typically amounts to between 7 and 8 percent of the value of their prior year's assets.

Public foundations are often population- or cause-specific, such as local women's foundations, Jewish federations, or disease-related funds.

Community giving programs are not endowed, but should be included in a comprehensive proactive search for potential funders.

From Foundation Center—2005 Growth and Giving Trends

In this climate of uncertainty, overall private giving by individuals, foundations, and corporations grew a modest 5 percent to an estimated $248.52 billion in 2004. For the more than 66,000 U.S. grantmaking foundations, estimated giving increased 6.9 percent to a record $32.4 billion.

Of the roughly 66,400 grantmaking foundations tracked in the Foundation Center's database in 2003, close to 34,000 indicated that they give only to preselected organizations and do not accept unsolicited grant proposals.

By law, independent and corporate foundations must pay out each year in charitable distributions at least 5 percent of the value of their assets in the preceding year. Smaller independent foundations generally exceed this rate because many of them maintain minimal endowments and instead the foundations serve as pass-throughs for charitable giving by their donors. In these cases, the donor's total gift to the foundation is granted in the same year, rather than invested in the corpus.

Community giving programs include United Way, community trusts, and other programs. Through annual fund-raising campaigns, these organizations raise money that is subsequently distributed through grants. Unlike foundations with endowed assets, the funding for these grants generally passes through them to nonprofit organizations.

Asset Size

Asset size generally plays a significant role in the staffing and structure of a foundation's grantmaking. The one thousand largest foundations in the U.S. account for nearly one-half of all annual grantmaking. While these larger foundations are governed by boards of directors, often called trustees, who make the final decisions regarding grant awards, most also have staff. Staff includes program or grants officers or program directors who are the first contacts for grantseekers and whose subsequent interest and support is necessary. Staff members generally bring to the trustees only those grant proposals they think will be of interest to the decision makers.

Small foundations may have few or no professional staff. In these cases, the trustees act as both program staff and decision makers. Through necessity, these foundations steer away from complicated grantmaking and often fund a small number of grantees over a long period of time.

Foundations That Fund Only Preselected Organizations

A large number of smaller foundations make grants only to selected charities. Their goal is to ensure ongoing support for the organizations, which often have played an important role in the lives of the donors (i.e., their church, a health-care organization, or institutions with some other personal affiliation). These foundations often serve as pass-throughs and are governed by the donor and/or his or her family members and are sometimes overseen by a banking executive. These foundations generally do not accept unsolicited proposals. Unless you know the donor or have another means to break through, your letters to the foundation or the contact person at the bank will go unnoticed and probably unread.

Program Areas

The more sophisticated grantmaking organizations understand their role in the grander scheme of multiple types and sizes of donors and prefer to focus their donations on specific targeted goals or what they call "program areas."

A report on trends in giving among the 1,010 largest U.S. foundations in 2003 indicated that foundation program areas include, in descending order by the share of foundation grantmaking dollars, education, health, human services, public affairs/social benefit, arts and culture, environment/animals, international affairs, science and technology, religion, and social sciences. These are aggregates and speak only to the largest foundations in the U.S. Most foundations have three to five program areas, though some have only one and others have many more.

Crafting a Proactive Grantseeking Strategy

The first step in proactive grantseeking is identifying the needs for funding at the nonprofit organization: what is the mission and what are the goals of the nonprofit? What programs is it launching or sustaining? What are the important outcomes of those projects? Who are the project beneficiaries and what are their outstanding needs? When you understand the organization's potential uses for grant money, you can use that information to find foundations that share those goals and, therefore, might be interested in reviewing a grant proposal.

Foundation Searches

When you search for foundations, there are many factors to consider. For instance, if you searched for all foundations that do educational funding for your nonprofit's school district, you may begin with a list of twenty thousand foundation names. As you cull through the list, you will eliminate those foundations that don't accept unsolicited proposals, limit their funding to a geographic area other than yours, focus their educational grantmaking in a way that is incompatible with your organization's focus, and/or have precommitted program funds for large, social change efforts (while you're searching for funding for a small program).

In the end, you may end up with fewer than a dozen real prospects. That's normal. In fact, five or six good prospects is much more important to a successful proactive grantseeking effort than a list of a thousand about which you know little or nothing.

Begin locally. First, learn all you can about local foundations and other grant resources: do you have a community foundation or United Way, and if so, what do they fund? What other foundations have made grants in your community or region, and what do the beneficiaries of those grant funds have in common? If you have a regional association of grantmakers (RA), contact them for a catalog or CD listing of foundations in your state or region.

Later, expand your search to regional or national funders, but only if yours is a project that has some special importance to that particular foundation.

A great resource for learning more about foundation donors is the Foundation Center (www.fdncenter.org). You can use the search function on the Center's web page to find foundations based on city and state and/or name of the foundation. The Center then provides a complete listing for the selected foundations that includes its address, contact person (if available), email, phone and fax numbers, type of foundation, deadlines for submissions (some only meet to consider proposals annually or biannually), assets and total annual giving, web page URL, and a link to its most recent IRS filing (990-PF for private foundations, 990 for community foundations), which can provide information on grants funded the year of filing. IRS 990s are also available at www.guidestar.org, where you will also find tax information about nonprofit organizations and businesses in your community.

Foundation Support Organizations

Several large national organizations provide education, advocacy, and other support for foundations. They include the Council on Foundations, Independent Sector, Forum of Regional Associations of Grantmakers, and the Foundation Center. In addition, there are approximately thirty regional associations of grantmakers (RAs), which provide education and support to foundations located in their regions.

While these organizations exist to serve their member foundations, there are two things a grantwriter should know about them: they do not make grants, and each provides directories or other information on funders that grantseekers can use to identify local grantmakers, review program areas, and find contact information. The Foundation Center and RAs are especially good resources for grantseekers.

Also, through exploring the websites of these organizations, you may find affinity groups. These are groups of foundations (some regional, some national) that share a focus on grantmaking in the same program area (e.g., funders in the arts, funders for early education, etc.). Affinity groups discuss shared problems and strategies for grantmaking. On occasion a small number of affinity group members will develop a regional effort with joint funding and goals for their program area. A grantseeker should be interested in affinity group lists as means to identify funders in the appropriate program area and to follow trends in grantmaking.

Foundation Staffing

Foundations do not have a commonly recognized system of staffing, staff responsibilities, or staff titles; however, here are a few clues for understanding people with whom you will want to have contact:

Foundations with staff generally have program-related staff who are responsible for reading and analyzing grants, doing background searches (due diligence), and making grant recommendations to the decision making body. When there are multiple program staff they are often divided by program area; e.g., arts or environment. Common titles include program officer, program director, grants officer, program manager, community investment officer, program assistant, or program associate. Another group of staff with whom you might have contact are those with grant administration duties. They are responsible for ensuring that reports, documentation, and grant files are in order and for processing grants once they have been approved. Common titles include grants manager, grants associate, and grants administrator.

Foundations with few staff members commonly have a president or director and his or her assistant, and/or a finance officer, with the president performing all the duties typically associated with program staff.

It is important to remember that unless you are dealing with the sole trustee, and thus the sole decision maker of a foundation, the final decision on granting funds is a board process involving a number of players. While staff may have influence, they make recommendations, not decisions. Does that mean you should skip the staff and go straight to the trustees? You do this at your own peril. As one foundation trustee put it, one of the primary motivators for hiring staff was to avoid being "hit up for a grant" every time he went downtown.

Once you locate the foundations in your community, go to their web page and look at their grantmaking guidelines. If the foundation does not have a website, telephone them or write a letter requesting that the guidelines be mailed to you.

Reading Grantmaking Guidelines

Guidelines can be very simple such as this sample from a geographically focused foundation:

Sample: Grantmaker Guidelines

Healthy communities have a high quality of life. The Family Foundation believes that managing growth and capitalizing on the natural environment contribute greatly to the quality of life in our community. For this reason we place a major emphasis on land protection. We encourage environmental preservation and seek to maintain a balance between open land and well-planned development in our target communities of western State.

Our grantmaking priorities include:
- Preserving and restoring high quality lakes and streams
- Expanding recreation trails and greenways
- Protecting and preserving critical lands—including farmland, parkland and natural areas of rich biodiversity
- Beautifying scenic transportation corridors, including gateways and the control of billboards

If, for instance, your organization's project is related to environmental protection but focuses on saving an endangered species or improving air quality, you know from reading these guidelines that such a project would not likely interest a funder like this one that emphasizes land use planning and protection.

Other guidelines can be more complex and detailed such as the sample from a national funder on the next page.

Once again, though you may find that your organization shares a goal with this foundation for improving the environment, this would not be a match for an environmental protection organization doing its work in the U.S.

Sample: Grantmaker Guidelines

Through rapid growth in population and increasing demand for resources, the world is in danger of losing much of its genetic, species, and ecosystem diversity. To address this challenge and to increase understanding of the strong relationships between the health of the biosphere and the welfare of human communities, the Foundation has established the Conservation and Sustainable Development area. This area is dedicated to conserving biodiversity, to enhancing knowledge of how to use natural resources sustainably over the long term, and to promoting environmentally sustainable economic growth benefiting those living in or near sensitive areas.

Purpose

The area's exclusive focus is on dealing with the problems of endangered tropical ecosystems. These are the regions with the greatest degree of species diversity but which are also plagued by acute human poverty and are often experiencing rapid population growth.

Strategies

The major categories in which the Foundation awards grants for conservation and sustainable development follow from a conceptual map that indicates a flow of influences on natural resources, beginning with threats in specific places, which can be addressed with a combination of conservation tools. The framework for Conservation and Sustainable Development grantmaking is based on geographic priorities. The Foundation will consider proposals that address significant threats to biodiversity within priority regions.

Geographic Priorities

The Foundation focuses its conservation and sustainable development work in a small number of tropical biogeographic zones. These zones, chosen for their richness of species diversity, endemism, limited institutional capacity, and the level of threat, are:

Latin America and Caribbean

- *Southern Tropical Andes*. The eastern slopes of the mountains in Peru and Bolivia
- *Northern Tropical Andes*. The eastern slopes of the mountains in Ecuador and Colombia and the Chocó from northwestern Ecuador to the Darién in Panama
- *Insular Caribbean*. Terrestrial and coastal ecosystems in the Greater Antilles (Cuba, Hispaniola, and Jamaica) and in selected islands of the Lesser Antilles

Asia and Pacific

- *Eastern Himalaya*. The mountain ecosystems of eastern Nepal, Bhutan, Northeast India, and Yunnan
- *Lower Mekong*. Forest regions of the Mekong basin in Lao PDR, Cambodia, and Vietnam
- *Indo-Melanesia*. Coastal and marine areas of Papua New Guinea, Solomon Islands, Fiji, and eastern Indonesia

Africa

- *Madagascar*
- *Lower Guinean Forest*. The coastal forest of Cameroon, Equatorial Guinea, Gabon, and Nigeria (particularly the Niger Delta)
- *Albertine Rift*. The highlands area of western Uganda, Rwanda, Burundi, and eastern Congo

Within each of these geographic regions there are a range of conservation tools that will be effective in countering the threats to biodiversity, including:

- Direct Protection: Includes establishment and management of parks, reserves, and protected areas, and development of innovative financial mechanisms for such areas
- Law and Policy: Includes the development of environment law and policy as tools for conservation
- Conservation Training and Education: Includes both formal and informal education to improve the capacity of institutions in tropical countries to protect their biological diversity
- Conservation and Sustainable Economic Development: Includes programs that address the economic forces affecting tropical biodiversity

Conservation ultimately depends upon the capacity of individuals and institutions in each region. Development of local capacity to implement projects and programs will be an important criterion in evaluating all requests. The Foundation defines capacity as the ability of institutions to conduct effective conservation science and natural resources management. Specific sets of skills that are required for effective conservation vary among the regions in which the Foundation is active. An effort will be made to identify those needs in some detail through a process of consultation in each region.

Contacting a Program/Grants Officer

Once you have a short list of potential funders, begin contacting program officers to discuss your project. Before you contact a program officer in any foundation, be sure you have done as much homework as possible. Don't just call and ask if they'd be interested in funding your organization. Call only when you have the project details committed to memory so you can respond if they ask you follow-up questions. Use the same etiquette you would use in contacting a business about a job or a sale. Do not call a program officer for answers to simple questions such as deadlines for submissions; instead ask the receptionist or grants manager such questions if you cannot find the information in the literature or on the website. Also, never contact a grants officer with an emergency question. Sometimes it can take weeks for these busy people to return your call.

> **When searching for potential grant-making sources, be sure to check for the following information:**
>
> - Program goals that complement your organization's work
> - Geographic limitations
> - Eligibility requirements
> - Average number of grant awards
> - Average amount of grant awards
> - Limitations (e.g., no religious purposes)
> - Timing of decisions—will it fit within your timeframe?

If you are serious about becoming a grantwriting resource to your employer or community, try to get an appointment with a program officer at your local community foundation. These individuals can provide a great deal of guidance and information about philanthropies in your region and the best ways to approach them. Once you've proven your skills, they might even lead you to organizations that need grantwriting services.

Using Email Communications with Program Officers

Email is both a blessing and a curse, and you need to know how and when to use it in contacting program officers. For the most part, foundations are not yet prepared to field email pitches for grants. When a grant proposal or concept paper comes in the mail, it can be routed through a grants manager who will assign it to the most appropriate program officer, track its review, and/or send you a polite decline letter. Email circumvents this well-established process and sometimes lands your proposal with people who can least help you.

If you've worked with a program officer before and have an easy, less formal relationship, you can email him or her with an idea before developing a concept paper or proposal and expect a relatively quick response concerning the program officer's interest. If you have never contacted the program officer before or have never met him or her, do not send an email. Instead, follow instructions (if any) for contacting the foundation described in its guidelines, or use established channels such as letters or telephone calls.

Tip: Be sure that your email address is professional and, if possible, gives some clue as to your organization (e.g., lindalavin@orionpublicschools.edu). Do not send an email from an address like blondebabe@internetfun.net. If your email address does not give a clue about who you are, put such information in your subject line so the recipient knows your note is not spam.

Preproposal Interviews/Discussions

If at all possible, try to schedule a meeting or phone call with a grants officer before submitting a proposal. This is especially important when you are planning to submit to a local foundation.

If you don't know who might serve as grants officer for your proposal, call the foundation to ask the receptionist for the name of the person who manages grants within the program area your proposal would fit. Do your homework so that you've identified which foundation interest area would cover your proposal.

If you don't know the grants officer well, treat your call or letter as you would any sales cold call. Briefly introduce yourself then ask if you could set a time (fifteen minutes maximum) to discuss a proposal you would like to submit. For example, "My name is Jody Fields and I work with Tomorrow's Hope, which provides remedial education services for children in Clark County. We have a project that we think you would find interesting. Would you have ten to fifteen minutes in the next week in which I could discuss this project with you?"

If you do know the grants officer, the gist of the contact—whether by phone, email, or letter—is similar. Briefly introduce the project and ask for a time to discuss it.

It's more than likely that the grants officer will ask you to send something in writing ahead of the conversation. Be sure to ask what he/she would like to see—a synopsis, outline or draft—and send the items accordingly.

The resultant conversation is not the time for a dog and pony show (i.e., bringing along several staff people and influential board members or developing an elaborate presentation). If the foundation has interest in the proposal, the grants officer may invite a presentation later. Instead, you want this to be a time to present the highlights of what you are proposing and ask for some candid feedback on where it might fit into the foundation's plans for grantmaking.

Before you leave, ask if you can submit a proposal and ask about deadlines for the next grantmaking cycle. Follow-up by writing a thank you note and providing any information that was requested during the discussion. If you make promises, such as exploring a partnership the program officer has suggested, be sure to fulfill them. Send an email or letter describing your results and incorporate an update into your grant proposal.

Letters of Inquiry

Many foundations now require a letter of inquiry (LOI) before they invite a full proposal. This differs greatly from the letters of intent described in chapter 2. The foundation grants officers then review the letter and determine whether or not the proposal has a chance for success and, if so, what sort of tips they might provide that will give your proposal a better chance of being approved by their trustees.

Think of the letter of inquiry as a concept paper or a minigrant proposal. Include four of the five essential components of a grant proposal: the statement of problem or need, the project description, the evaluation plan, and the budget. A general LOI sample follows.

Sample: Letter of Inquiry

March 20, 2006

Anna Smith, Program Officer
Corporate Foundation
Builder Way
Anytown, USA

Dear Ms. Smith:

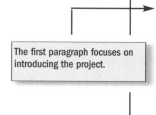

I write as a representative of a community collaborative addressing the health concern of lead poisoning in children. This multisector collaborative includes organizations approaching lead poisoning through data collection and analysis, hazard reduction, education, and advocacy. While important work is ongoing in each sector, this project will integrate that work to improve efficiency and reach more children earlier.

The first paragraph focuses on introducing the project.

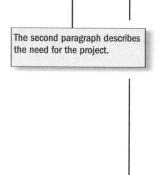

The toxic effect of lead poisoning is a well-known fact. The federal government banned lead as an additive in residential paint in 1978, yet nationally twenty million homes have unsafe exposure to lead. There are an estimated 35,717 homes with lead contamination in the City. Low income households in the central city are more likely to be affected by lead exposure. The County Health Department tests all children receiving Women, Infant and Children (WIC) benefits. The findings indicated the following prevalence of children with elevated blood lead levels (>9.9 ug/dL) by zip code:

The second paragraph describes the need for the project.

> 00001: 36 percent
> 00002: 27 percent
> 00006: 27 percent
> 00008: 26 percent

Medical research indicates that prolonged elevation at levels greater than 9.9 ug/dL will result in irreversible neurological damage. The implications for academic achievement and future employability potential are obvious.

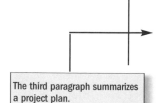

Lead poisoning is a treatable environmental health issue. The collaborative intends to address the issue through the Integrated Community Lead Hazard Reduction Plan that we have developed over the past five months. The County Health Department and City Office of Children, Youth and Families are currently identifying a Pilot Area to recommend for a three-year intensive investment of resources. Under the guidance of a project coordinator employed by the Leadership Institute, the work of education, hazard reduction, data collection and analysis, and advocacy will be carried out in that geographic area. The City Housing Rehabilitation Office will focus its Community Development Block Grant funds in the area as will the State Department of Community Health (SDCH). A key component in the education sector is the establishment of a CLEARCorps chapter in the city. This entity, to be housed in Nonprofit Housing Repairs, will utilize AmeriCorps members to take lead education to the households throughout the city, with particular focus on the Pilot Area. Education—which includes training in lead-safe home cleaning techniques and nutrition for lead risk reduction—is a recognized strategy for hazard reduction. The Integrated Plan seeks to test all children (not only those receiving WIC) in the Pilot Area, and will use AmeriCorps members to do finger-prick blood draws in the homes. The data collection in the Pilot Area, to be carried out jointly by the Health Department and CATCCH, a

The third paragraph summarizes a project plan.

health data project of Major Health, will provide a picture of the population such as we have not had. In fact, the SDCH indicates that such an aggregation of data would be unique in the state.

While the methodology of this project is rather sophisticated, its goal is simple: to eliminate the risk of exposure to lead for children in the city. We will begin to accomplish that goal through the Pilot Area project, expanding to a citywide effort should our evaluation after three years warrant such an expansion. Achieving the goal in the Pilot Area will require an integration of the work in all four sectors. We will attempt to reach all Pilot Area children with testing. We will attempt to reach all at-risk Pilot Area households with education. We will attempt to remediate all Pilot Area houses with children having elevated blood lead levels. We will initiate a citywide awareness campaign. We will advocate for state and federal funding. We will promote local and state legislation. The Integrated Plan uses a Log Frame (or Logic Model) approach to project implementation. The Log Frame includes goals, objectives and activities to accomplish goals. It also includes indicators and a measuring methodology. The Integrated Plan calls for Participatory Evaluation that includes the engagement of collaboration partners with Pilot Area residents and organizations in designing the Log Frame. Furthermore, the Integrated Plan budget includes funding for an outside professional evaluator to work with a Continuous Evaluation Team.

> This paragraph discusses the goals of a pilot effort.

The time frame for this project is three years at a total cost of approximately $300,000. We are hoping that the Foundation will invite a proposal for $100,000 to enable us to launch this pilot effort and gather the data necessary to support its expansion.

> The writer gives the cost of the project and asks for an invitation to apply for a grant. The writer may have considered attaching a line item budget to indicate where the $300,000 would be spent.

We will be seeking funding from multiple sources in addition to the Foundation and would welcome your counsel and assistance in securing other funders.

> It's important to point out that the organization does not expect one foundation to fund the entire pilot project and that it will be seeking other funders to share the risk of investing in this effort.

Sincerely,

Joanne Abernathy
Executive Director
For the Collaborative

This second sample is a bit different. The funder, in this case, has provided an outline for its letters of inquiry and wishes the potential grantee to respond to the questions in the outline. The foundation wants the grantee to describe how the project meets the goals and values of the foundation before it will consider requesting a full proposal.

Sample: Letter of Inquiry

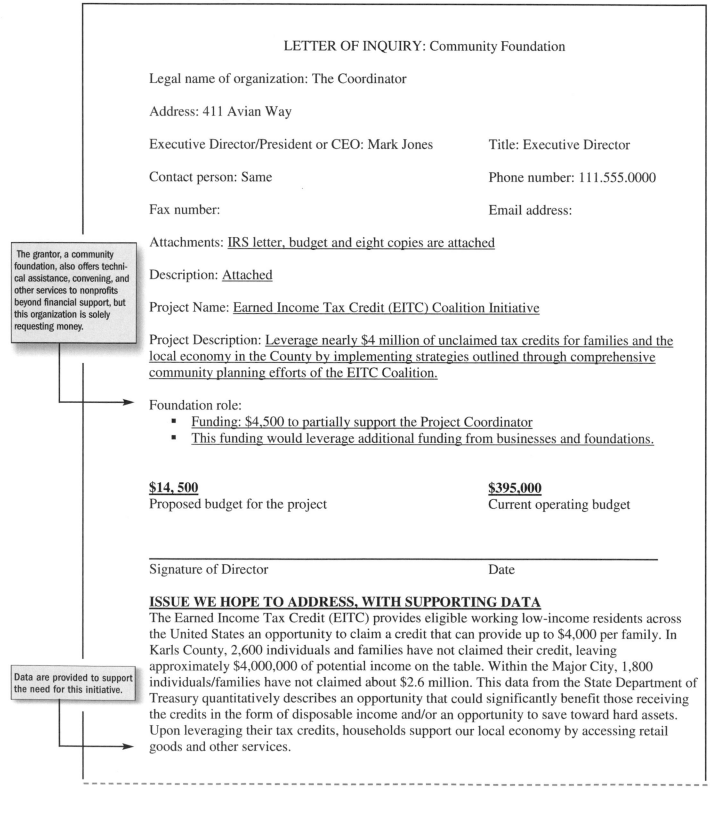

LETTER OF INQUIRY: Community Foundation

Legal name of organization: The Coordinator

Address: 411 Avian Way

Executive Director/President or CEO: Mark Jones   Title: Executive Director

Contact person: Same   Phone number: 111.555.0000

Fax number: Email address:

Attachments: IRS letter, budget and eight copies are attached

Description: Attached

Project Name: Earned Income Tax Credit (EITC) Coalition Initiative

Project Description: Leverage nearly $4 million of unclaimed tax credits for families and the local economy in the County by implementing strategies outlined through comprehensive community planning efforts of the EITC Coalition.

Foundation role:
- Funding: $4,500 to partially support the Project Coordinator
- This funding would leverage additional funding from businesses and foundations.

$14, 500
Proposed budget for the project

$395,000
Current operating budget

_____
Signature of Director   Date

ISSUE WE HOPE TO ADDRESS, WITH SUPPORTING DATA
The Earned Income Tax Credit (EITC) provides eligible working low-income residents across the United States an opportunity to claim a credit that can provide up to $4,000 per family. In Karls County, 2,600 individuals and families have not claimed their credit, leaving approximately $4,000,000 of potential income on the table. Within the Major City, 1,800 individuals/families have not claimed about $2.6 million. This data from the State Department of Treasury quantitatively describes an opportunity that could significantly benefit those receiving the credits in the form of disposable income and/or an opportunity to save toward hard assets. Upon leveraging their tax credits, households support our local economy by accessing retail goods and other services.

The grantor, a community foundation, also offers technical assistance, convening, and other services to nonprofits beyond financial support, but this organization is solely requesting money.

Data are provided to support the need for this initiative.

Our EITC Coalition's goal is to increase the number of households in Major City accessing their Earned Income Tax dollars. The EITC Coalition intends to accomplish this goal with modest financial resources and solid commitments from willing volunteers. Upon completion of the 2005 tax year and a successful, broad-based collaborative, an institutional home will be identified for the program. Currently, there is no institution that sees this as their mission across the community. An institutional home for the collaboration will help in recruiting and training volunteers, as well publicizing the benefit of EITC to possible eligible tax filers.

In years past, there have been a number of EITC sites, managed by AARP, and several other neighborhood sites. Last year, our EITC Coalition, facilitated by The Coordinator and the Family Independence Agency, established one site at the FIA that processed about two hundred returns.

We are currently preparing to collect data citywide from cooperating sites to determine our baseline achievements to date. Three measures will be included in that data: numbers of returns filed at free sites, size of received credit, and savings from not using commercial tax prep sites. We have retained a project coordinator over the course of the summer to identify additional sites based on geographic areas with dense populations of low income households and to develop contacts with possible sources of volunteers.

> Goals for the project are established.

Consistency with the Community Foundation's Principles
Accountability: Tracking which credits are utilized is a relatively easy task and one that will be pursued. This project provides quantitative, measurable benefits to recipients and the community. In addition, the willingness of an institution to take our demonstration project under its wing for the future is very measurable.

> The foundation has listed its values or the principles that it holds important in all funded projects. While this information is not requested in the grant proposal, it is in the LOI. The principles/values should apply to any project (to somewhat varying degrees) regardless of which program area applies.

Collaboration: Since the beginning of our Coalition in July of 2004, we have exhibited a collaborative approach: eight organizations are represented in the EITC Coalition. Additionally, the collaborative partners with neighborhood sites, colleges, volunteer groups, etc.

Diversity: One of the criteria for site selection is diversity of organizations (and staff), because we recognize the need to provide locations and contacts that are diverse. Both individuals we are considering for project coordinator are people of color. We will do our best to identify volunteer tax preparers who represent racial and ethnic diversity in our community, although this may be a bigger challenge.

Justice: This project is about social justice—ensuring that those who are legally entitled to some relief of their low-income status are helped to obtain income. All eligible participants are welcome at the sites.

Prevention: The EITC Coalition will link EITC customers to information and resources that will assist them in acquiring hard assets (homes, education, etc.) and thereby increasing their ability to achieve healthy lifestyles. We are not directly tying financial literacy training, IDAs and other incentives for acquisition of hard assets into this program at this time, however it is hoped that upon this year's success we can expand the program in coming years.

Social Capital: This project provides the volunteers and participants an opportunity to connect with each other and learn about each other's lives. If possible, we intend to align a source of volunteers and a CPA firm with each site or two sites with the hope that they will return next tax season to the same location(s). This will strengthen their connections and mutual learning.

Systems Approach: From the beginning of the Coalition's work, participation across sectors in the community has been essential and is consistent with The Coordinator's principles, as well.

Proposal for Addressing the Issue

We intend to hire a part-time (twenty hours/week for twenty-six weeks) project coordinator to implement the objectives of the EITC Coalition. Staff will be supported by the coalition as well as The Coordinator's public relations resource.

> The writer describes why the initiative needs funds and what it would use funds to accomplish.

Briefly, this plan includes
- Recruiting volunteers
- Ensuring that sites meet IRS-recommended computer hardware requirements
- Identifying a site coordinator for each site
- Ordering software from the IRS
- Developing and distributing publicity, including working with businesses, neighborhoods and human services organizations to get the word out
- Collecting the baseline data
- Scheduling training with IRS trainers
- Troubleshooting problems during the tax season.

Anticipated Accomplishments/Evaluation

We intend to:

> These will be written as planned outcomes in the grant proposal.

- Track progress from the 2005 tax season (January 15-April 15) as compared to 2006 for all sites that have baseline data
- Increase our Coalition's number of sites from one to six
- Increase those receiving credits from our Coalition's sites from 200 to 400
- Increase the amount of credits received proportionally
- By next fall, identify an organization or a very stable collaboration that sees EITC work as part of its mission
- Track numbers of those persons eligible in The County and Major City based on State Department of Treasury numbers, if they are collected

Evaluation will be relatively straightforward, as we can manage all data collection through our planned process.

Proposed Timeframe

The main part of the project will run from November 1-April 30 (aligned with tax season), with the possibility of extending if the need surfaces. We will have data on the tax season results by May 30, 2006.

EITC BUDGET: 2005-2006

- **Coordinator**
  @ $15/hour; 20 hours/week; 26 weeks $7,800

- **Office supplies, mileage, and other expenses** $1,000

- **Promotional materials** $500

- **The Coordinator supervision (along with the FIA)** $2,500

- **Coalition Team Facilitation** $3,000
  @ $50/hour; 10 hours/month; 6 months

                                       Total   **$14,800** ◄

> While the writer in this case includes a budget with breakdown, he or she failed to request an invitation to apply for a grant or to break down the income side of the budget so that the foundation staff could easily determine how much money the Coordinator would be requesting and how much it would seek from other funders.

Learning More

Theory of Change

Often the most fundable proactive programs are grounded in the theory of change. A theory of change is the product of a series of critical thinking exercises often mapped in a logic model (see chapter 7) and is used by some of the largest foundations to develop strategies within their program areas. To develop a program based in the theory of change, use the following steps:

- Identify your long-term goal or outcome. (What are you trying to achieve?)
- Work backwards from the goal by identifying the conditions necessary to achieve it (actions, people, setting).
- Identify the interventions you will need to perform to create these preconditions (actions).
- Develop indicators that describe how you will know when each precondition is met (evaluate).

Remember, having the greatest need among your target population does not entitle you to grant money; having the clearest understanding of the problem and the most innovative and achievable plan for addressing the problem is a far more fundable approach.

Foundation Non-negotiables

Every foundation has a number of things about which there is simply no negotiating. These might be as clear as geographic boundaries, or "fund only charitable 501(c)(3) organizations or government agencies." They also may be as unclear as the statement "we fund community-based projects," offered without a definition of "community-based." Thus, it is important not only to read foundation guidelines carefully, but also to listen carefully during meetings with grants officers. Learn from your discussions the items that raise flags with the foundation trustees, those things that will prevent funding, no matter how great your project. Some of these rules are unwritten. Listen for clues such as "the trustees have been increasingly concerned about project sustainability."

Be careful not to drive your organization over the bridge in making project or organizational changes to get around these non-negotiables. Be absolutely sure that what you agree to is supportable in the long run.

Twelve Principles of a Great Proactive Grant Proposal

Taken from A Great Grant Proposal by Dr. Joel J. Orosz, formerly W. K. Kellogg Foundation.

1. Try a new approach. If all the world's problems could be solved by tried and true methods, there would be no problems.

2. Have both expertise and outside help. The most successful organizations are those with a lot of know how and those that recognize and have a plan to address their weaknesses.

3. Be determined. Never say "if you don't fund this, the project will die." Funders want to know that this means something to you, that the work is so important to the agency that it will get done no matter what.

4. Do your homework. Ask questions, learn what others in the field are doing, dig deeply to find out as much about the funder as possible.

5. Work with others. It's critical that whatever you plan to do, you do it with rather than to the people you are trying to help. Invite their input into the program design and evaluation.

6. Improve human well-being. Even capital projects should have goals for programs that will improve the human condition. Address the external needs in your community rather than the needs of the proposing organization.

7. Invest your own money. If a nonprofit is willing to invest its own scarce funds into a project, it demonstrates the importance of the project.

8. Make it comprehensive. Complex problems require holistic solutions.

9. Collaborate. The most effective projects mobilize a variety of organizations to address a problem.

10. Evaluate. Grantors are learning all the time. Proposals should include a plan for capturing the lessons learned in the project and sharing them with funders and other nonprofit organizations.

11. Plan for sustainability. Foundations like to provide seed money, nurture a project through its formative years, then move on to other new projects. Before you get money, you must plan how you will grow your project to become a healthy, independent "adult."

12. Look for broader impact. Address the ways in which your project has the potential for replication (with or without modification for individual differences) elsewhere.

CHAPTER 4
Thoughtful Planning

There are several concepts that the nonprofit applicant must consider before writing a grant proposal:

- sustainability
- community involvement
- inter-agency cooperation

Though they are not the scope of the grantwriter (unless you are writing as director of the agency), the grantwriter needs to understand how these important concepts affect grant outcomes.

Planning for Sustainability

A critical, but often neglected part of planning a project is sustainability. You must incorporate into the project the ways that you will keep the project going after the grant runs out.

For instance, imagine that your neighborhood association wants to reclaim a vacant lot and turn it into a basketball court for young people in the neighborhood. You successfully apply to the community foundation for $10,000 for paint for foul lines and lumber for benches and for paving the empty lot once it's ready. The project gets the neighbors excited and they come out in force to clean up the lot, build the benches, and tackle the painting. One of them even finds a contractor who paves the lot for less than commercial price.

So, can you write your progress report and call the project complete and a success? Not yet. What happens next season? Who will repaint the foul lines next year? Who's going to store the paint between seasons and what facilities do they need to do that? Who's going to keep the court free of debris?

While the project seemed relatively simple and straightforward on the surface, you can see that underneath are all manner of questions and potential problems that must be resolved before you can write a grant proposal.

Funders rarely want to give an organization grant after grant for the same project. Ideally, they would prefer to share their resources with other groups and other projects. Therefore, for better or worse, they want nonprofits to stand on their own merits, to find ways to be self-sustaining to the greatest extent possible.

Because this is a major concern, foundations and government funders are becoming reluctant to fund projects that don't take sustainability into consideration in their design. One-time costs like capital or equipment, project evaluation, and similar items may be approved if they are needed to make the project successful. But if you also need additional staff and benefits, administration and operation costs, or stipends and payments to other service providers, funders likely will want to know when and how you expect to incorporate them into the agency's annual budget. This is their way of ensuring that the positive outcomes from your project can be sustained beyond their grant.

Thus, when funders ask for a sustainability plan, they are really asking how the project will continue and where you will find necessary resources after the grant period.

If your grant program is as simple as the previous one, you must address the issues and resolutions to them in your proposal. When your project is more complex and has potential for changing a social condition or problem in your community, you will need to plan for the project's sustainability. For example, will it be institutionalized into the operations of collaborative organizations and other stakeholders in your community?

Multi-year Funding

Projects that have many renewable expenses are good candidates for multiyear funding opportunities. In these cases, you might ask for a three-year grant with declining grant awards each year in order to give the agency time to incorporate the renewable costs into its budget. If, for instance, you are requesting the annual salary for a fund development specialist, you might ask for 100 percent of his or her wages in year one, 60 percent in year two, and 30 percent in year three, and show that, as the person raises more money for the organization, the position can pay for itself.

Who Are the Stakeholders?

Broadly, stakeholders are those affected by the direction and actions a nonprofit takes. Stakeholders can range from board and staff members to the population served to fellow service providers and other community representatives, businesses and organizations. From a strategic planning perspective, they are all important, but the level of their involvement (based on the effect the project has on them) will vary from project to project.

Community Involvement

Nonprofit organizations need to involve stakeholders, particularly those who will be directly affected by its programs, in planning to solve problems that affect them. This will not only result in stronger project plans and greater likelihood of success, but will convey the message to the target population that they have power, that they have a voice in their own lives and conditions. After all, the point of every social change effort should be not just to help people, but to help people help themselves. You can't do that by foisting unwanted projects and initiatives on an unengaged population.

Community involvement, no matter how you define "community," is critical to the success of any nonprofit effort.

Why? Consider this: let's say the copy machine at the nonprofit organization jams frequently and copies sometimes have streaks. It's annoying but not unmanageable. Knowing this, a board member surprises you with a new machine. It does everything, but because it does, it is complicated to operate and requires you to make arrangements for a half-day training program for yourself and staff members. It comes with one toner cartridge, but it is used faster than your old machine and replacements are expensive. Plus, you wonder what you will do with the stockpile of supplies you have to operate the old machine.

Think of how differently things would have turned out if your board member had simply asked you first. It might have spoiled the surprise, but you would have had time to consider the pros and cons and you might have found a new machine that better fit your needs.

Of course, this is a very simple representation for what can happen in very complex relationships between a nonprofit organization and its target population. The thing to remember is that just because the heads of the nonprofit think that people need something doesn't mean the people agree. And, providing something that people don't want, and sometimes even forcing it on them "for their own good," can make them resentful.

When you are designing a school curriculum, it's likely that funders will want to know if you've asked students how they learn best. When you are promoting a smoking cessation program, they will wonder if you've asked smokers what will draw them to attend. If you are trying to reduce unemployment, have you asked the unemployed what they need to secure and keep their jobs? Has anyone listened? It may be that you want to make the case for a new literacy project as a way to address unemployment, but the unemployed people all tell you that they read perfectly well and what they really need are cars to get to and from the available jobs. Since providing cars or rides is not a part of the literacy organization's mission, you need not pursue funding for something that you have learned is not necessary and would not work.

Identifying and Involving Other Organizations

Sometimes in reactive grantseeking, collaboration is mandated by the grantor. Some even identify which types of organizations you must work with. For example, the federal Safe Schools, Healthy Students project is offered jointly by three departments of the government: education, health and human services, and justice. It, therefore, requires three organizations to apply jointly: a school district, a mental health service provider, and the local police or sheriff's department.

No nonprofit is an island unto itself. Whether collaboration is mandated or encouraged, it's generally a good idea for applicant organizations to work with other organizations when they design a project. Many nonprofit organizations comprise a collaborative simply because they know what certain organizations can bring to the problem-solving process or project design. The resources that each of them brings to the design process can shape a unique project—one that has a better chance of making a real change in the problem you are addressing.

> ***TIP***
>
> Remember, most funders understand that your organization is probably not the only game in town. If you fail to mention other organizations and your working relationships with them, it can raise a red flag in the mind of the funder.

When considering which other organizations to involve in a collaborative project, a freelance grantwriter can sometimes have an edge over one who works as staff to a nonprofit. Staff people have to know everything they can about their own organization, its strengths and weaknesses, and its needs and the needs of its target population. So, sometimes, when they need to build relationships, they may tend to call only on organizations they have worked with before. Freelancers, on the other hand, work for several nonprofit organizations and may have a more objective view of the nonprofit landscape in the community. Because they don't belong to any nonprofit, they can think outside the organizational culture and sometimes suggest very creative relationships.

As a grantwriter, you can help the nonprofit organization identify and involve other organizations in a proposed collaborative by writing a brief concept paper describing the problem and the proposed solution. The concept paper is used to set the stage for a discussion among potential collaborators to, at minimum, determine if it's something that interests them. If the leadership of a nonprofit organization does not know who does what in the community, you can help by calling your local United Way or community foundation and asking for suggestions.

Communicating with Collaborators

Throughout the writing process, the grantwriter will need input and cooperation from all the participant organizations on a number of things: the plan of work and its goals and objectives, the budget, and the support letters or interagency agreements, to name just a few.

Keep the lines of communication open whether through team meetings or sharing draft proposals. Be sure that before you finalize a grant proposal, every nonprofit leader and those in his or her organization who have responsibilities for carrying out the plan has read and understands the work plan. If you have mapped out a plan of work for a nonprofit organization—whether the applicant or a collaborator—you must be sure that they know what they have agreed to do and are willing to perform at the level described for the money that was budgeted. Remind them that, if the grant for the collaborative is awarded, they are entering into a contract and will be held accountable for their individual and collective organizational performance.

TIP

It's a big mistake to treat support letters as an afterthought. Whether your project is a formal collaborative or simply provides complimentary services, support letters are an important part of any proposal. You must plan from the beginning to ensure that the letters are ready to attach to your proposal on submission day.

Letters of support can be drafted by the grantwriter or written by the director of the collaborative organization. They must be signed by the executive director or board chair of the nonprofit organization and printed on letterhead from that agency. You can choose to address the letter to the applicant organization or to the potential grantmaker.

Letters of Support

It is critical to have members of a collaborative send signed letters of support with the grant proposal. These letters must confirm the scope of work that each organization has committed to provide and ensure the grantor that the organization is engaged and ready to work when the grant is made.

Every foundation program officer you talk with can tell you of a time in which he or she received a grant proposal that touted an exciting and creative collaborative project but was missing letters of support from the collaborators. Some can even tell you that, when they went about their due diligence review of the proposal, they found that the partners were not consulted during the project design or the grantwriting process. They weren't asked for letters of support and knew little or nothing about the project under consideration.

In those cases, you can guess what happens: the foundation stops the grant review and sends an immediate decline letter to the proposing organization.

Remember, a grant proposal is like a bid and a grant is a contract. You cannot have a binding contract unless all the parties know and agree to its terms.

Sample letters of support follow:

Sample: Letter of Support

May 1, 2006

Chief of Police
Big City Police Department
Anystreet NW
Anytown, USA ZIP

Dear Chief:

The Community Mental Health and Substance Abuse Network of Anytown supports the BIG project and recognizes the importance of mental health and substance abuse services to serve the individuals participating in this program for former prostitutes. A collaborative effort was made over the past two years to provide support to the BIG social workers and their clients.

CMHSA agrees to provide clinical consultation and supervision to the BIG social workers. The supervision will be provided by a clinician with experience in assessing and treating substance abuse and/or mental health issues. We agree that by providing community based supervision for these staff, we may be able to improve coordination and access to other community services.

We look forward to working with you and your staff on this matter.

Sincerely,

Dr. Shrink
Executive Director

This letter is addressed to the applicant organization and comes from a collaborative agency—one that has a stake in the proposal and work plan.

The letter indicates that the mental health organization has been involved in the project for two years and supports the case for "stakeholder involvement."

The writer affirms that he or she understands the scope of work in the project plan and the reason that this agency was selected to provide the service.

Sample: Letter of Support

May 15, 2006

State Department of Community Health
Office of Drug Control Policy
Capital City, USA

Dear Mr. Grubbs:

The Suburban Police Department last year received nearly eight hundred calls for service from a local hotel on the border of Suburban and Big City. The hotel is known for renting rooms by the hour to prostitutes and johns.

The problem is so profound that we recently received a grant to allow us to assign one community police officer to the three-and-a-half blocks surrounding the hotel. The officer reports that he has made some contacts with the prostitutes and has tried to assist them in getting help; however, current support services do not appear responsive to the needs or lifestyles of prostitutes. For instance, one woman told the officer in January that she had an appointment for drug rehabilitation scheduled for April but lacked transportation to the site and had failed to reschedule.

The problems of prostitutes and prostitution are not bounded by jurisdictions. Both the chief of the Big City Police Department and I are convinced that prostitution is a problem that requires not only coordinated efforts on behalf of social service agencies but also coordinated law enforcement. The Suburban Police Department plans to link its Community Police Officer with BCPD's BIG program so that prostitutes working on this side of the city limits receive the same assistance as those working within Big City.

I strongly endorse BCPD's application for a Byrne grant to support the pilot BIG program and believe that, working together, our departments can develop effective practices to reduce prostitution and its negative effects on our communities.

Sincerely,

Chief Don Donaldson
Suburban Police Department

Margin notes:

This letter is going directly to the granting agency and is provided by the police chief of a nearby jurisdiction. His community is not providing services but plans to coordinate and assist the Big City effort. The suburban department will not be receiving grant funds to coordinate with the Big City.

The writer confirms the need and expands on what is related in the grant proposal with anecdotal evidence of need.

The commitment to coordinate and support does not indicate that the suburban department plans to be a part of the Big City's work plan (or the budget for the grant), but such support is attractive to funders since they understand that the target population will receive the services they pay for even if they cross city lines.

CHAPTER 5

Before You Write

Planning is critical to writing successful proposals. Be sure to schedule tasks and develop a framework and outline before you write.

Planning the Process

The steps involved in planning to write proactive and reactive grant proposals differ. Before the grantwriting can begin in a proactive grantseeking approach, you need to assess funding needs, identify potential funders, research their guidelines, meet with foundation staff if possible, and, sometimes, write letters of inquiry.

The planning process for reactive grantwriting includes reviewing the RFP, determining the fit between the nonprofit organization and its programs and those outlined in the request for proposals, and planning a comprehensive response that meets both the funder's requirements and the nonprofit's mission and goals.

Further, there is a process to writing grants that is both similar to and different from the process for most other types of writing. The writing process for either a reactive or a proactive proposal will include most of the components that follow:

- Gather information on the organization and its target population and/or the problem it is addressing. Study it so that it's familiar to you. Find out what industry-specific terms mean so you can explain them to others, if needed.
- Outline the grant proposal. Use every header in the instructions as your own and keep the headings in the specific order given.
- Develop a schedule for writing, review, completing forms, and securing signatures.
- Request letters of support from collaborators or draft an interagency agreement for review by all partners.
- Write as complete a first draft as possible.
- Meet with the design team or client to review the draft.
- Write a second draft.
- Recruit an outside reader, someone who is unfamiliar with the agency or project and who can let you know what they understand about the project and when they have questions.
- Complete the final edits based on input from readers and the design team. Ensure time for thorough review and approval by all collaborators.

- Complete all forms and schedule times for securing the signatures of required parties (usually the executive director and/or board chair of the nonprofit).
- Put the grant proposal packet together and make copies. Generally, you will send the original and a requisite number of copies (this always varies) to the funder and reserve one for each of the involved agencies and one for your own files.
- Ship, upload, or deliver the grant in whatever way needed to ensure that it arrives before the deadline.

Scheduling to Meet the Deadline

All RFPs have deadlines. They are absolute and final. If the proposal arrives an hour late, it will be thrown away or returned unread. Even if you submit electronically through grants.gov, you must have the document and attachments loaded and ready to submit before 5:00 p.m. eastern time on deadline day. The government provides a warning that if their website crashes on deadline day and you miss the submission time—even though it's not your fault—they will not consider your proposal. The government makes no guarantee that the electronic submission process will work at all hours, so you must plan ahead. There have been a few, rare exceptions in which extensions have been offered—in the aftermath of major disasters such as 9/11 or Hurricane Katrina, for example. These extensions were only available to people directly affected by such an event.

Foundation deadlines are as absolute as the individual foundation makes them. Some have no deadlines, but provide in their guidelines the dates they make grant decisions and request that you submit thirty to sixty days in advance of those dates. If a foundation offers a request for proposals, the deadline for submissions will be firm and late submissions will not be considered. Sometimes, if you have a good relationship with a local funder, they will give you a one- or two-day grace period on a submission when they already expect the proposal and you can provide a strong reason for not meeting the original date. If you don't allow yourself to get a reputation for late submissions, they will likely look more kindly on the rare instance that you must request an extension.

As a preliminary to writing a proposal, you should build a schedule so the rest of your team (clients, collaborating agencies, staff, etc.), knows what to expect and when they will be asked to contribute. Work backwards from the deadline to ensure ample time for reviews and crisis management. It's Murphy's Law that the tighter the deadline, the more apt you are to have a time-consuming crisis arise during the process.

Following is a sample schedule for a grant that is due approximately five weeks from the start date:

Sample: Grantwriting Schedule of Tasks

Due May 16

Date	Task	Responsibility
ASAP	Find out if state gets MHTSIG (Mental Health Transformation Infrastructure Grant) and EECM (Education Emergency Response & Crisis Mgmt). Must coordinate with them if they do. Find out how and what's expected.	School district
ASAP	Identify Juvenile Justice authority to participate in project	School district
4/11	Develop interagency agreement	Writer with team review
4/12	Gather and send to writer all data for needs section (e.g., # & type of problems in schools, # & type of problems seen by juvenile justice, annual report—basic numbers and test scores from district, # of suicides or other profound problems, disciplinary actions, anything else you can think of)	District, mental health provider, law enforcement partner
4/13 or 14	Team meeting, flesh out program plan	All
4/15	Develop draft project budget	Writer, partners, and district finance dept.
4/20	First draft completed	writer
By 4/24	Comments due to writer	Team
By 4/24	Draft all letters of support and submit to district office (district office to follow up on expected letters that have not arrived by this date)	Collaborators
By 5/1	Second draft for review; final budget review	Writer
By 5/5	Second draft sent to 3rd-party reader for review	
By 5/5	Comments due to writer. Full team meeting to discuss and resolve any issues	Team
By 5/8	Final draft; copies to partners for last review and approval.	Writer
By 5/12	Complete all cover sheets, forms and budget forms	Writer
5/13	Review by 3rd party reader	
By 5/14	All forms, interagency agreement, and support letters signed and ready. Compile all parts of proposal and make requisite number of copies.	Writer (team members to sign as appropriate. Documents held at district office 5/12-5/14)
5/15 or before	Overnight ship original and five copies of proposal.	Writer

Reviewing Drafts

It is critical that you build draft reviews into your grantwriting plan. As you write, you will have to make judgments about the work that needs to be done. Those who will be doing the project work must understand what you are assigning and agree that staff can and will carry out the work plan and that the budget for the work plan is reasonable. Further, if there are collaborating agencies involved in the project, they must all agree that their assignments and budget allocations are reasonable. These review sessions are not meant to be about correcting grammar and spelling errors in your draft, although you may receive such corrections during the meeting. Keep notes about these edits and try to keep the meeting focused on the big picture—the plan of work for the project, the proposed outcomes, and the budget allocations.

It's always helpful to get a "cold reader" before you finalize the grant. This person should be unfamiliar with the organization and project. Give him or her the RFP or guidelines and ask the person to read and score the grant proposal based on the criteria or rubric provided in the RFP. If possible, ask someone to be responsible for proofreading the final draft. Generally, the writer will have become too close to the work to do a good job of proofing, so it's better to assign this work to the cold reader or a willing team member.

The Framework

Following Directions

Guidelines and RFPs are really directions for what needs to be included in a grant proposal. You, as the grantwriter, must follow those directions exactly. It may be as simple as following the outline provided and presenting the information in the order requested in the outline. Alternately, the directions may be quite detailed, prescribing the font and size type you must use, page limits, margin sizes, line spacing, type of paper to use, use of bindings or staples, and much more. This is particularly critical when it comes to government grants. There are actually people sitting in government offices who measure your margins with a micrometer and look through papers to make sure that not even one line is single-spaced when the RFP says to double space. Picture those folks dancing with glee when they catch an error and can send your proposal straight to the reject pile.

Being disqualified for a technical error is heartbreaking, but there is a reason beyond that for following the directions. Government grant reviewers are given score sheets and a stack of proposals to review. If they have to work to find whether you've responded adequately to a section of the proposal, they will reduce your score. If they can't find the section because you've put it in the wrong place, they will assume that you missed it. On the very rare occasions that a section of a proposal is not applicable to your organization, you must still enter the headline and write "not applicable" or risk having the reviewers reduce your score because they assume that you chose not to respond.

Once again, you will find that foundations are more forgiving. It is not unheard of to have a program officer or grants manager call you if you forget to attach your IRS letter or board roster to a proposal or to ask you to submit additional narrative information after the deadline. Nonetheless, because it's a reflection of your professionalism, you should follow the outline provided in the foundation guidelines and deliver complete grant proposal packets by the submissions deadline.

Outlining Your Proposal

To ensure that you follow the directions, always outline the entire proposal (or paste it into a new document if the RFP or guidelines are electronic). Include the point value for each section so you can concentrate your narrative on the parts that the grantor deems most important. Make notes for yourself about special information you may need to gather or strategies you need to incorporate into the narrative. The outline on the next page was created from the RFP for the Safe Schools-Healthy Students program offered by the federal government:

Sample: Grant Proposal Narrative Outlines

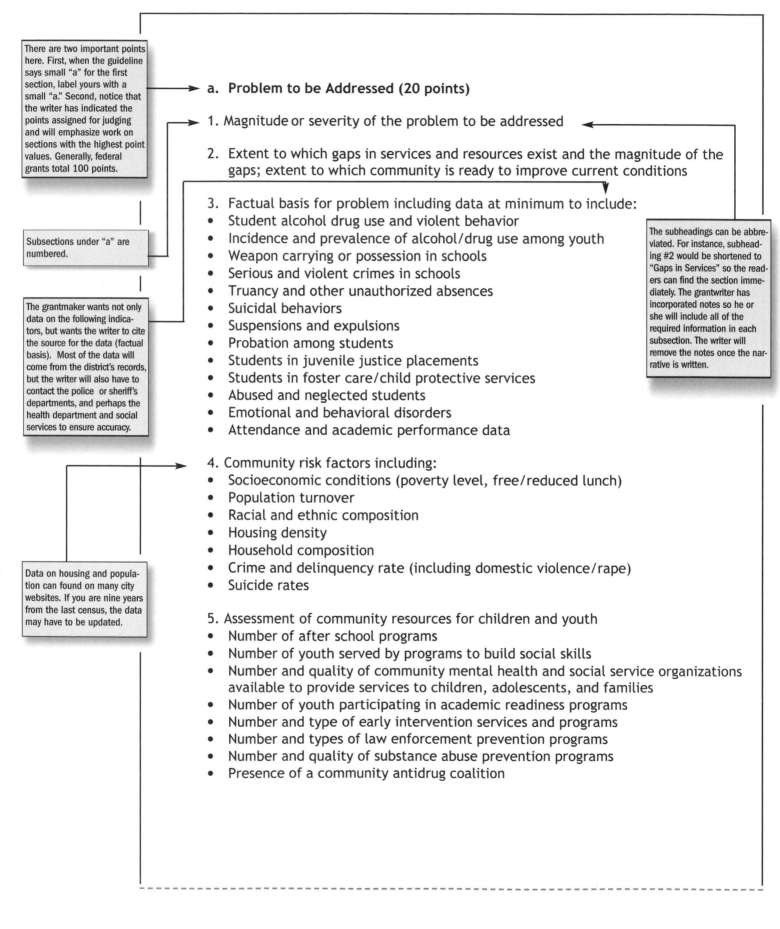

There are two important points here. First, when the guideline says small "a" for the first section, label yours with a small "a." Second, notice that the writer has indicated the points assigned for judging and will emphasize work on sections with the highest point values. Generally, federal grants total 100 points.

Subsections under "a" are numbered.

The grantmaker wants not only data on the following indicators, but wants the writer to cite the source for the data (factual basis). Most of the data will come from the district's records, but the writer will also have to contact the police or sheriff's departments, and perhaps the health department and social services to ensure accuracy.

Data on housing and population can found on many city websites. If you are nine years from the last census, the data may have to be updated.

a. Problem to be Addressed (20 points)

1. Magnitude or severity of the problem to be addressed

2. Extent to which gaps in services and resources exist and the magnitude of the gaps; extent to which community is ready to improve current conditions

3. Factual basis for problem including data at minimum to include:
   • Student alcohol drug use and violent behavior
   • Incidence and prevalence of alcohol/drug use among youth
   • Weapon carrying or possession in schools
   • Serious and violent crimes in schools
   • Truancy and other unauthorized absences
   • Suicidal behaviors
   • Suspensions and expulsions
   • Probation among students
   • Students in juvenile justice placements
   • Students in foster care/child protective services
   • Abused and neglected students
   • Emotional and behavioral disorders
   • Attendance and academic performance data

The subheadings can be abbreviated. For instance, subheading #2 would be shortened to "Gaps in Services" so the readers can find the section immediately. The grantwriter has incorporated notes so he or she will include all of the required information in each subsection. The writer will remove the notes once the narrative is written.

4. Community risk factors including:
   • Socioeconomic conditions (poverty level, free/reduced lunch)
   • Population turnover
   • Racial and ethnic composition
   • Housing density
   • Household composition
   • Crime and delinquency rate (including domestic violence/rape)
   • Suicide rates

5. Assessment of community resources for children and youth
   • Number of after school programs
   • Number of youth served by programs to build social skills
   • Number and quality of community mental health and social service organizations available to provide services to children, adolescents, and families
   • Number of youth participating in academic readiness programs
   • Number and type of early intervention services and programs
   • Number and types of law enforcement prevention programs
   • Number and quality of substance abuse prevention programs
   • Presence of a community antidrug coalition

b. **Goals and Objectives (10 pts.)** ◄──────────

> Goals and objectives most often are presented as a part of the work plan. In this case, they are separate sections of the proposal.

1. Measurable, definable, and attainable

2. Lead to healthy childhood development, positive mental health, safe, disciplined and alcohol- and drug-free learning environment

3. Measurable action steps to achieve goals

c. **Design of Proposed Strategy (30 points) (emphasize #9...ten points for it alone)** ◄────
   1. Represents comprehensive network that addresses, incorporates, and integrates all elements of the Initiative
   2. Intervention is appropriate to age and developmental levels, gender, and ethnic and cultural diversity of population
   3. Describes programs, activities, and services
   4. Linkage between activities and objectives
   5. Identify performance measures for short-term, intermediate, and long-term objectives
   6. Coordination with similar or related efforts and linkages with appropriate agencies and organizations (including community, state, and federal resources)
   7. Plan to collect data related to violence from a variety of sources such as mental health services, social services, schools, law enforcement, and juvenile justice
   8. Potential support after grant period ◄──────────
   9. Evidence-based research to support elements 2, 3, 4 ◄──────
   10. Ease of replication (documentation)
   11. Meets goals and objectives of the community's comprehensive plan

> The writer has looked at the scoring and inserts a reminder to emphasize #9, meaning that research that supports the design of the project should be included.

> The RFP requests information on sustaining the project after the grant period.

d. **Evaluation Plan (10 points)** ◄──────────

e. **Management and Organizational Capability (20 points)**

f. **Budget (10 points)**

> When the writer responds to 2, 3, and 4, he or she will have to cite research and source material that supports selection of the program model.

> There is less detail under the following three points. There are no subheadings, and the grantor provided little information for what to include, assuming that the points were understandable without specific instructions.

> Here the writer will emphasize the strength of the applicant organization and its history of managing large grants.

Common Grant Applications

Most foundations provide an outline of the grant proposal in their guidelines. Some say that they accept "common grant applications," which are generic applications developed by a group of foundations or various regional associations of grantmakers (RAs) for use by their foundation members. The RA will also provide grantseekers a list of the foundations that accept the common grant application.

The sample outline on page 57 comes from the Minnesota Regional Association of Grantmakers and is available, along with several other common grant applications for different regions, at the Foundation Center's website (www.fdncenter.org) or from individual RA web sites.

Sample: Foundations' Common Grant Application

Minnesota Common Grant Application Form
PROPOSAL NARRATIVE
Revised December 2000

Please use the following outline as a guide to your proposal narrative. Most grantmakers prefer up to five pages, excluding attachments, but be sure to ask each individual funder if they have page limitations or any additional requirements. Also, include a cover letter with your application that introduces your organization and proposal and makes the link between your proposal and the mission of the grantmaker to whom you are applying.

> Most foundations appreciate a cover letter like the one described here. Submissions to the federal government rarely require a cover letter.

I. ORGANIZATION INFORMATION

> Number section one with "I" and its subsections as "A," "B," "C," and so on.

A. Brief summary of organization history including the date your organization was established.

B. Brief summary of organization mission and goals.

> In this case, the organizational description is first. More often, however, this information comes last in the proposal.

C. Brief description of organization's current programs or activities, including any service statistics and strengths or accomplishments. Please highlight new or different activities, if any, for your organization.

D. Your organization's relationship with other organizations working with similar missions. What is your organization's role relative to these organizations?

> The RA suggests that you have communicated with the individual funder and learned of its specific requirements. If so, you should add points to your outline so you remember to include that information in your narrative.

E. Number of board members, full-time paid staff, part-time paid staff, and volunteers.

F. Additional information required by each individual funder.

II. PURPOSE OF GRANT

> There are two different formats included here, one for those seeking operational support and the other for those seeking program or project support. Some funders also have different narrative requirements for small and large grant requests, and some have different narrative requirements for capital projects than for program support.

- General operating proposals: Complete Section A below and move to Part III - Evaluation.
- All other proposals: Complete Section B below and move to Part III - Evaluation.

A. General Operating Proposals

1. The opportunity, challenges, issues, or need currently facing your organization.

2. Overall goal(s) of the organization for the funding period.

3. Objectives or ways in which you will meet the goal(s).

> Note that the foundation will want to make sure that if it provides operating support, your organization knows that it should be looking elsewhere for ongoing funding so you don't appear to become dependent on their support alone.

4. Activities and who will carry out these activities.

5. Time frame in which this will take place.

6. Long-term funding strategies.

7. Additional information regarding general operating proposals required by each individual funder.

If your organization were making an application for operations, you would delete section B from your outline; for a program proposal, delete section A, and begin your narrative with the heading, "B:.

All Other Proposal Types

1. Situation

    a. The opportunity, challenges, issue, or need and the community that your proposal addresses.

The foundations want to know who the stakeholders are and how you involved them in the program design.

    b. How that focus was determined and who was involved in that decision making process.

2. Activities

    a. Overall goal(s) regarding the situation described above.

    b. Objectives or ways in which you will meet the goal(s).

Sometimes the proposing organization will carve out a financial niche for each funder, asking one for an educational component, another for evaluation assistance, etc., in keeping with the different foundations' interests. However, if the foundation does not ask this question, let them choose how they want to support the organization.

    c. Specific activities for which you are seeking funding.

    d. Who will carry out those activities.

    e. Time frame in which this will take place.

    f. How the proposed activities will benefit the community in which they will occur, being as clear as you can about the impact you expect to have.

    g. Long-term strategies (if applicable) for sustaining this effort.

They are asking for planned outcomes.

III. EVALUATION

A. Please describe your criteria for success. What do you want to happen as a result of your activities?

B. How will you measure these changes?

C. Who will be involved in evaluating this work (staff, board, constituents, community, consultants)?

What will you do with your evaluation results?

The funders want to know if the evaluation will be ongoing and will be used to revise the project when it's not working, and whether a final evaluation will be shared with others.

ATTACHMENTS

Generally the following attachments are required:

1. Finances
   - ☐ Most recent financial statement from most recently completed fiscal year, audited if available, showing actual expenses. This information should include a balance sheet, a statement of activities (or statement of income and expenses) and functional expenses. Some funders require your most recent Form 990 tax return.
   - ☐ Organization budget for current year, including income and expenses.
   - ☐ Project budget, including income and expenses (if not a general operating proposal).
   - ☐ Additional funders. List names of corporations and foundations from which you are requesting funds, with dollar amounts, indicating which sources are committed or pending.

2. List of board members and their affiliations.

3. Brief description of key staff, including qualifications relevant to the specific request.

4. A copy of your current IRS determination letter (or your fiscal agent's) indicating tax-exempt 501(c)(3) status.

5. If applying to a corporate funder only: if an employee of this corporation is involved with your organization, list name and involvement.

Be sure to check each funder's guidelines and use discretion when sending additional attachments.

CHAPTER 6

The Five Core Components of Every Grant Proposal

Most grant proposals, whether reactive or proactive, contain five core sections:

- An abstract or executive summary
- The statement of need or problem
- The project description
- An evaluation plan
- A budget

Though there may be additional sections, it is critical that a serious grantwriter master these components—learn the expected content, where to find information, and how to craft a clear, concise response.

The first three of the five core components are illustrated with sections from one grant proposal. It was written in response to a federal RFP that seeks to support organizations classified by their states as local workforce development boards with experience providing skills development to help unemployed people find and retain jobs. The federal government further wants the applicants to use a portion of their grant award to regrant to small faith- and community-based organizations (FBCOs). Although this sample proposal would be classified as reactive, you will see many of the same key components in many foundation guidelines that you approach proactively.

Executive Summary or Abstract

The executive summary (also called an abstract) can range in length from one paragraph to one or two pages. Each funder will have specific length requirements for this section.

The executive summary is your reader's first impression of the work. To make a good impression and leave the reader eager to read the body of the proposal, craft this section carefully. Pull out the most salient information and highlight the strength of your project and organization. Tell the reader up front what you are going to do and what you want the grantmaker to do.

The primary points in the executive summary will succinctly cover the other four basic sections of the grant proposal. Discuss the need or problem, the approach you will take or other key information from the project description, how you'll evaluate the program, and what it will cost. You'll also introduce your organization, state your grant request, and discuss how the project meets the grantmaker's stated goals.

Always write the abstract or executive summary last. That way, you can pull information from the proposal narrative and highlight only the most critical items. It is presented here first because it is the first thing the grantmaker reads. A sample executive summary follows:

Sample: Executive Summary

The applicant is introduced. The statement additionally speaks directly to the federal grant focus on FBCOs.

A mandate contained in the RFP is that grant money cannot be used to assist sex offenders or violent criminals in becoming employed.

This statement summarizes the need for services.

The organization's status as a participant in a regional initiative is noted.

The grantee will be ESS, the local branch of the state's workforce development board, as these agencies are the only ones qualified to seek grant funding for this offering.

The number of individuals who can be served with grant funds and the total grant request from the budget is provided.

The writer briefly highlights key services from the project description and confirms that the model for service has been tried and proved successful.

Summarizes the planned outcomes and method of evaluation for the proposed project.

Briefly confirms grant eligibility requirement that ESS will regrant funds to relevant local faith- and community-based organizations reserving only a portion of the funds for oversight.

Executive Summary

The Recidivism Reduction Team (RRT) in Keller County, Midwest State, is a collaborative effort among more than 40 businesses, faith- and community-based organizations, local funders, law enforcement agencies, and probation offices. Its mission is to coordinate the many services, such as housing, mentoring, job training, job search and placement, transportation, emergency services, and/or drug/alcohol treatment that exoffenders need to adjust successfully to living in the local community. The existing collaborative was a key deciding factor for Keller County's selection as one of eight Midwest State Prisoner Reentry Initiative (MPRI) pilot projects to begin this fall in Midwest State.

On behalf of the RRT, Employment Service System (ESS) seeks a federal grant of $660,000 to address the needs of approximately 250 nonviolent/nonsexual offenders, parolees, and probationers in the coming year. Qualified RRT member agencies will receive portions of grant funds for providing employment training and placement and mentoring; remaining funds will be used to fund coordination of wrap-around support services and indirect costs for the lead agency.

The RRT is establishing an exoffender Employment Resource Center (ERC), which will provide a forum for collaboration among private businesses, nonprofits, faith-based organizations, and government organizations to coordinate the resources and services that promote self-sufficiency. The Center is modeled on a successful pilot workforce development initiative, The SEED, which has successfully moved dozens of individuals along progressively higher-pay and higher-skill career tracks in its two years of existence.

Performance outcomes for the initiative will include the examination of variables impacting the central issues of recidivism and community benefit. In the assessment of recidivism, such variables will include comparative analyses of 1) rearrest (broken down by crime severity and time-to-crime information), 2) completion of program training and/or treatment, and 3) compliance with parole rules. An examination of community benefit outcomes will include 1) employment (e.g., attendance, retention, and changes in earning), 2) housing (e.g., levels of transience and property ownership), 3) family dynamics (e.g., reconnection with children, payment of child support), and 4) payment of restitution.

Statement of Need or Problem

Once, the "statement of need" was just that. If your target population was poorer, had more illness or more school failure, or lived in more substandard housing than another program's target population, you could prove the greatest need for grant money. Those with the greatest need were often first to receive grant funding.

Today, this section is most often called the "statement of the problem," and it is where the proposing organization clearly identifies the problem as it exists in its community. In its analysis, the grantmaker will be looking for those programs that hold the most promise for addressing the problem.

It's a subtle but important distinction. Grantwriters who continue to approach grantwriting with the old thinking tend to write grants that sound like the organization is entitled to the money because it has the most need for money. Consequently, they often do not present the most creative or innovative solutions to problems.

> ### Six Things a Grantmaker Looks for During Proposal Analysis
>
> - Does the proposal fit within the funder's strategic objectives?
> - Is the plan of work reasonable given the proposed time frame, staffing, and budget?
> - Are the characteristics that are important to the funder, such as model of practice, demonstrated in the proposal?
> - Are the goals, objectives, and work plans aligned and clear?
> - Is the proposed work a good fit with the applicant's mission and expertise?
> - Does the proposal seek funding in an amount appropriate to the funder?

Dealing with Awkward Narrative Order

Can you imagine having a conversation with a stranger in which you spend an hour telling them why you plan to do something before you ever tell them what you're going to do? It seems odd, but that's exactly the order of information in most grant outlines. First you tell them why, then you tell them what.

Once you get used to it, it becomes a natural way to approach grantwriting. As discussed earlier, grantmaking follows certain trends. Years ago, it was appropriate to have the need statement come first because it was the most important criteria for judging which organizations and projects were most necessary to a community and which communities had the most need for funding. Today, the statement of need comes first precisely because identifying a problem is the first step in problem-solving models. The grantwriter must demonstrate a thorough understanding of the problem and later in the narrative connect the solution (project plan) back to the problem statement.

Grants often are given for the most pressing issues, but as funders have grown more sophisticated, they are responding to those issues with the most creative and need-responsive programs. In these cases, the depth of need, while still a consideration, becomes secondary to the strength and responsiveness of the program.

Introducing the Organization

To further complicate things, try to imagine telling both why—and what—before you tell the person listening who you are! Because the order of grant proposal sections listed in RFPs tends to leave organizational descriptions for the end of the proposal, it may appear that you should wait until the end to tell the reader about your organization. Savvy grantwriters get around this by introducing the organization in the first one or two sentences of the problem or need statement.

The introduction should be very brief and should be necessary to the statement of need or problem. For instance, you could provide a descriptive phrase as in the following: "The Central Media Group, a collaborative of public access radio, television, and print media, serves the population of Conroy, Nevada." In instances such as that illustrated by the sample proposal, because there are very few qualified applicants, it instead introduced the location of the applicant and the service population.

TIP
Do not use the need section to discuss the needs of the applicant organization. Use it to discuss the needs of the community in which the organization works.

Using Data

In many cases, the RFP will dictate what sorts of information the funder wants about the community in the statement of need, for instance, poverty rates, high school graduation rates, number of minority families, or percentages of people affected by a medical condition. In other cases, the funder leaves open which data you will present to make the case.

Context is important. If your community problem is a high incidence of poverty in an isolated neighborhood, your antipoverty project will, of course, focus on the isolated neighborhood. If you intend, instead, to pilot an anti-poverty effort in a place of need, but not necessarily the greatest need, you might select a more economically diverse neighborhood that promises a greater likelihood of success. In the latter case, you should also describe why you selected that neighborhood over another.

Data include both numbers (hard data) and testimony or input from participants (soft data). Hard data are not difficult to find. Census data are collected and updated every ten years and often can be updated from local sources. Practically every business and nonprofit organization now collects data. The difficulty comes in sifting through the wealth of information to find the right data to support your case.

Use the most current data you can find. If the data are critical to making your case, but are not current, consider having them updated by a local university or market research firm. With outdated data you risk appearing as if you are behind the curve, developing a response to a problem that may already have changed. For instance, in the early 1990s, the nation's unemployment rate was around 2 percent, and many nonprofits tried to help businesses recruit and retain scarce employees by offering training programs, mentoring initiatives, and similar development efforts. The 2000 census data still indicate a relatively low unemployment rate, but today's newspaper headlines tell an entirely new story. In the past five years, the unemployment rate has risen rapidly, particularly in communities that have a large number of manufacturers. Today, a nonprofit organization could best help these communities by designing programs to retrain displaced workers or to attract new employers to the region.

When you use sources outside your organization for data, you must cite those sources either with footnotes or within the narrative as in "according to the local health department…"

The primary purpose of the needs or problem statement is to lay the foundation for the case you are building for funding. Use data as your primary tool to state your case.

Sample: Statement of Need

Keller County, in southwestern Midwest State, has long been known as a manufacturing center, but today is becoming known for its growing rate of unemployment. In 2000, the County had a population of 574,335, approximately 35 percent (197,800) of whom live in the central City of Green River, Midwest State's second largest urban center. In the City, approximately 40 percent of the population is of a minority ethnicity, while in the County, ethnic minorities account for approximately 20 percent of the population. Poverty is also concentrated in the City: nearly 16 percent of City residents live in poverty, according to the 2000 Census.

The author introduces the community in which the project would be implemented and cites the resource (2000 Census) for data.

Since the last census, family incomes in Keller County have decreased overall. The jobless rate climbed from 2.2 percent in early 2000 to 8 percent in March 2004, exceeding the then-5.7 percent national jobless rate. With 2005 rates fluctuating around 8 percent, according to the Green River Press, Midwest State now has the highest unemployment rate in the U.S.

This statement is risky. If unemployment for average citizens is on the rise, there is apt to be even greater difficulty putting exoffenders into jobs.

The economic mainstay in Midwest State has always been manufacturing, but in the past few years, thousands of individuals have become unemployed. Part of the problem is that manufacturers are moving offshore, but a bigger issue is that those manufacturers that remain in the community require higher level skills—skills that few in the existing workforce have developed. Other growing economic sectors—healthcare, information technology, hospitality, and biomedicine—recruit from outside the community to find applicants that meet their requirements.

It's a good idea for grantwriters to subscribe to a local newspaper and clip articles that contain updated data about local problems.

This would be an argument for providing training to potential workers currently living in the area.

When the unemployment rate was low, employers recruited employees from nontraditional sources. Manufacturers seemed to have a near unending need for people they could train and struggled to find appropriate placements for individuals with disabilities, limited English proficiency, or long-term welfare dependence, Today, however, even individuals with strong employment histories search for jobs alongside those who face barriers to employment.

This example points to a community in economic transition.

Even before the recent and dramatic rise in unemployment, it was difficult to ameliorate the many barriers faced by those just released from jail or prison. They need jobs to build new lives, but when released often have little or no support from family or friends, no housing, transportation, work history, or healthcare; they have limited education and training and few workplace-appropriate skills. Often, they are addicted to drugs or alcohol, suffer from a mental illness, or have other difficulties socializing, and most are unaware of the "hidden rules" that Ruby Payne in "Understanding the Culture of Poverty," claims help middle-class working Americans obtain and retain employment. The Midwest State Department of Labor and Economic Growth (MDLEG) estimates that 75 percent of armed-services veterans seeking work through a one-stop have an offense on their records and have found no one resource that is tailored to their needs.

The author cites an expert source rather than the writing team's opinion.

This is state-level data that likely reflect the local situation.

"One-stop" is a term familiar to the proposal reader.

Currently, there are approximately 5,685 exoffenders in Keller County; approximately 4,500 of whom are on probation or parole. Another two thousand prisoners are released into the community each year. If past trends continue, more than 48 percent of those released this year will return to prison or jail within three years.

The data in this statement come from the probation department, a collaborator to the project. Nonetheless, the grantwriter should have cited the source.

For many years, several small and large faith- and community-based organizations grappled by themselves with the issues surrounding exoffender reentry. In 2002, they approached a

These individuals and organizations identified a community problem and have been working together for two years to solve it—long before the RFP came along. This fact demonstrates broad-based community support for the initiative, a factor that is critical to success. It also demonstrates that this collaborative is not developing programs simply to respond to RFPs.	community organization, The Convenor, to help them identify and bring together others to discuss shared problems and solutions. Together, more than forty organizations have formed the Recidivism Reduction Team, a collaborative effort among businesses, faith- and community-based organizations, the Workforce Development Board (WDB) local funders, law enforcement and probation, and the Midwest State Prisoner Reentry Initiative (MPRI), to develop a new system for assisting individuals in building law-abiding, self-sufficient lives after incarceration.

Economically, Keller County cannot afford to ignore the problems of exoffenders. Unemployment robs the County of income taxes; increased or repeat crimes cost victims, police, courts, and the larger community; and the cost of incarceration robs the community of scarce resources. The cost of incarceration exceeds the cost of assistance that might prevent it: residential substance abuse, for instance, costs an average $45 a day compared with $77 a day for prison.

These data are provided, again, by a collaborator to the project. The source should be cited.

Neither can Keller County afford to lose the potential contributions of many parolees and probationers. While entry-level manufacturing jobs are becoming more scarce, last year, healthcare providers sought to fill more than 1,000 entry- and mid-level jobs. Those manufacturers that have stayed in west Midwest State are seeking workers with specialized and/or technological skills—skills that could be developed, under the new Recidivism Reduction Team model, among prisoners while they are still incarcerated.

Project Description

The project description is the heart of your grant proposal. In it, you will describe the purpose of your project, present the strategies you have selected, and lay out your plan of work. The project plan comes from a team of organizational staff, and sometimes collaborators, who determine a course of action that addresses the problem or need and accept organizational responsibility for implementing the effort.

Responding to the Stated Need

Each section of the grant proposal narrative should build from the previous section and lay the groundwork for the next. The project description, then, must derive from the problem or need statement and set up the evaluation plan.

Make deliberate links throughout the narrative, describing the project plan with references to the statement of need or problem. Begin these statements with "because," as in "because there are x number of arrests in the pilot neighborhood for domestic assault, our nonprofit organization plans to collaborate with an organization that provides communication training, anger management, and dispute resolution workshops."

Strategies

Within the narrative, you will describe the strategies the organization (and its collaborators, if relevant) has selected to approach the problem or remediate the need. You will want to cite when the strategies are proven effective as the grantwriter in the sample does when he or she suggests that the exoffenders will use a process similar to the proven SEED model to develop job skills and move workers from entry-level jobs to more highly skilled and higher-paying jobs.

Alternately, the team may have designed an entirely new approach to an old problem. In this case, describe the strategies they plan to use, why they were selected, and the ways in which the approach can be replicated elsewhere if it proves successful. In the sample, if the SEED model did not exist, you might write, "EES has established a new model for moving individuals from unemployment to full employment in good-paying jobs. The model involves a series of three certification levels…" and go on to describe the method involved in employee certification as well as the employer interest in the model.

Following is a brief section of the project description from the sample grant proposal, which describes the methodology the organization will use to select subgrantees, the faith- and community-based organizations that will receive grants and report to ESS:

Sample: Project Description

Subgrantee Selection Methodology: ESS will use an RFP process to identify and select subawardees among faith-based and community organizations that will form the support system for ex-offenders.

In the RFP process, ESS will ensure that applicants meet eligibility requirements for small FBCOs . It will also, with assistance from the Recidivism Reduction Team, identify the services needed by exoffenders and solicit applications from at least two each of providers of mentoring, child care, transportation, housing, substance abuse treatment, job skills development, life skills, education, money management, and other needs. It will set forth the goals established in this proposal. The RFP will contain reporting requirements and deadlines, which will be reiterated and agreed on before a financial subaward is made.

Notice of the availability of RFPs will be mailed to members of the Recidivism Reduction Team and to other identified faith- and community-based organizations and will be published on ESS's website and in area newspapers. GRACE, an organization that provides services to thousands of area churches and synagogues, will announce availability of the RFP and its deadlines in its newsletters to congregations and through a Listserv.

ESS and other members of the Recidivism Reduction Team will hold two workshops to assist potential applicants with their responses to the RFP and to explain the reporting requirements and legal uses for federal dollars. They will continue to work with subawardees to ensure accurate and timely reporting throughout the grant period.

> This is an established model understandable to the reader.

> A larger organization like ESS cannot provide the one-to-one assistance that the smaller faith-based and community-based organizations can.

> The regrant awards will provide a mix of services that the applicant stated in the last section were needed by exoffenders.

> ESS will develop grants contracts with all subawardees to ensure that it can report to the federal government.

> This statement describes how faith- and community-based organizations will learn of the funding opportunity.

> Many small FBCOs have no experience applying for federal grants, so they will require assistance in this. The workshop must also explain reporting requirements so the FBCOs know exactly what they are committing to before they apply.

Components of a Project Plan

Most project plans include a narrative explanation of how the project will be implemented and several specific sections, which may be placed into a table, written as narrative, or sometimes a combination of both. They include, depending on the proposal instructions, some combination of the following:

- Goals of the project
- Objectives
- Planned outcomes
- Action steps
- Timelines
- Resources needed
- Evaluation indicators

Goals: What Will You Accomplish?

A goal is a broad statement about what you hope to accomplish with the project. It need not be measurable. The goal is not a restatement of the nonprofit organization's mission but should be a means of bringing the mission to life.

The purpose of your project should derive from your problem statement and be translated into a primary goal for the project. In the case of reactive grantseeking, you must have the same purpose as that stated in the RFP. When you are seeking grants proactively, the purpose of your project must further the mission and goals of the nonprofit applicant *and* match the programmatic goals of the potential funder. State the purpose of your project in your goal(s).

Objectives: Steps to Meeting the Goals

Objectives are the means by which the organization will meet its goal(s) for the project. Objectives must be measurable or provable. Though it goes against writing rules, you can think of your goal statements as sentences beginning with the infinitive "to" and objectives as beginning with the word "by," as in "to accomplish A by doing a, b, c, and d."

Objectives form the framework for your evaluation plan. You can and will be held accountable for each of your objectives whether or not your project achieves its goal or its outcome. Your evaluation plan will be easier to write if you spend time writing careful, understandable, measurable, and achievable objectives.

Outcomes: What Will Change?

Outcomes are statements that tell what will change as a result of your program. Outcomes must be stated as measurable, as in "the project will reduce recidivism by 50 percent."

Outcomes are most often used to describe changes in the participants or the environment. If you plan for outcomes, the project will generally be more successful as every contributor will have in mind the change that they are attempting to make.

Objectives and Outcomes— What's the Difference?

In general, objectives tell how many or how much. How many people will attend a seminar or participate in the project? If your objective is to have thirty people attend a seminar, you are successful if thirty or more attend.

But so what? What will they learn? How will their new knowledge change their behavior or habits or lives? The outcome statement answers the question, "So what?" An outcome of the project to help high school graduates prepare for good jobs would be that, when they leave school, they will go into employment or they'll stay in the community.

Following is a brief section of the project description from the sample grant, containing its goals, objectives, and outcomes:

Sample: Project Description

The overarching goal of ESS's proposed program is to deploy and build the collective resources of the Recidivism Reduction Team (RRT) in order to provide wrap-around services to exoffenders seeking self-sufficient living. ESS holds the following targets (objectives) for service development and delivery:

> The goal is a broad statement of purpose derived from the problem statement:

> Be sure that all objectives can be measured or proved through documentation.

- Identify at least fifty community organizations (approximately ten new organizations) and FBCOs involved in providing services for exoffenders and invite them to join the RRT.
- Ensure that all targeted services are available through at least one FBCO or other RRT member.

> The services referenced have been identified in the proposal narrative.

- Employ a full time contract administrator to assist FBCOs in applying for funds, implementing their work plans, and reporting their expenditures and outcomes.
- Working with the ERC, recruit at least eight new businesses and industries to the RRT by providing compelling case statements for hiring exoffenders.
- Working with the RRT members, recruit at least three hundred exoffenders to the Employment Resource Center.

> The grantmaker indicates in the RFP that it wishes the WDB applicants to carefully monitor the work of the FBCOs. It is appropriate, therefore, to make an objective of hiring a person to concentrate on this activity.

- Working with subaward FBCOs, assist at least 250 exoffenders in becoming employed and ensure that at least two hundred are employed for at least ninety days.
- Working with the ERC and FBCOs, ensure that at least fifty workers receive Level One certification before the end of the grant period. Further ensure that at least fifty workers advance to a higher wage/status job before the end of the grant period.
- Working with the ERC and FBCOs, ensure that at least twenty workers receive Level Two certification before the end of the grant period.

> The grantseeker expects that not all participants will be successful. They will recruit three hundred, help find employment for 250, and expect two hundred to continue employment. It is important to be realistic when assessing potential outcomes.

The planned outcome of ESS and the RRT's work is to reduce recidivism by one third in the eighteen months beginning July 1, 2005. By December 31, 2006, 32 percent or fewer of participating exoffenders will be reincarcerated.

> The outcome tells what will be different by the end of the grant period. It is more specific than the goal and must be measurable.

Action Steps: How Will You Achieve the Objectives?

Most goals have several objectives, and most objectives have several action steps. Action steps are the things that an organization will do in order to achieve its objective. While they may be written into the narrative description of the strategy, they may also be included and summarized within a timeline or a table of goals and objectives. Action steps, especially when incorporated into a timeline, help focus the nonprofit on what it needs to do next after the grant is made and it is ready to implement the project.

Timelines: When and Who?

Most funders request a timeline for implementing your project. Include in the timeline the specific steps you'll take to achieve the objectives (action steps), the deadline for accomplishing the steps, and the person or organization responsible for accomplishing each task.

The timeline must correspond to the time limitations of the grant. If you are funded for one year, the timeline must cover the entire year. If the proposal is for a project that will continue for more than one year, you should include a detailed timeline for year one and a less detailed project timeline for later years. A regular evaluation review should also be included in the timeline, As the project unfolds, the nonprofit should look regularly at the evaluation criteria to determine if they are on track or if something needs to be strengthened or changed.

The timeline that includes the action steps from the sample grant follows:

Sample: Timeline

Timeline must correspond to funding timeframe: eighteen months in this case.

These are the action steps.

The first step is to hire a staff person to oversee the regranting process and to supervise the subawardees.

These are the essential functions of the project and will have to be continuous in order to achieve the promised objectives.

The ERC will coordinate the employment component. Note that the ERC is not yet established as its development is one step in the timeline.

The timeline extends months from notice of funding.

This refers to Employment Service System, the applicant organization.

These internal steps indicate to the grantmaker that the applicant organization is led by an intergovernmental group. This goes back to the eligibility criteria for applicants.

This task will be accomplished by the Recidivism Reduction Team rather than by the applicant organization. However, the applicant (ESS) retains responsibility, in the grantmaker's view, for all components of the workplan, including those that are assigned to collaborating organizations.

Timeline: A timeline of activities for the eighteen-month project period follows:

Date	Task/Activity	Responsibility
Upon award notice	Write job description for contract administrator and post opening	ESS
Ongoing	• Recruit ex-offenders to participate • Recruit and train mentors • Recruit employers and FBCOs to RRT and Employer Resource Center (ERC) • Monthly meetings of sub-awardees	ESS & RRT members
July 1, 2005	Draft RFP for subawards and review with RRT members	ESS
July 30	Have RFP approved by governing board and WIB; release to prospective grantees	ESS
Aug. 1-15	Hold at least two workshops for RFP applicants	ESS, RRT MPR coordinator
August 30	Deadline for applications from potential sub-awardees	FBCOs
Sept. 15	Complete review of applications and select sub-awardees	ESS
Sept. 15-30	Hold pre-award conferences with all sub-awardees to ensure terms are understood and agreed to.	ESS, subawardees
September 30	Finalize and sign all subawardee contracts	ESS, subawardees
By October 1	Establish Employment Resource Center (ERC)	RRT coordinator
By October 1	Begin inreach in jails and prisons	RRT
July, 2006	Present Level One certification to 6-month employees	ERC
December, 2006	Present Level two certification to 12-month employees	ERC

Putting it All Together

Goals, objectives, outcomes, and action steps are related and can be placed into hierarchal order to express their relationship as the following outline illustrates.

Goal: Broad statement of purpose

Objective 1: measurable statement describing how the goal will be met

Action step 1.a.	Time frame	Responsibility
Action step 1.b.	Time frame	Responsibility
Action step 1.c.	Time frame	Responsibility

Objective 2:

Action step 2.a.	Time frame	Responsibility
Action step 2.b.	Time frame	Responsibility
Action step 2.c.	Time frame	Responsibility

Outcome: Describes what will be different as a result of achieving the objectives.

Sample Project Description Narrative

Tables illustrating goals, objectives, outcomes, and timelines are just a part of the project description. You must fully explain what you intend to do. In the sample grant, the overall approach was broken into several components, including developing business partners, making subgrants to FBCOs, providing inreach to individuals before they are released from jail or prison, and developing and implementing the employment model.

The following excerpt from the sample grant describes the resources and services that will be delivered under the terms of the grant proposal, an integral part of a narrative project description.

Sample: Project Description

Points to an existing and successful model that has worked to employ hard-to-place and hard-to-advance individuals.

Describes coordinating the small organizations into a systemic approach to helping exoffenders become self-supporting and successful.

Services The Recidivism Reduction Team (RRT) is establishing an Employment Resource Center (ERC) for exoffenders by July 2005. The Center will provide a forum for collaboration among private businesses, nonprofits, faith-based organizations, and government organizations to coordinate the resources and services that promote self-sufficiency. The Center is modeled on a successful pilot workforce development initiative, The SEED, which has successfully moved dozens of individuals along progressively higher-paying and higher-skill career tracks in its two years of existence.

Under the adapted SEED model, the ERC will identify small FBCOs (faith- and community-based organizations) to provide life skills, mentoring, housing (or transitional housing), tutoring, instruction in the hidden rules of the workplace, clothing, etc. The Team is recruiting businesses willing to hire and train exoffenders and to certify them as employable, based on skills and work habits, after six months of employment. This Level One certification is the exoffenders entrée into other employers' firms—where they can enter into more highly skilled work and receive higher wages. The exoffenders can receive three certifications, each linked to skill development or training such as Level One's QS 9000 or conflict resolution; Level Two's ergonomics, money management, or lean enterprise, and Level Three's home ownership or car purchase. A Level Three employer is one that hires skilled workers and pays commensurately. That employer is assured that its new hires have completed at least two years' employment with other participating companies and that the employee has demonstrated strong work habits and has mastered the skills necessary to work in advanced manufacturing or other skilled fields.

Throughout the certification process, the exoffenders will require support provided by small faith- and community-based organizations. This will ensure that the exoffenders remove the barriers to retaining and advancing in employment.

The existing Exodus program (contracted by ESS) provides case management, intake, and orientation to the Midwest State Works! system, assessment, job search and placement assistance, individual employment plans, career counseling, job skill development, job club (communication skills, conflict resolution, professional conduct, work habits, etc.), and individual counseling. New Hope receives funding from the Department of Corrections to provide intake and vocational assessment, employability skills development, cognitive behavioral therapy, job training, vocational case management, placement and retention services.

This describes existing resources and sets up the next paragraph that explains how gaps in existing services can be filled by small organizations that are funded by regrants.

Gaps in needed support for exoffenders will be filled by small FBCOs. Needed services include low-cost child care, transportation assistance (rides, bus passes, etc.), mentoring, substance abuse treatment (in- and outpatient), transitional and permanent housing, job training, soft skills development (as job club, above), education and/or tutoring, mental health and health/dental care.

TIP

Foundations, like governments, are challenged to account for the impact resulting from their grantmaking. With all the billions of dollars invested in communities, what has changed? Many have responded to the challenge by tightening their funding strategies. They still want to fund change and change agents, but they also look at the propensity for success—projects that follow proven models or proposed new models with promise for replication.

Evaluation Plan

The Language of Evaluators

Few grantwriters or nonprofit staff are professional evaluators, and most struggle a bit when it comes to writing an evaluation plan. It may seem a little technical, but all you need are analytical skills and an understanding of evaluation language.

A few words you'll need to know include:

- Baseline: The measure against which the evaluator will measure change; the current measure or status. Baseline measures are often described in the need or problem statement.
- Context: The environmental factors affecting a project and its chances of success.
- Formative: Evaluation of the implementation of a project (also called a process evaluation).
- Impacts: The ways in which the outcomes create societal change over time.
- Implementation: The plans and activities required to move the project from concept to reality.
- Indicator: An agreed-on measure of change. Indicators for determining whether or not a neighborhood has been improved through a project might be reduced arrests, increased housing prices, community participation at a neighborhood event, or cleaner streets.
- Inputs: The resources necessary to implement a project or take a logical step in the process.
- Logic Model: A flow chart that defines issues to be addressed and illustrates how inputs and actions interact to produce outcomes and impacts. (See chapter 7 for a sample logic model.)
- Longitudinal: A study of change over time, usually a year or longer.
- Outcomes: Measurable results of a project; the change in the environment or people who participate in the project.
- Outputs: The tangible products of activities; e.g., reports, programs, capital projects.
- Pre- and Post-: Measures status or numbers before and after an activity as in pre- and post-tests or pre- and post-surveys.
- Qualitative Evaluation: Measures the qualities within the project's objectives and/or outcomes. It is more concerned with an examination of processes, meanings, properties, or characteristics that are not easily quantified in terms of measurements. How well did people learn a topic? What are people's opinions of the project? What stories have they told? Qualitative evaluations collect soft data, that is, data that may be expressed in numbers, as in results from an opinion survey, that are based on experience and thought instead of on facts.
- Quantitative Evaluation: Measures quantity within project objectives or outcomes. It is more concerned with numerical data analysis. How many people attended? How many completed a class? How much are people earning? How much lower are blood sugar levels? Quantitative evaluations collect hard data, or the facts without interpretation.
- Summative: Evaluation of the outcomes of the project (also called an outcomes evaluation).

An evaluation should be designed so that it gets to the heart of the matter: how will you know if the organization has achieved its planned objectives? How will you know if there's an outcome or result from the project? What does the organization hope to learn from the project? How will it share what it learned so that others can replicate a successful project or take another path if a project has not achieved what it set out to achieve?

TIP

A good resource for a grant-related glossary is the Nonprofit Good Practice Guide from the Johnson Center for Philanthropy and Nonprofit Leadership at www.npgoodpractice.org.

You've probably heard the old saying that nothing you learn from is wasted. That's true of grant-funded programs, too. Even if a grant fails to achieve its goals and outcomes, when the grantor and grantee learn from the effort, it is not a failed grant. A grant fails only if the nonprofit organization fails to deliver on its objectives or fails to implement the project as it agreed to do in the grant contract.

Your work plan forms the basis for your evaluation plan. Look at your objectives and ask how you'll know if you've achieved them. How will you measure whether or not they've been achieved? Look too at your outcomes and ask how you'll know the results from your project. If you cannot determine a method to evaluate your success, you could consider consulting with a professional evaluator at a local university or research center, or you may just need to take a closer look at your work plan and ask yourself if the objectives and outcomes are truly measurable.

> ***TIP***
>
> In a nutshell, an evaluation should prove what you have accomplished and capture what you have learned during the project implementation.

Internal or Third-party Evaluation?

An internal evaluation is one performed by the nonprofit applicant; an external evaluation is one performed by a professional evaluator who is not on the staff of the applicant organization.

In the case of reactive grantseeking, the RFP will often dictate whether you use an internal or third-party evaluation, and sometimes a foundation grantmaker will want to learn something specific from your project and will ask for a third-party evaluation to capture those lessons. For instance, when a grantmaker is doing a cluster evaluation (a collective evaluation of similar projects) it might assign its own evaluator to your project.

When it is not predetermined, the format you select depends on what the organization wants to learn and needs to prove through the project. Even complex projects can be assessed internally when the questions and data necessary to evaluate success are straightforward and clear from the inception of the project.

You probably don't need an external evaluator to come in and tell you whether or not a project to teach non-English speaking residents how to balance their checkbooks was a success. You could design and carry out your own evaluation with pre- and post-tests of checkbook balancing skills, surveys of participant satisfaction, and/or self reports from participants regarding how many opened a checking account after the class.

Types of Third-party Evaluations

Third-party evaluators are experts that you should bring in when your project evaluation is mandated, when the evaluation is complex and/or lengthy, or when you are implementing a demonstration project designed to test a theory or service model.

Third-party evaluators can design and carry out the following types of evaluation studies:

- Scientific: Relies on quantifiable data with rigorous and replicable analytical methods.
- Experimental: Related to the scientific approach but is more rigorous; includes the use of a control group, double-blind studies, and/or longitudinal study over many years.
- Impressionistic: The most simple (and least expensive) evaluation; essentially an informed opinion provided by a knowledgeable observer. It does not include quantifiable data.
- Anthropological: Primarily uses extensive stakeholder interviews to capture important lessons.

Sample Evaluation Plan

In the sample grant proposal from ESS used throughout this chapter, the grantwriter merely reiterated the measurable objectives stated in the program description and used them as a plan for an internal evaluation process. This is possible when objectives are clearly measurable at the outset.

The sample that follows is from a different proposal and provides an example of a planned third-party evaluation. Note that the writer identifies the evaluator and provides a list of questions that the evaluator will address with a comprehensive approach to project evaluation.

When to Bring in an Evaluator

If you will be using an outside evaluator, involve him/her in the project as early as you can—during the project design process if possible. An evaluator can save your organization extra work, such as collecting unanticipated data, and help you establish procedures that keep the project on track and develop processes by which you can gauge progress and change direction if an activity is not yielding sufficient results.

Sample: Evaluation Plan

All Safe Schools-Healthy Students grant-funded projects will be evaluated by a professional under contract with the federal government. Each individual project must also have a local evaluator to help the grantee gather and report necessary data to the national evaluator and help the grantee stay on course for achieving the objectives of the project.

This line is taken verbatim from the RFP, which requires applicants to make a statement about their willingness to participate in a national evaluation.

The applicant has worked with an evaluator in the development of the proposal and this section and can describe her credentials as an evaluator.

Much of the project plan is built around increasing assets and reducing deficits. The Search Institute information, then, is critical to determining the effects of the community/student interaction aspects of the project plan.

In this case, to "operationalize" means to make the qualities measurable with indicators for progress.

KPS and its local partners to the project agree to participate in a national evaluation of the Safe Schools-Healthy Students Initiative, which will collect data on student risk indicators and outcomes of the programs implemented across sites on an annual basis. Further, our local evaluator will:

- help KPS strategically plan activities that will achieve the program goals and objectives;
- respond to the direction of the national evaluator to ensure the collection of high-quality core data;
- design and implement a process evaluation of the local program with assistance from the national evaluator to show results achieved, as appropriate;
- provide KPS with data that can be used to make adjustments in service delivery and improve the overall program; and
- design and conduct an outcome evaluation to determine whether an intervention is producing its intended effects.

Specifically, the local evaluator, Debra Vandyke of Green Valley State University's School of Public Administration and director of the Office of Community Research, will assist the partnership in all forms of interim, annual, and final evaluations and will teach staff how to gather and log appropriate data to track the progress of the KPS Safe Schools-Healthy Students Initiative and all KPS students. Academic and other appropriate data on all students will be gathered continuously by KPS staff as advised by the local evaluator and reviewed quarterly in reports to the project partners to ensure immediate responses to weaknesses in the plan.

The Search Institute survey of assets was given to Kanyon 7th, 9th, and 11th graders in 2003 and in 2005 and is scheduled to be given again in 2007. In this way, KPS is able to gather comparative data on cohorts of young people (i.e., the 9th graders tested in 2005 were mostly the same 7th graders tested in 2003). The asset survey responses for 2007 will provide a baseline measure of assets early in the proposed process of involving the entire community in building assets. A fourth survey (second during the grant period) in 2009 will measure the effect of the community process on the youth.

Healthy Communities-Healthy Youth, a program of the Search Institute, has compiled the following list of fifteen characteristics of Asset-building communities. The local evaluator will operationalize these characteristics to establish benchmark measures for the Kanyon community in the first year of the grant. By the end of the three-year process, KPS and its partners will have demonstrated progressive development in each of the characteristics listed:

1. All residents take personal responsibility for building assets in children and adolescents.
2. The community thinks and acts intergenerationally.
3. The community builds a consensus on values and boundaries, which it seeks to articulate and model.
4. All children and teenagers frequently engage in service to others.
5. Families are supported, educated, and equipped to elevate asset building to top priority.
6. All children and teenagers receive frequent expressions of support in both informal settings and in places where youth gather.
7. Neighborhoods are places of caring, support, and safety.
8. Schools—both elementary and secondary—mobilize to promote caring, clear boundaries, and sustained relationships with adults.
9. Businesses establish family-friendly policies and embrace asset-building principles for young employees.

10. Virtually all youth ten to eighteen years old are involved in one or more clubs, teams, or other youth-serving organizations that see building assets as central to their mission.
11. The media (print, radio, television) repeatedly communicate the community's vision, support local mobilization efforts, and provide forums for sharing innovative actions taken by individuals and organizations.
12. All professionals and volunteers who work with youth receive training in asset building.
13. Youth have opportunities to serve, lead, and make decisions.
14. Religious institutions mobilize their resources to build assets both within their own programs and in the community.
15. The community-wide commitment to asset building is long-term and sustained.

Within the first six months of the grant period, the local evaluator will design a plan for evaluating all components of the Initiative, including, but not necessarily limited to:

- a longitudinal study of the effect of 9th grade retreat camp on the students' high school careers and number of assets;
- a sample population study of at least thirty toddlers from high-risk families and the effect of parent training/counseling and educational intervention on development and/or kindergarten readiness;
- a comparison of all sociological and academic data gathered in each of the three years of the grant project indicating reductions in such things as truancy, expulsion, dropping ou disputes in schools, teen depression, teen pregnancy, experimentation with alcohol and drugs, juvenile crime, and reports of abuse/neglect, and increases in SEAP scores and academic performance against KPS' outcome standards;
- a sample study of at least ten high-risk teens identified as potentially violent and the effect of intervention services on behavior and attitude; and
- a comparative study on reported feelings of "safety" among students in each of the building levels: elementary, middle, freshman, and high school.

> While agreeing to participate in the national evaluation and identifying a local evaluator were important parts of the RFP, a full and formal evaluation plan is not necessary at this point. Nonetheless, the grantwriter needs to be sure that the right questions (i.e., what do we want to learn) get incorporated in the proposal planning

This formal evaluation plan, incorporating all components of the program and addressing the three priority objectives described above, will be submitted to the granting agencies for approval or further recommendations by the end of year one of the grant.

Budget and Budget Narrative

The grant proposal budget lays out the costs (expenses) and income (revenue) for the project you are proposing.

The budget is interdependent with the project description: that is, everything described in the plan of work that costs money must be called out within a line item in the budget, and everything that is in the budget within a line item must be described in the plan of work. The budget narrative (also called budget justification) should clarify what is included in each line item using language, where possible, that matches the project description narrative. For example, if you discuss hiring consultants in the project description, don't call them independent contractors in the budget narrative.

The grantwriter does not and should not have to develop a budget by him or herself. The grantwriter, however, should have input into the budget as he or she is the person most familiar with the plan of work. Work closely with the finance officer, the executive director, and any collaborators to compile a list of expenses and revenues that are necessary to implement and carry out the project.

Learning the Language

As in developing an evaluation plan, there is a vocabulary that the grantwriter needs to understand to read an RFP or guidelines and to write a budget narrative. Terms include:

- In-kind Support: Portions of the budget that are offered by the applicant in the form of existing products, space, equipment, and similar items.
- Multi-year Requests: Multi-year requests are grant proposals for more than one year. Such proposals must have a budget that spans the project period and provides annual breakdowns of costs.
- Indirect Costs/Charges: Costs a nonprofit can add to the budget to help cover the grant's management functions (e.g., the portion of accounting, supervision, etc. related to the project) are called indirect costs/charges. The federal government is now requiring that many of its applicants have a preapproved percentage for indirect costs. If not, they are disallowing this line item.

How Much Can You Request?

Most RFPs contain a ceiling amount on the grants they intend to fund—the amount that the grantor believes it will take to do the job as they envision it. For instance, an RFP may state that the government estimates making forty grants with a ceiling of $200,000 on each grant. A tip—this doesn't mean you should ask for precisely $200,000, but that you should ask for an amount of money less than or equal to $200,000 that will enable you to fulfill your obligations under the grant contract.

When you seek grants proactively, the amount you can ask for is far less clear. Examine annual reports, grantmaker guidelines, 990s, and directories of grantmakers for guidance on this. Look for the average amount of grant awards in the program area; find out if the foundation makes many small grants or a few large ones. If the documents do not yield the information you need, be sure to add a question about funding parameters into your preproposal interview.

There are other considerations in determining what you can request:

- Is the foundation willing to fund a project all by itself or does it want you to seek funding from a variety of sources? The latter situation is most often the case, and some foundations even put a formula on it, indicating, for instance, that you may not receive more than one-third or one-quarter of the necessary funds from them.

- How much is your organization willing to commit? Some grant opportunities require matching funds. In order to qualify for grant funds, the organization must commit a percentage of the project costs from its own coffers or other sources. And, whether a match is required or not, it always looks great to see that the nonprofit grantseeker is so committed to the project that they are also investing scarce dollars into its launch.

Meeting Funder Instructions for Budget Formats

Every proper budget has two sides: expenses and revenues. Only occasionally, as in the case of some RFPs that offer grants without matching dollars or other commitment by the nonprofit, can a grantwriter focus exclusively on the expense side of the budget. Every foundation funder wants to know both the expense line item allocation and who else is helping to fund the effort.

Some grantmakers will define in their guidelines what sorts of expenses are allowable and what sorts are not. For instance, lobbying is not an allowable activity or expense for private foundations. Some will not fund capital purchases, so you cannot, for instance, purchase a computer or a van to use in the project. Others will not fund operations, so you must make sure that nonproject-related overhead such as electricity, gas, rent, and similar expenses are allocated as in-kind contributions to the project and will come from the organizational budget to the project budget.

Further, some grantmakers require that you create a project budget that matches their format; others allow you to present it in your own organizational style. Whether the grantmaker requires you to use it, a sample format, if available, will tell you a lot about what a foundation considers acceptable expenses and what its funder is looking for in terms of revenues. The following is a sample budget format from a common grant application:

Return on Investment

The way a foundation might examine a project budget is similar to how a business might look for a return on its investment. On one hand, a project budget should be realistic; on the other hand, the total costs should appear reasonable. If, for example, the per-person service costs appear quite high, you should prepare to explain why and how this investment will pay dividends; for example, if the foundation invests $10,000 per person in prevention services, participants and their communities will benefit by saving $20,000 in treatment costs that they would otherwise incur without the investment in prevention.

Sample: Foundation Budget Form

GRANT BUDGET FORMAT

Below is a listing of standard budget items. Please provide the project budget in this format and in this order.

Fiscal years do not necessarily correspond with calendar years. They are any twelve-month period for which the nonprofit organization budgets its resources and audits its books.

A. Organizational fiscal year:_____

B. Time period this budget covers:_____

Enter the project duration (e.g., six months, one year, three years, etc.)

The funder recognizes that a capital budget has different line items than those provided for a project budget.

C. For a CAPITAL request, substitute your format for listing expenses. These will likely include: architectural fees, land/building purchase, construction costs, and campaign expenses.

D. Expenses: include a description and the total amount for each of the following budget categories, in this order:

You will add a description of each line item and an explanation for calculating the total in the budget narrative.

Use column one to indicate the portion of funds that will be requested of the grantmaker and column two to indicate expenses that will come from other sources (other grants, the organization itself, etc.).

Salaries	$_____	$_____
Payroll Taxes	$_____	$_____
Fringe Benefits	$_____	$_____
Consultants and Professional Fees	$_____	$_____
Insurance	$_____	$_____
Travel	$_____	$_____
Equipment	$_____	$_____
Supplies	$_____	$_____
Printing and Copying	$_____	$_____
Telephone and Fax	$_____	$_____
Postage and Delivery	$_____	$_____
Rent	$_____	$_____
Utilities	$_____	$_____
Maintenance	$_____	$_____
Evaluation	$_____	$_____
Marketing	$_____	$_____
Other (specify)	$_____	$_____
Total amount requested $_____	**Total project expenses** $_____	

The nonprofit applicant should have a formula for calculating the percentage of salary that is allocated to fringe benefits, such as health insurance, 401(k), and similar items.

When the project is complex enough to warrant an outside evaluator, this cost most often is charged to the grant.

These are fees specific to the project and will be spent under contracts with providers, so the nonprofit does not incur the ongoing expense of hiring a staff person and providing benefits. This option is often a good one for grant-funded programs because the organization can use expert services without a long-term commitment.

E. **Revenue**: include a **description and the total amount** for each of the following budget categories, in this order; please indicate which sources of revenue are committed and which are pending.

You would only include the amount that you know will be earned from this particular project, not the amount that the applicant earns annually from events or publications. These project revenue amounts would fall into the pending column, as they have not yet been earned.

	Committed	Pending
1. Grants/Contracts/Contributions		
Local Government	$_____	$_____
State Government	$_____	$_____
Federal Government	$_____	$_____
Foundations (itemize)	$_____	$_____
Corporations (itemize)	$_____	$_____
Individuals	$_____	$_____
Other (specify)	$_____	$_____
2. Earned Income		
Events	$_____	$_____
Publications and Products	$_____	$_____
3. Membership Income	$_____	$_____
4. In-Kind Support	$_____	$_____
5. Other (specify)	$_____	$_____
6. **Total Revenue**	$_____	$_____

Pending means that the organization has applied for funding but has not heard yet whether it received a grant or not. Committed funds, of course, are those that are confirmed, if not already in hand.

This is a project budget. All expenses and all revenues should describe only those items, spaces, people, and other resources necessary to achieve the objectives and outcomes in the project proposal. An organizational budget is a separate document that the applicant would attach to its grant proposal.

Balancing Your Budget

Just as with any budget, the expenses and revenues must match up. You cannot, for instance, raise $60,000 in grant funds to launch a project that will cost $20,000. Guessing at revenues can be even more difficult than estimating expenses. If you cannot be reasonably certain that you can raise the necessary funds to launch a project (from the pending grant and other grants, collaborators, program income, or organizational budget), take another look at the project costs to see if it would still be feasible to implement it with less money or wait to implement the project (holding any secured grant funds) until you raise all the necessary funding. Do not, under any circumstances, plan deficits by starting a $20,000 project with a $5,000 grant. Wait until you have raised the money you need to do it right. If that means you end up returning the $5,000 grant because you can't raise all the money you need, then that's what you must do.

Writing the Budget Narrative

The budget narrative (or justification) explains the calculation you used to figure costs and describes what is included in each line item (e.g., for the staffing costs line item: how many staff will be funded, for how long, and how much will they be paid?). Although the project description should have established why all costs are necessary to implement the grant, do not be afraid to add this detail to the budget narrative as well.

> ### Two Things Grantmakers Look for in Budgets
>
> Is there a correlation between the budget and the project description? For example, are there line items in the budget not mentioned in the project description and vice versa?
>
> Does the scope of the budget seem both reasonable and sufficient? Grantmakers don't want to risk over-funding a project; neither do they want to risk project failure because the budget did not adequately estimate critical costs.

The budget narrative should also cover the source of revenues and the calculations used to provide any estimates of revenue. For instance, if you expect that an event will generate $10,000 that you can use to support a project, you should say that you can safely estimate a $10,000 revenue because in years past that event has always raised at least that amount.

The following sample budget narrative comes from the ESS grant proposal used as a sample throughout this chapter. Although the grantseeker was not required to produce income or match funding, it does have contributions from other sources to dedicate to the project.

Sample: Budget Narrative

Headings in the justification should correspond to the headings in the line item budget.

The state funding for additional personnel is attributed as an in-kind contribution to the overall project costs.

Some funders require that their grantees travel to a conference of others funded for the same project and that the cost of travel be included in the budget.

When you do not have a fixed cost, estimate the cost and say that it's an estimate.

This line item is not fully described, rather it's implied that supplies include paper, ink, pens, etc.

This statement reiterates the services for which ESS will contract with FBCOs to provide.

Indirect costs contribute to the overall costs of operating ESS.

The applicant will use $10,000 of the grant award to contract with an auditor and to contract with people to provide a grantseekers workshop to local FBCOs. The remainder of grant funds must, under federal mandate, be provided as regrants to FBCOs.

Budget Justification

Personnel: ESS requests salaries for 1-FTE contract administrator ($32,000 annually x 18 months) for $48,000, and .5-FTE supervisor at $20,000 annually for 18 months or $30,000. Total line item requested of federal grant funds is $78,000. The state of Midwest contributes a $60,000 annual employee under the MPRI program as the RRT coordinator. A $90,000 salary is credited as a State allocation for the 18 months of the federal project.

Fringe Benefits: ESS estimates benefits as 30 percent of salaries. For 18 months' employment, this includes $14,500 in fringe benefits for the contract administrator and $10,000 for the supervisor.

Travel: Travel is estimated at $2,500 to cover mileage for in-reach services at prisons and jails, and to cover travel to at least one conference on reentry programs.

Equipment: Equipment is estimated at $3,000 to cover the cost of computer and office furniture for the new hire, contract administrator.

Supplies: Estimated cost of $2,000 for supplies directly related to the project.

Contractual: This line item includes $5,000 for an audit of grant funds and expenditures; $5,000 for training for FBCOs before and after the RFP process to determine subawardees, and $350,000 (70 percent of grant funds) to be subawarded to small faith-based and community organizations. Subawards will be made to organizations that provide mentoring, case management, life skills training, job training, substance abuse treatment, and/or behavioral health.

Indirect: ESS requests $25,000 in indirect charges (approximately 5 percent of grant funds).

CHAPTER 7
Beyond the Basics

Though the five core components described in Chapter 6 are required in most grant proposals, grantmakers can and do often ask for more information. The sections in this chapter describe the most frequently encountered requests for additional narrative information:

- Collaboration/partnership agencies and their roles
- Interagency agreements
- Staffing qualifications
- Management plans
- Similar projects/agencies
- Constituent involvement
- Review of literature
- Sustainability plans
- Organizational history
- Logic models

Collaboration/Partnership Agencies and Their Roles

A section on collaborations or partner agencies is always a part of RFPs that mandate a collaborative project and is often a part of grantmaker guidelines. Thus, any time you collaborate with another organization, you should describe that organization, its mission, and the services it will provide to the project.

Grantmakers value collaboratives, but not those convened for convenience sake. The collaborative should make sense—the two (or more) organizations that work together should bring diverse skills and abilities. Their shared expertise should strengthen the program design and improve its chances of success. For instance, in the Safe Schools-Healthy Students proposal in the previous chapter, the school district is using two very different mental health services. Were they not different, the mental health service would be redundant, fiscally irresponsible, and confusing for participants.

To write this section well, gather brochures of the different collaborating organizations to describe their history and capacity. You should also interview a staff member from each collaborating organization and ask them to describe four reasons or benefits they expect from being part of the project. Their roles in the project should be clear in the project description section. You might also consider using this section to discuss how the different organizations will work together to form a whole from the sum of their parts.

Sample: Collaborative Organizations and Their Roles

This statement was written to a local grantmaker. If you were describing a collaborative to a grantmaker who is unfamiliar with your community, it would be a good idea to add more about the longevity of each of the collaborating agencies, their capacity to deliver on the work plan, and to highlight some of their achievements.

This passage discusses the necessity of each collaborator and the role it plays in the project.

FTE is a standard abbreviation for "full time equivalent."

The strength and innovation of the "Get the Lead Out!" initiative lies in three things: concentrating efforts to eradicate lead hazards in one area of the city, ensuring a data-driven evaluation and study, and collaboration. The collaboration crosses public/private sectors; nonprofit/for-profit sectors and includes health organizations, higher education institutions, home rehabilitation contractors, and advocates for rental property owners, children, environmental justice, and racial justice.

Each participant makes a unique contribution to the project. Housing Fix-It Services, with its depth of experience in home renovations for low-income individuals and families will manage the CLEARCorps function. The County Health Department and the CATCCH Project of Major Hospital will collect and analyze data obtained from the project. Further, the Health Department plans to contribute .75-FTE Public Health Nurse to manage the blood-lead testing of children from the Pilot Area and will provide a .25-FTE Environmental Health Officer. The City Housing Rehabilitation Department will continue providing inspection services, development of rehabilitation specifications, and funding of rehabilitation by private contractors. The City Office of Children and Families will provide awareness outreach and education as a part of its "Safe Homes-Safe Kids" project within the Pilot Area. University School of Nursing intends to work with the County Public Health Nurse to establish referral sources and a continuing care component for children in the Pilot Area. The Community Leadership Initiative, the applicant for these grant funds, will serve as project coordinator, employer of record for project staff (other than CLEARCorps), and fiduciary for project funds other than LISC and CLEARCorps-USA.

This collaboration is open-ended and will undoubtedly expand. Early in May, a local congregation began a dialogue with Get the Lead Out! about providing support services to parents of children with lead poisoning in the Pilot Area. The County FIA and Regional 4-C are new participants in the past month.

Interagency Agreements

Federal and state governments are increasingly requesting interagency agreements among collaborating organizations, particularly when the collaboration is a requirement for funding. Interagency agreements are formal documents similar to contracts, though they are not reviewed by an attorney before submitting them with a grant proposal. Like management plans, the agreement should outline the manner in which the organizations will work together, how they will resolve disputes, communication among the organizations, and which will be responsible for oversight of grant funds and staff. All members of the collaborative should read and sign the interagency agreement before it is submitted.

The following sample was attached to the same proposal that illustrates management plans in this chapter. The two are similar, but the interagency agreement is a formal document that ensures that all the collaborating agencies understand the goals of the project and agree to abide by rules for operating that they have developed jointly.

Sample: Interagency Agreement

The goal of the KPS Safe Schools-Healthy Students Initiative is to create a school and community environment that leads to healthy early childhood development, promotes positive mental health among young people, and ensures that all KPS school buildings are alcohol- drug- and violence-free safe havens of learning for all students. Toward this end, the proposers hold the following objectives:

1. Increase the number of assets and decrease the number of deficits among KPS students in the Search Institute Survey (surveyed every two years in 7th, 9th and 11th grades).
2. Increase depth and availability of mental health counseling services in the schools and community. Increase feeling of safety in school and community among all students as self reported on student surveys. (Actions are inter-related.)
3. Improve academic/developmental performance for all students as measured on the SEAP test, kindergarten entrance tests, grade reports, or other standardized tests.

Kanyon Public Schools will be responsible for dispersing funds to other partners in the project and for filing progress and financial reports with the granting agencies. Kanyon Public Schools will be the fiscal agent for the grant monies, which will be held in a separate account and administered by the Finance Director, Greg Newman. All partners will be paid in units of service (e.g., weeks of camp, number of workshops) or FTE in the case of a social worker and mental health counselor provided by Archer Circle.

The District will hire, employ, and supervise the work of the 1-FTE Volunteer Coordinator, 1-FTE Student Service Administrator, 2-FTE Social Worker/Mental Health professionals, and .5-FTE support staff, and will confer with partners regarding performance of its own staff and the staff of other partners to the Initiative.

Partners will retain the responsibility for supervising their own staff, but will establish a mutually agreed-on process for evaluating staff performance on the project and for addressing employment or performance issues among all project staff. Kanyon Public Schools as lead agency will have final authority over such personnel issues relating to the project if they are not resolved within the administrative team to every partner's satisfaction.

The District will ensure maintenance of all equipment purchased for the Initiative and will retain such equipment at the end of the project. The District will be responsible for fulfilling contractual obligations with any consultants hired by the partnership, including consultancies from the partner organizations.

The School District will coordinate the gathering of data and, with the assistance of the local evaluator, the compilation of data relevant to the project at least quarterly. All other partners to the project will cooperate with each other in the gathering of data and in the development and implementation of action plans to address slow progress.

Any personal disagreements among or between the partners or any two partners shall first be brought to the attention of the administrative team, composed of members of all partner agencies and any subsequent partners to the effort. If the team cannot arbitrate an agreement between individuals, the matter will be referred to the Superintendent of Kanyon Public Schools for final decision making. Any disputes between the School District and any member of the partnership, except those regarding dispersal of grant funds, will be referred to a third-party facilitator for discussion and settled by majority vote of all partners. Dispersal of grant funds is the sole responsibility of the Kanyon Public Schools and is not subject to partner control. Should a partner suspect financial impropriety, he or she must submit that concern in writing to the full

This provides an alternative for a collaborating agency to dispute the lead agency's handling of finances.

partnership and, if it is not resolved to the partners' satisfaction, to the national evaluator and/or granting agencies for final decision making.

All members of the administrative team (Directors of partner organizations, Superintendent of Schools, and other staff as requested) will meet quarterly to review progress reports, discuss potential improvements, and finalize future plans for service delivery.

All partners must sign the interagency agreement. Their signatures indicate that they have jointly planned the project and agree to the terms that will be in the grant agreement.

Monica Jones
KPS Superintendent

Ron Meyer
Kanyon Chief of Police

John Deacon
CEO, Archer Circle

This narrative was written by the leader of Archer Circle both because it was a requirement of the grantor and because it further assured his understanding of the proposed project.

Agreement for Mental Health Services

Kanyon Public Schools and Archer Circle Corporation mutually and individually agree to the following terms and conditions with respect to the KPS Safe Schools-Healthy Students Initiative.

KPS school staff and/or mental health care providers will refer all students and/or families requiring mental health evaluation/care to the KPS mental health liaison, who will in turn refer the student/family to Archer Circle staff for student assessment. The student assessment plan will form the basis for an individual/family mental health care plan that incorporates all necessary services for the student and/or family and the provider (Archer Circle or a community agency). Archer Circle staff will ensure appropriate referral and follow up with all community agencies involved with the family. The KPS mental health liaison will participate on the case planning team and ensure, on behalf of the schools, access, transportation, and payment for all mental health services provided to the student/family.

This statement describes the way the two organizations will work together with the same population

KPS and Archer Circle shall individually retain supervisory responsibilities for their mutual staff and will meet at least quarterly as an administrative team to review the process and personnel. The two organizations will draft and adopt a mutually agreeable staff evaluation process and form for all mental health providers to the program.

In addition, under the terms of the agreement to perform in this project, Archer Circle will provide at the agreed-on cost:

Archer Circle has seen the budget and is now stating in writing what services the district will purchase with the grant funds allocated. Later, if Archer Circle is asked to do more or to provide other services, it can make the case for additional funding, which would come from the school district's general budget. If it came from grant funds, it would have to be preapproved by the grantmaker.

- Early identification and outreach to families of infants and toddlers to include assessment of infant/toddler needs based on developmental measures, development and/or parent training assistance, and coordination of services and referral to systems and/or appropriate providers.
- Assignment and supervision of trained mentors or parent aides for at-risk parents; aides will assist in skill building, positive role modeling, and will build relationships with new or at-risk parents.
- Substance abuse counseling programs in the schools and for families in the community; family intervention and mental health counseling; case management for school and home-based services, and violence intervention mental health services.
- Social work consultation with school representatives in all buildings, participate in child-study team, troubleshoot, coordinate community services provided to families, and provide assessment, referral, and follow up.

- Treatment groups and psycho-educational groups on substance abuse prevention, early intervention, violence prevention, self esteem, sexual restraint, etc.; participation in first-time offender treatment plan; in-services for teachers on mental health topics.

KPS' mental health liaison will be responsible for coordinating all services provided in the schools by Archer Circle and for ensuring that services are provided equitably to all students and/or families as needed.

_____   _____

Monica Jones   John Deacon
KPS Superintendent   CEO, Archer Circle

> The third collaborator, the police department, is not a party to this separate agreement between the district and the mental health service provider.

Staff Qualifications

Highlighting the qualifications of nonprofit leaders is especially critical when writing a proposal to a non-local grantmaker. If you are both grantwriter and leader of one of the applicant organizations, approach this as you might a brief resume for you and key staff members. If you are writing this section on behalf of others, ask for their resumes and take highlights from those documents to construct the section. You might also interview the individual leaders to expand on points you want to make about their qualities and qualifications. While you should not inflate people's experience or expertise, you cannot be modest either. Leaders who have passion and commitment to the mission of their organization help the organization weather difficulties, which is an especially important quality when launching a new project.

When you are proposing a new project and plan to hire staff to fill leadership positions, the applicant organization should prepare a job description. Use that job description as the basis for your description of the responsibilities and qualifications the organization will look for in its new employee.

Sample: Staff Qualifications

The name has been changed.

This executive director is a nationally recognized expert in the field of community media, a selling point that may provide the grantmaker a greater assurance of the project's success. In fact, when this grant proposal was funded, the only condition was that the grantmaker wanted to be notified if the leader left the organization before completing the project implementation.

This statement provides some indication that the organization has staff capacity to implement the proposed project.

It is important to discuss the racial/ethnic composition of staff, especially if the target population is ethnically diverse.

This passage briefly defines job responsibilities for a person not yet hired.

Often, you are asked to describe the person who will lead the project long before they are hired. In this case, the writer should have better defined the educational and experiential qualifications the organization would look for when hiring its project coordinator.

Technology Services is a part of the applicant organization.

Dan Kennedy is executive director of the Community Media Center (CMC), which oversees the operations of all CMC affiliates and programs. Kennedy was a founder of CMC and has been with the organization since 1981. He has been named by the Green River Jaycees as one of the top five leaders in the City and in the State, has been a guest on such national television programs as *Good Morning America*, and has published hundreds of articles on community media, free speech, and/or democratic principles. Kennedy has been keynote speaker at several national and international symposiums and has traveled throughout the world advising third-world nations on issues surrounding democracy and the media. He has worked as a juror for the National Arts Technology Exhibit and has participated in the NEA Open Studio Arts and Internet Project, the Arts Integration Team for Local Botanical Gardens and the Arts Integration Team for Neighborhood Arts Academy.

The CMC employs ten full-time staff, three of whom are racial minority; three staff members are women. Its Board of Directors is also composed of diverse individuals: ten are majority race; two members are minority; three members are women. The CMC has a written and understood policy for hiring individuals who have traditionally been underrepresented in the sector. Its personnel policy states: "CMC provides equal opportunity to all applicants without regard to race, color, religion, age, sex, physical or mental disability, national origin, marital status, sexual orientation, or any other legally protected status. In addition to complying with the letter and spirit of this policy, CMC practices policies of recruiting, hiring, training, management development, promotion, and compensation based only on an equal opportunity basis."

The Project will be staffed by one full-time project coordinator and two assistants. Equipment repair and linkages will be maintained by Technology Services, which has a staff of two. The project coordinator will be responsible for scheduling the training van's stops and visits, for developing curricula and deploying it to the Web, for marketing the services available from the Project with other local nonprofit organizations, particularly those serving at-risk populations, and for reporting progress toward goals to the Executive Director and the CMC Board of Directors. This person is not yet hired. The CMC will make every effort to recruit a minority and/or woman for the project coordinator position. At least one of the Project assistants, both of whom will work most closely with program participants, will be a person of color.

Management Plans

Management plans describe the existing structure of an organization and responsibility assignments; in other words, a narrative and detailed organizational chart. If you are proposing a collaborative project, it also describes the way the organizations will work together, who will manage staff members, and who will manage the finances and make payments to the others. A management plan can also include information about project implementation (a timeline with responsibilities defined), and an organizational reporting chart.

Sample: Management Plan

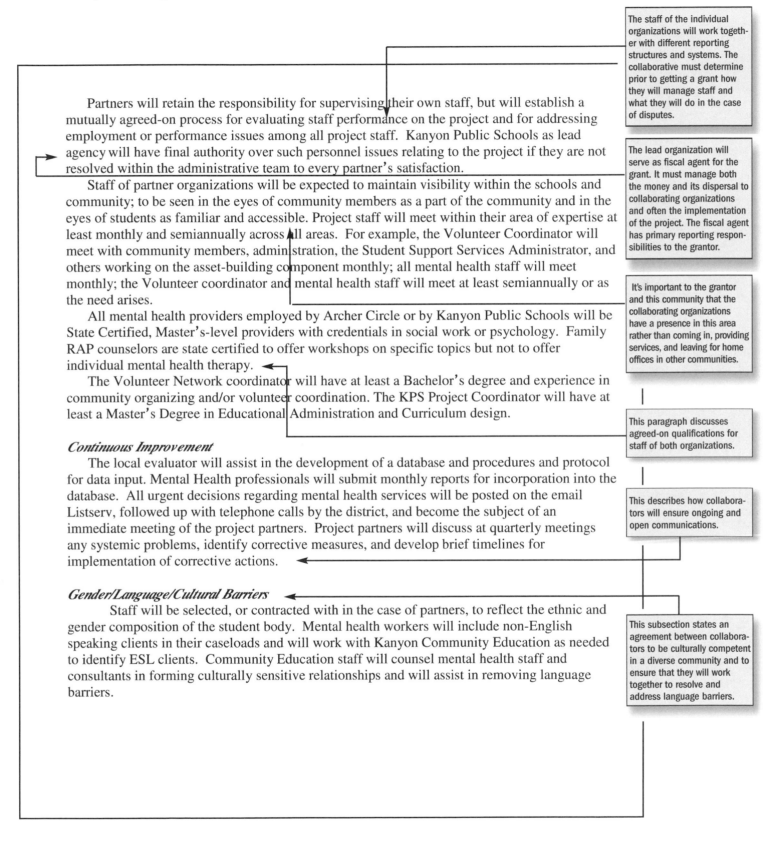

Partners will retain the responsibility for supervising their own staff, but will establish a mutually agreed-on process for evaluating staff performance on the project and for addressing employment or performance issues among all project staff. Kanyon Public Schools as lead agency will have final authority over such personnel issues relating to the project if they are not resolved within the administrative team to every partner's satisfaction.

The staff of the individual organizations will work together with different reporting structures and systems. The collaborative must determine prior to getting a grant how they will manage staff and what they will do in the case of disputes.

Staff of partner organizations will be expected to maintain visibility within the schools and community; to be seen in the eyes of community members as a part of the community and in the eyes of students as familiar and accessible. Project staff will meet within their area of expertise at least monthly and semiannually across all areas. For example, the Volunteer Coordinator will meet with community members, administration, the Student Support Services Administrator, and others working on the asset-building component monthly; all mental health staff will meet monthly; the Volunteer coordinator and mental health staff will meet at least semiannually or as the need arises.

The lead organization will serve as fiscal agent for the grant. It must manage both the money and its dispersal to collaborating organizations and often the implementation of the project. The fiscal agent has primary reporting responsibilities to the grantor.

All mental health providers employed by Archer Circle or by Kanyon Public Schools will be State Certified, Master's-level providers with credentials in social work or psychology. Family RAP counselors are state certified to offer workshops on specific topics but not to offer individual mental health therapy.

The Volunteer Network coordinator will have at least a Bachelor's degree and experience in community organizing and/or volunteer coordination. The KPS Project Coordinator will have at least a Master's Degree in Educational Administration and Curriculum design.

It's important to the grantor and this community that the collaborating organizations have a presence in this area rather than coming in, providing services, and leaving for home offices in other communities.

Continuous Improvement

The local evaluator will assist in the development of a database and procedures and protocol for data input. Mental Health professionals will submit monthly reports for incorporation into the database. All urgent decisions regarding mental health services will be posted on the email Listserv, followed up with telephone calls by the district, and become the subject of an immediate meeting of the project partners. Project partners will discuss at quarterly meetings any systemic problems, identify corrective measures, and develop brief timelines for implementation of corrective actions.

This paragraph discusses agreed-on qualifications for staff of both organizations.

This describes how collaborators will ensure ongoing and open communications.

Gender/Language/Cultural Barriers

Staff will be selected, or contracted with in the case of partners, to reflect the ethnic and gender composition of the student body. Mental health workers will include non-English speaking clients in their caseloads and will work with Kanyon Community Education as needed to identify ESL clients. Community Education staff will counsel mental health staff and consultants in forming culturally sensitive relationships and will assist in removing language barriers.

This subsection states an agreement between collaborators to be culturally competent in a diverse community and to ensure that they will work together to resolve and address language barriers.

Similar Programs/Agencies

In many communities, several organizations offer similar services and/or target the same population. In the latter case, grantmakers prefer to see collaboration—or at the very least, cooperation—among service providers working with the same population. In fact, it's likely that the population would prefer not to have three or more different staff people from different organizations to work with.

Working in the same community with another organization that provides similar services can be harmful to the grantseeking efforts of both, as this appears to be duplication. For instance, many cities have numerous summer camp programs for core-city children. They tout the advantages of getting children out of the hot and sometimes dangerous city and into nature for three days or a week, and they put different emphases on their various strengths: some are faith-based, some provide education or conservation training, others include challenge courses, and still others provide mentors to keep kids from getting involved in illegal activities at home. While each has its own value, think about how you would feel if you were paying taxes to support several camps that were providing similar services to similar and sometimes identical populations. That's the way grantmakers may feel too—torn between selecting one good program over another good program, yet determined that they cannot and should not attempt to support them all.

> ### Duplication
>
> Duplication of services is a red flag for many grantmakers. While exact duplication is rare, it is often difficult for the grant reviewer to discern differences among service providers. The worst case is when a grantmaker receives multiple proposals promising what appears to be the same set of services in the same area. Avoid this situation by describing the service landscape and your organization's place within it.

If your organization could be seen as having duplicate services, you must use this section of the proposal to highlight your differences from them and to underscore your organizational strengths. Do not ignore the fact that there is competition, but don't dwell on it, either. You don't want the grantmaker to assume that you don't even know about other organizations doing similar work. It's best if leadership from competing organizations have discussed similar problems and possible collaboration. If they have, report reasons why they have determined that collaboration is not a viable option in this case.

Sample: Similar Programs/Agencies

In the first sample, the agency is one-of-a–kind.

There are no programs or agencies similar to Pediatric Asthma Network (PAN) in the County and only a handful of such programs in the nation. In fact, at a recent convention for healthcare professionals who specialize in asthma management, the local program was highlighted for several of its features: its broad partnerships, which cross the entire spectrum of healthcare providers in the community; its focus on research, education, treatment and evaluation; and its statistically significant results achieved in a relatively brief time. ◄———

> This statement not only assures the grantor that there are no competitors, but takes the opportunity to offer statements about the uniqueness and strength of the organization.

It is the vision of PAN's Advisory Board to become "the State model organization for asthma care, offering education, professional expertise, and advocacy resources to control this serious illness. Through stronger collaboration with institutions of higher education and health care, PAN will improve the lives of infants, children, and adolescents with asthma." Furthermore, PAN aims to "become a nationwide model making its experience in research, education, and treatment available for replication by any and all interested professionals and organizations." (Long-Range Strategic Plan)

The second sample comes from a grant for a camping program, of which there are several programs with similar populations and services.

Camp Orleans was the first of its kind in the State of Midwest to provide summer camping for low-income youth. Today, it knows of several camps providing experiences for at-risk and/or low-income children and youth, including Boy Scouts, Camp Tall, Med Children's Camp, Camp Indian Guides, and Pines Island Camp. ◄———

> This sentence names the competition within the region.

Camp Orleans has always been unique in that police officers participate with youth at camp as day counselors and coaches. To further its unique appeal and use to the larger community, Youth Service Organization plans a year-round facility with challenging programs designed to develop leadership skills in young people. All specialty camps are available on a sliding fee from $20 to $200 depending on what families can afford.

> This paragraph describes how this camp is different and how it will be further differentiated with new programs.

Constituent Involvement

Stakeholders are all the agencies, leaders, members of the target population, staff, and others who will be affected by a program or initiative. When a grantmaker asks about constituent involvement, it is asking whom you brought in to the project design and/or whom you will work with to design and deploy an evaluation. They expect the "who" to include members of the group that will benefit or be most affected by your project.

Sometimes, nonprofit organizations don't ask first. Sometimes, they want to pilot something they believe will work and get input later. While this is common practice, it makes this particular section difficult to write.

This is how one organization that did not seek specific information from the target population handled the question:

Sample: Constituent Involvement

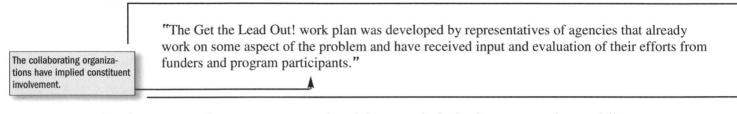

The collaborating organizations have implied constituent involvement.

"The Get the Lead Out! work plan was developed by representatives of agencies that already work on some aspect of the problem and have received input and evaluation of their efforts from funders and program participants."

Another response for an organization that did a great deal of information gathering follows:

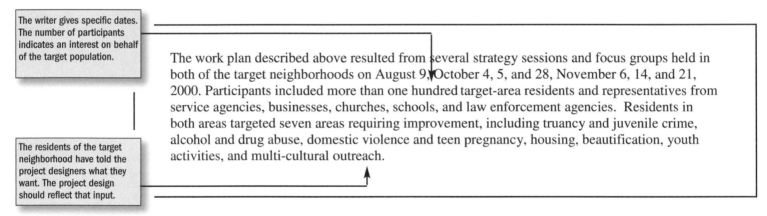

The writer gives specific dates. The number of participants indicates an interest on behalf of the target population.

The residents of the target neighborhood have told the project designers what they want. The project design should reflect that input.

The work plan described above resulted from several strategy sessions and focus groups held in both of the target neighborhoods on August 9, October 4, 5, and 28, November 6, 14, and 21, 2000. Participants included more than one hundred target-area residents and representatives from service agencies, businesses, churches, schools, and law enforcement agencies. Residents in both areas targeted seven areas requiring improvement, including truancy and juvenile crime, alcohol and drug abuse, domestic violence and teen pregnancy, housing, beautification, youth activities, and multi-cultural outreach.

Review of Literature

Grant opportunities in the areas of medicine/health care, science, and/or new technology often require a section called review of literature. You will rarely encounter this section in a foundation grantmaker's guidelines unless they are focused on a research, technical, or scientific project. The grantmaker that requests this information is testing the applicant to determine its level of expertise and its familiarity with current research in the field. If the section is requested in a federal government grant, one or more of the grant reviewers will be an expert in the field. RFPs that have a review of literature often require your project have a principal investigator (PI), as the person leading the project. His or her credentials are important to the success of the grant proposal.

When you are called on to write a review of the literature, you must locate and read all available work and be sure that it is as current as possible. Structure the narrative response to discuss both how the literature supports your approach and how it does not. When the literature does not support your approach, you must also address why your organization is determined to take an alternate approach.

Sample: Review of Literature

Research has shown that lead poisoning has a pervasive impact on the human body, impacting most of the physiological systems. Those most affected include the central nervous system, reproductive system, kidneys, and others. At higher levels, lead poisoning also can cause comas, convulsions, and even death, but even at lower levels, the presence of lead in the blood can severely limit a child's development. Some of the most significant consequences include diminished intelligence, limited neurobehavioral development, diminished physical growth and stature, and impaired hearing.

A review of existing literature on lead hazards results in numerous publications on risk analysis, lead hazard control, primary prevention strategies, and global prevention strategies. Little literature exists on the development of broad-based collaborations to ameliorate exposure and risk or on the potential for effectiveness of such collaborative efforts.

The "Get the Lead Out" Collaboration builds on the lessons learned across the country by bringing together actors from state and local government, national development organizations, nonprofit organizations, and community-based groups, as well as private citizens. The collaboration also features the direct involvement of hospitals, community health centers, and research institutions. In this regard the collaboration has the capacity not only to make an unprecedented impact in remediating environmental hazards of lead poisoning but also to conduct research at the ground level. Through its diverse membership, researchers working with the lead collaboration will have the opportunity to engage in new levels of inquiry relating to the factors contributing to lead exposure and the long-term implications for child development, and will be uniquely positioned to evaluate the effectiveness of a comprehensive community partnership to address this health issue.

> It is not critical that the writer cite sources here because all the research on the issue agrees.

> The research supports that something must be done about lead hazards in homes, supporting the statement of need.

> The writer claims that the review of literature yielded few relevant results.

> The writer makes an offer to become a test site that would assist in building the body of literature available to other community efforts—a way for others to learn from this collaborative's lessons.

Sustainability Plans

Most grantmakers now include a question regarding the long-term sustainability of new initiatives and projects or for organizations as a whole. Grantmakers receive far more proposals than they can ever hope to fund in a given year, regardless of their assets, so they hesitate to launch even more efforts that they will have to sustain through grants from their foundation. The long-range sustainability should be integral to the project design and should be called out in this section of a proposal.

Sample: Long-Term Strategies for Funding

HK 2010's current annual funding partners include the Keller County Health Department, Majority Health, and the State of Midwest, which, together, provide support of approximately $400,000 per year. Launching the I-Team activities is projected to require an additional $150,000 per year for the next three years. The outcomes of the implementation teams' work will be measured, and successes used to market Healthy Keller 2010 and its work to major HMOs and other health insurers and to area businesses to demonstrate effective reduction of health care problems and resultant costs.

> The organization has ongoing operational support that is not threatened.

> The proposed project will cost $150,000 annually and is not a part of the organization's budget.

> The organization's plan for sustainability is to market its efforts to for-profit businesses that have a business interest in the work.

In the next example, the organization is applying for a one-year grant to launch a program. Its sustainability plan indicates where money will come from to sustain the ongoing operations of the project:

Sample: Long-Term Strategies for Funding

The organization describes the stability of its annual sources of revenue to assure the grant-maker that it will have a means to incorporate ongoing program costs into its budget.

Much of the cost of launching the Mobile Lab (ML) and its programs is requested from the year-one grant. Ongoing costs include maintenance and fuel for the van, staffing, software/hardware upgrades, and an annual student video production competition.

CMC is prepared to incorporate the estimated annual cost of maintenance, repair, storage, and gasoline for the MML into its annual budget and has already done so for year one programs. The cable franchise fee recently negotiated provides CMC with both cable-access television support and some Internet support for the next fifteen years. Because part of the cable franchise fee will come from a portion of the cable company's "At Home" Internet subscribers, the money may be used to sustain the cost of operating and maintaining the ML.

The organization has calculated ongoing costs. This is a good practice to incorporate into the grantwriting planning process.

The remaining ongoing costs come to approximately $120,000 (staffing and awards dinner) and approximately $20-$30,000 annually for equipment/software purchase/upgrades or a total of $150,000 needed each year to operate the MML and its programs. CMC will encourage agencies and schools that use the ML regularly to include in year two and beyond budgets a fee for service based on the number of hours requested and based on positive evaluation and need for continuation. It will also charge fees for service at large community meetings and events and will seek local funding of ongoing costs until the program is subsidized entirely by fees for service.

The applicant believes that funding will come from several sources rather than relying on funding from one foundation.

CMC plans the following mix of funding sources for years one through four:

Year One: **$432,500 Budget**
45% local funding   CMC annual budget - $75,000
                           Fees for service - $3,000
                           Existing grant - $80,000
                           Donations and discounts - $40,000

The remainder of the seed funding is assumed to come from the grant if this proposal is successfully funded.

Year Two: **$175,000 Budget**
100% local funding: CMC annual budget - $25,000
                           Local grants - $100,000
                           Fees for occasional services - $5,000
                           Fees for regular service - $25,000
                           Local underwriters (competition/awards) - $20,000

Note that the sources of funding remain the same, but the amounts change over time as the project gains strength and supporters.

Year Three: **$175,000 Budget**
100% local funding   CMC annual budget - $30,000
                           Local grants - $75,000
                           Fees for occasional services - $10,000
                           Fees for regular service - $35,000
                           Local underwriters - $25,000

Year Four: **$175,000 Budget**
100% local funding   CMC annual budget - $50,000
                           Local grants - $35,000
                           Fees for occasional services - $15,000
                           Fees for regular service - $50,000
                           Local underwriters - $30,000

Organizational History

This is generally the easiest section of any grant proposal because it usually exists in brochures, past grant applications, and many other places, including institutional memory of staff. Once written, it can be cut and pasted into other grant applications with only minor updates. Each time you reuse this section, be sure that you revise it so that it speaks to the qualities of greatest interest to the potential funder. Focus this section on the mission and strengths of the organization, and use the section to highlight recent accomplishments such as a successful project or an award made to a program or staff member. As with staff qualifications, this is not a time to be modest, but don't overstate the case, either.

Sample: Organizational History

The introduction provides information about longevity and structure.

The Community Media Center (CMC) was founded as Cable Access Center in 1981. Today the CMC houses TECH services, a computer service provider for nonprofit organizations; a laboratory that provides scheduled classes and free use of computer equipment; CityTV television studio and video editing; WYWY, a community radio station; and Institute for Information Democracy (IID), a program that teaches media literacy around social issues and that logs and reports local media election coverage.

Until this section, the proposal has centered on goals for the project or initiative it is proposing for funding. Now it focuses on broader organizational goals that are a part of most organizations' strategic plans.

Mission and Goals
The affiliates and all of their programs work together under a shared mission of "building community through media." Goals for the coming year were established by the Board of Directors and include:
• Developing an overall partnering and collaborating strategic plan
• Establishing partnership with the Public Schools and continue building on successes with SU and CC
• Identifying community technology classes and other groups for future marketing
• Pursuing cross-marketing opportunities with these groups by sharing and cross-promoting class information and organization information
• Cross-promoting between affiliates
• Establishing budget for marketing
• Creating an All-Affiliates annual event for recognition, education, awareness, fund-raising, etc.
• Developing a strategic/feasibility plan for radio equivalent of CityTV, space needs, content sharing, and print media
• Reviewing and assessing Help Desk effectiveness and expansion possibilities
• Adding CMC links to and from Chamber of Commerce sites and other organizations
• Reviewing feasibility of online newsletter
• Further defining and developing CMC services and educational areas and cost (e.g., NPO database and newsletter, informational brochures, public forums, etc.)

Although you are probably eager to tell of all the organization's accomplishments, try to keep this section brief. A page or less is desirable.

Current Programs, Activities, and Accomplishments
Currently, CMC is working with Southtown to establish wireless connectivity for all nonprofit tenants and to exchange services for reduced rent for our educational staff. Other recent projects include partnering with the Museum, City, and County to provide technology services, including oral history production at the new Community Research and Archive Center; an effort to assist a California city in replicating the CMC/library model; and an effort to build a media center in Ghana. CMC and its affiliates continue to look for new ways to partner and/or to serve the community with instruction and assistance in all forms of media communications.

This highlights only the most recent accomplishments.

Organizational Chart
An organizational chart is attached.

Focus on organizational capacity and structure.

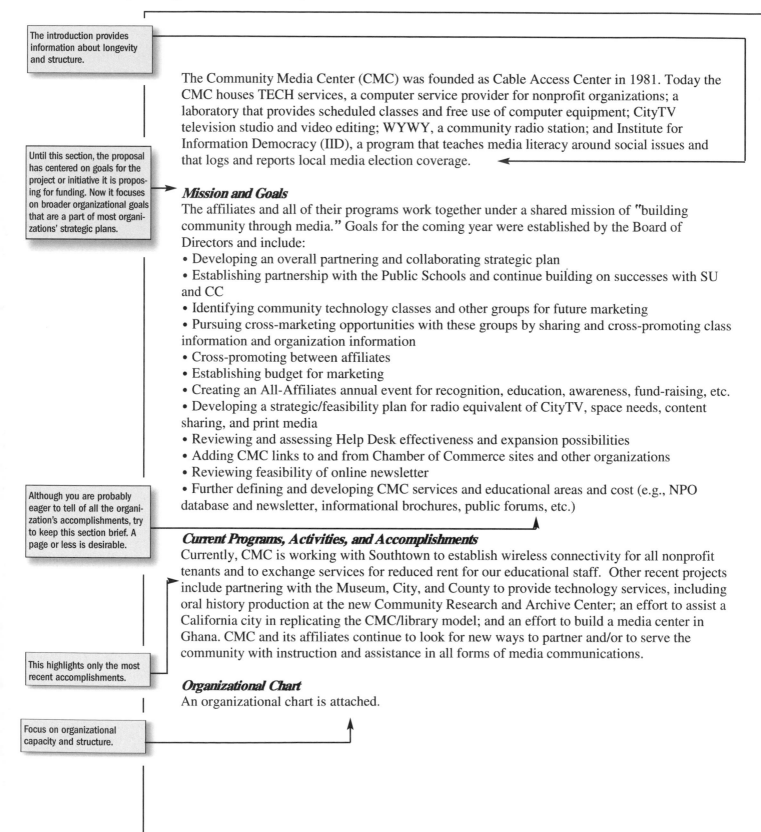

Logic Models

Logic models are a means to present an integrated project and evaluation plan. They are often selected by applicants as the best means to illustrate the synergy between the two plans. Nationally, most United Way organizations require proposals for funding to include a logic model.

Writing a logic model is not difficult, but they often intimidate nonprofit leaders because they require a vocabulary lesson to explain the sections.

- Inputs are the resources (money, time, equipment, etc.) the organization needs to undertake the activities.
- Outputs are the measurable/tangible effects of the activities.
- Outcomes are the changes that will come about because of the project and its activities. They are defined as initial (immediate), intermediate (within the year), and long-term (possibly after the grant period).
- Indicators are the data the organization will use to determine whether it met the planned outcomes of the project.

Sample: Logic Model

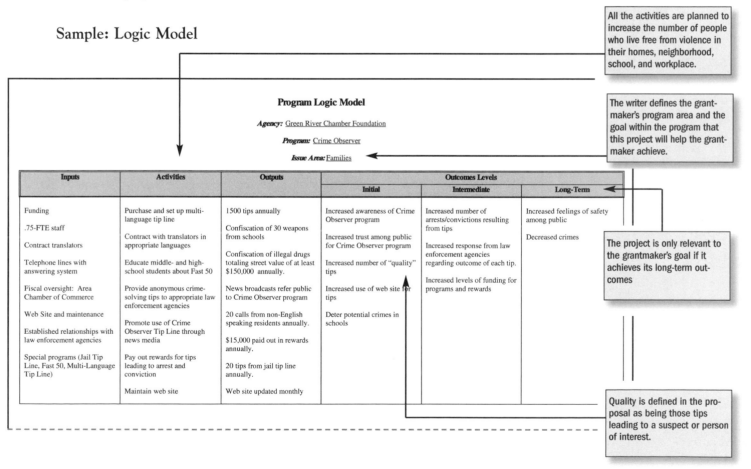

Program Logic Model

Agency: Green River Chamber Foundation

Program: Crime Observer

Issue Area: Families

Inputs	Activities	Outputs	Outcomes Levels		
			Initial	Intermediate	Long-Term
Funding	Purchase and set up multi-language tip line	1500 tips annually	Increased awareness of Crime Observer program	Increased number of arrests/convictions resulting from tips	Increased feelings of safety among public
.75-FTE staff		Confiscation of 30 weapons from schools	Increased trust among public for Crime Observer program		Decreased crimes
Contract translators	Contract with translators in appropriate languages	Confiscation of illegal drugs totaling street value of at least $150,000 annually.	Increased number of "quality" tips	Increased response from law enforcement agencies regarding outcome of each tip.	
Telephone lines with answering system	Educate middle- and high-school students about Fast 50	News broadcasts refer public to Crime Observer program	Increased use of web site for tips	Increased levels of funding for programs and rewards	
Fiscal oversight: Area Chamber of Commerce	Provide anonymous crime-solving tips to appropriate law enforcement agencies	20 calls from non-English speaking residents annually.	Deter potential crimes in schools		
Web Site and maintenance	Promote use of Crime Observer Tip Line through news media	$15,000 paid out in rewards annually.			
Established relationships with law enforcement agencies	Pay out rewards for tips leading to arrest and conviction	20 tips from jail tip line annually.			
Special programs (Jail Tip Line, Fast 50, Multi-Language Tip Line)	Maintain web site	Web site updated monthly			

> All the activities are planned to increase the number of people who live free from violence in their homes, neighborhood, school, and workplace.

> The writer defines the grant-maker's program area and the goal within the program that this project will help the grant-maker achieve.

> The project is only relevant to the grantmaker's goal if it achieves its long-term outcomes

> Quality is defined in the proposal as being those tips leading to a suspect or person of interest.

The data source indicates what measures the organization will use to gather the indicators. The collection method indicates whether the organization will use surveys, reports, or other means to gather the data needed.

Outcome Measurement Framework

Program: Crime Observer

Outcome	Indicator(s)	Data Source	Data Collection Method
Increased awareness of Crime Observer program	Number of tips increases annually	Call counts	Internal
Increased trust among public for Crime Observer program	Number of tips increases annually	Call counts	Internal
Increased number of "quality" tips	Number of tips resulting in arrest/conviction	Law enforcement reports; staff follow up	Internal
Increased use of web site for tips	Number of tips reported on website	"hit" counter	Internal
Deter potential crimes in schools	Number of guns and drugs confiscated in schools	School administrators	State-mandated annual report by school administrations
Increased number of arrests/ bind overs resulting from tips	Number of tips resulting in arrest/bind over	Law enforcement reports; staff follow up	Internal
Increased response from law enforcement agencies regarding outcome of each tip.	Number of specific communications from law enforcement agencies	Computer software	Internal
Increased levels of funding for programs and rewards	Funding resources	Budget of revenues	Internal
Increased feelings of safety among public	Individuals reporting feelings of safety	Community Research Institute (GVSU)	Annual community survey and report
Decreased crimes	Number and types of crimes	Law enforcement agencies in Kent County	Law-enforcement reports

All initial, intermediate, and long-term outcomes are brought into a second chart and further explained.

CHAPTER 8
The Grantwriting Craft

Searching for grant sources, identifying appropriate alliances, talking with funders, totaling budget line items, while important, do not overshadow the need for a grantwriter to write, and write well. Central to writing well are knowing your audience and keeping in mind throughout the writing process what the audience wants and needs to know; secondary, but also important, are the grammatical, structural, and stylistic aspects of writing.

Write It Well

Many people have pet peeves about certain uses of grammar, trite sayings, or current jargon. One might be bothered by a split infinitive (inserting an adverb between "to" and a verb as in "to boldly go"); another might think, "If I read the phrase 'a seat at the table' one more time…"; and still another might be weary of the overuse of "youth" to describe teenagers or adolescents or the use of "impact" as a verb.

Every writer should keep his or her potential audience in mind during the writing process. Therefore, it is important to make yourself aware of unintentional habits that creep into your writing from the oral language. To your ear, it may sound perfectly acceptable to use phrases and words that people use all the time, but writing is a more formal mode of communication and merits your attention to correct usage. Keep stylebooks, writing manuals, grammar textbooks, and a dictionary close to your computer for frequent use. When your work is corrected by a professor or an editor, learn from your mistakes. Commit the error to memory so you don't repeat it.

When you write a grant, write simply and straightforwardly. State the ideas and concepts clearly, using shorter sentences, and selecting, when there are options, easily understandable words. Your writing won't have more authority because you use bigger words. It will have authority because you have a deep understanding of your topic. Remember, grant reviewers read several proposals a day. The easier yours is to read, the more quickly they can grasp the concepts and, ultimately, the more positive their response to the proposal will be. Good writing won't sell a bad program, but many good programs have gone unfunded because the proposal was poorly written.

Explain Acronyms and Terms

On first reference, spell out the name of the organization, project, or other item followed by the acronym in parentheses. Thereafter, try to write out the entire name once per page. Unless the acronym or abbreviation is commonly used and understood by the reader, try to use them minimally. No reader likes to have to turn back three pages later to recall what you mean by "BISCR." Use shortened versions of the formal name rather than alphabet soup. For instance, Keller School District can be called alternately by its full name, by KSD, and by "the district."

If there are terms specific to the nonprofit be sure to explain what is meant by each term. For example, "transfer" means to move something from one point to another, but it has a specific meaning to inventors. Similarly "advanced manufacturing" has a specific meaning to manufacturers, but means little to a lay audience. And, while "digital divide" is fairly well understood by most readers, you may have to describe what it means in your community.

Use the Active Voice

Good writers always use active voice construction and slip out of the active voice only for deliberate effect, as in the line from *Death of a Salesman* when Willie Loman's neighbor says, "attention must be paid." If you take nothing else away from this chapter but adopting the use the active voice in your writing, you will come away with improved skills for writing more readable and interesting proposals.

Active voice has a subject; passive voice doesn't. Note the difference between the following:

- Active: ABC Nonprofit served three hundred children in 2005.
- Passive: Three hundred children received services in 2005.

Taking the actor out of the sentence is not just poor and dull writing, it can also have a psychological effect on the reader. If your proposal is written in passive voice, the reader may get the impression that service is magical, that the nonprofit is unnecessary.

Many nonprofit leaders speak and write in passive voice. While they are often accountable for their mistakes, they rarely take credit for their accomplishments, and, as a result, they often hesitate to make themselves or their organization the subject of their sentences.

A grant proposal is not the place to be modest. Your mission is to convince the funder that the organization is strong, its staff is capable, and that the nonprofit has a track record of success. Your organization and its staff take the actions in your project—make them the actors in your sentences.

Tips from a Program Officer

- Set out the primary point of a proposal section in the first paragraph. Help the reader understand why you are making the supporting points.
- Don't make the program officer read through pages and pages before you get to your request. Tell the reader what you want up front.

TIP

If you select an acronym to name your project, try to select one that is a word and is, therefore, memorable to the reader. For instance, a planning committee called its technology on wheels project the MML for mobile media laboratory. Later, they changed the name to MoLLIE, for Mobile Learning Lab for Information Education. While the actual words used to create the acronym are longer than the original, the acronym MoLLIE is memorable to participants and funders alike.

First or Third Person?

The choice of first or third person narration is entirely the author's. First person narration uses "we" statements about the applicant. Third person refers to the applicant organization as an "it." The first person narration is friendlier and, therefore, perhaps less appropriate for a formal application to an unknown reader. On the other hand, as you develop relationships with local grantmakers, the third person may begin to feel too distancing or stiff. Either way, be sure that you are consistent in your usage throughout the proposal.

Speak with Authority

A good writer knows his or her subject matter. The writer must become an expert, not just in proposal writing, but in the subject, whether that topic is new cancer research, K-12 education, technology, counseling, or law enforcement. Depending on your background and ability to learn and absorb quickly, you may have to leave some grantwriting, such as that for medical research, to subject experts.

Will/Would

Use "will" in grant proposals, as in "ABC nonprofit will train tutors," or "DEF nonprofit will convene a meeting." The auxiliary verb "would" implies that the organization's action is conditional, that it will perform the action if, and only if, it receives grant money. Thus, it further implies a lack of staff commitment to the project.

Further, many grantmakers pull the objectives in your proposal verbatim to place into a grant agreement (contract). The use of "will" statements translate well into the contract, as in "ABC will serve three hundred children by December 2008."

Political Correctness

Politically correct terms change, so you must stay current and use the latest terms in your grant proposals. Once again, be sensitive to your reading audience.

Since people of Mexican, Korean, or African descent are fast becoming the majority ethnicities in communities, it is no longer accurate to use the collective "minority" race/ethnicity. Instead, use "people of color."

Try to use the actual country of origin when writing about segments of the population (e.g., Mexican American, Korean American, or people of Mexican descent.) If you group people within segments, the current politically correct terms are Latino/Latina or Hispanic, Asian ("Oriental" should only be used to describe furniture from the East), African American, and American Indian (a recent change from Native American).

Try to be gender inclusive. Use "he/she" for the singular subject or revise the sentence to use the plural "they."

When referring to individuals who are blind, deaf, or physically/mentally challenged, emphasize the person over the disability, as in "people with disabilities" or, even more in vogue, "people with different abilities." Don't sensationalize with phrases such as "afflicted with," "suffering from," or "victimized by."

Check Spelling, Grammar, and Punctuation

A writer becomes too close to a piece of work to be a good editor or proofreader; however, proofing and editing are critical functions. Ask someone who's never seen your proposal to read it just for spelling, grammar, and punctuation errors. Review their work to identify the errors you make frequently and then correct them permanently. Do not rely on your computer to proofread the work. It cannot identify your intent and will let pass words that are improperly used if they are spelled correctly. You may have meant to say "the organization is providing a full complement of services," but inadvertently used "compliment" instead.

Ten Essential Qualities of Grantwriters

1. Strong writing skills
2. Analytical and/or systems thinker
3. Ability to meet deadlines
4. Ability to follow instructions and pay close attention to detail
5. Analytical and intuitive reader (can read between the lines)
6. Skilled negotiator and facilitator
7. Knowledge and understanding of community and people
8. Knowledge and understanding of change theory
9. Empathy for reading audience
10. Accepts criticism well, doesn't personalize document feedback

---

Cover Letters and Abstracts—Write them Last

The last two things you should write before submitting a proposal are the executive summary or abstract and a cover letter. In many cases, this is where you make your first impression—and the concise writing required in these sections can be tough to do. If you wait until you've written all the other sections, you'll be better able to select the key points you need to bring out in the cover letter and abstract.

Some grantmakers, especially government agencies, throw out cover letters; other grantmakers require them as part of the proposal package. When they are required, cover letters serve two purposes: first they offer a summary of the project and a means to make the request up front, and second, but even more importantly, they offer the grantseeker a chance to thank the potential funder for their review.

Sample: Cover Letter

May 22, 2006

Mr. Alex Axle, Executive Director
Twenty-Two Foundation
4444 Thirty-Third St. SE
Anyplace, USA 55555

Dear Mr. Axle:

Thank you for the opportunity to submit the enclosed proposal for "Connective Media," a capital campaign to enable the Community Media Center to acquire the Historic Theatre, thus expanding communications access to the south quadrant of the city and "electrifying" the revitalization efforts of the Historic Street business district and its surrounding neighborhoods.

We have developed several new projects for the southeast neighborhood including a Drop-in Center (young filmmaker training), TVStudio (community street-front broadcast studio), and a neighborhood audio recording studio. These enable us to provide constructive youth programs that teach job skills, introduce people to creative computer-based applications, build self-esteem and social skills, improve literacy, and develop pride in the neighborhood.

We have already seen dramatic results from these activities and a ready acceptance of media technology by the community that lives near this media campus. Recently, the consultant evaluating the WI-FI pilot project of the City noted that the Historic Theatre area pilot was the strongest. We believe that's because the CMC called on partners to donate computers and wireless cards, which we were able, in turn, to donate to families who participated in CMC computer use training.

The CMC respectfully requests a Twenty-Two Foundation gift of $50,000 toward the $2.4 million campaign and would like to work with the Foundation trustees to determine the most appropriate naming opportunity to acknowledge your gift. Please contact me if I can answer any questions regarding this project. And, again, thank you for your interest.

Sincerely,

Director
Community Media Center

The letter begins by focusing on the reader rather than the writer, and it opens with a thank you. This is preferable over "I am enclosing...," which focuses on the writer first.

Although this name has been changed, it can be helpful to name all your projects with a name or acronym that is memorable.

Twenty-Two Foundation focuses funding on programs that serve young people and education. A request for capital must emphasize the ways in which the building and equipment will fulfill the foundation's goals for improving educational outcomes for young urbanites.

This sentence states the requested grant amount.

The grant request is not earmarked for any one specific activity or piece of equipment the CMC is purchasing. A naming opportunity provides the foundation with a way, if it chooses, to emphasize its program focus to the future visitors. This foundation might elect to have the CMC call its educational TVStudio the "Twenty-Two Storefront," to help build public awareness of its priorities.

This sentence offers to follow-up if needed.

Teamwork—Reviewing Your Proposal

It's critical to put together a grant proposal review team for every proposal you write. Representatives of organizations that will be performing the work described in the proposal must read and approve the work plan and any later changes to the work plan.

As you gain experience and success in grantwriting, often leaders of organizations with whom you are working will tell you they trust your judgment and skill. It may be true and nice to hear, but you cannot allow the flattery to turn into a shortcut. If you are unsure whether nonprofit leaders are taking the time, ask them to initial each page so you can be sure they've signed off on the proposal.

Though they won't be a part of the project design team, two other types of readers are critical: a third-party grant review person and a proofreader. The third-party reviewer should be someone entirely unfamiliar with the organizations and project. Give him or her the review criteria or rubric and the latest proposal draft and ask that they read and score the proposal. Ask for feedback on how they think you can strengthen the proposal. You should see this reviewer as representative of your reading audience, the grant reviewers. If the reader points out a flaw and you disagree, don't argue your point. You wouldn't have a chance to do that with a grant reviewer, would you? Instead, take in all the criticism and work diligently to strengthen your proposal. There's no place in professional proposal writing for a fragile ego. Get over it, and get on with it.

Finally, have a trusted person (an English major or someone known for their technical skill) proofread your final draft. This person, too, should come fresh to the process so their eyes catch your errors and help you make the proposal the best it can be.

Review Criteria

RFPs released by the government contain selection criteria and scoring parameters that will be used by the panel of independent reviewers. As you saw in the outline of the Safe Schools-Healthy Students grant in chapter 5, each section was assigned a point value so the writer knew what to emphasize in the proposal. Scoring grant proposals is subjective. In fact, you will often find that if you request reader comment sheets after a failed federal grant proposal (see chapter 12), that no two reviewers agree. One may award you nineteen points out of twenty on the need section while another awards only twelve.

In an effort to make the scoring more objective, some federal grants contain a rubric—a scale that helps them identify which range of scores they should award based on the content of the application. The rubric will be available to grantwriters as well. Use it during both the planning and writing process and provide it to your third-party reader. The following is a sample rubric for a Community Technology Center (CTC) grant, a federal grant program to address and correct the digital divide in many U.S. communities.

Sample: Rubric

Eligibility-Please answer yes or no to the following questions and provide comments as necessary.

Eligibility:		Comments:
Is the organization a CTC?	__ Yes __ No	
Is the organization a nonprofit?	__ Yes __ No	
Has the organization been in operation for a year or more?	__ Yes __ No	

If you answered no to any of the above questions, it is possible that this proposal is not eligible for consideration for the grant program. Please email or call Suzie Staff (555.555.5555) immediately to discuss its possible disqualification.

Proposal Rating-Please score the following sections using the criterion as a guide. If any element of the proposal does not receive a good or exemplary rating, please explain, in detail, the reason(s). Please use the following as a guide of scores for the sections below:

Out of 5 points	Out of 10 points	Scoring Guidelines
0-1	0-2	Information not provided or incomplete
2	3-4	Lacks sufficient information
3	5-6	Marginal (requires clarification or additional information
4	7-8	Good (clear and complete)
5	9-10	Exemplary (well conceived and thoroughly developed)

Before the grant reviewer reads the rest of the proposal, he or she must telephone the staff person to discuss eligibility. If the two find that the organization is ineligible, the proposal will not be read. The proposal writer must be sure to cover these eligibility criteria within the first paragraph of the proposal.

Criterion	Score	Comments
Organizational Capacity Applicant organization shows sufficient experience to carry out the proposed project. Project fits within organization's stated mission.	__ out of 5	
Need for proposed product/project Proposal clearly states a need for the proposed project. Proposal shows evidence that a literature review/needs assessment was completed by applicant. The stated need will be addressed by the proposed project. The proposed project will not duplicate other products/efforts that already exist. The proposed project will be applicable and beneficial to other community technology programs.		
Project Description Applicant provides a clear description of the proposed project. Proposed project will be suitable for widespread distribution. Applicant proposes the creation of adequate supports (instructions, documentation) to support use of project by CTC field.		
Project Outcomes Outcomes are clearly presented. Outcomes are desired by larger CTC field.		
Project Implementation The timeline of key implementation activities is clearly presented. The timeline of key implementation activities is realistic. There is a clear description of staffing requirements for proposed project.		
Budget The budget is realistic, given the project being proposed. All activities described in the budget are described in the narrative.	__ out of 5	

Criterion	Score	
Organizational Capacity Applicant organization shows sufficient experience to carry out the proposed project. Project fits within organization's stated mission.	__ out of 5	

Each section has a total point value of five or ten points. The range of scores reflects the scoring guidelines for both point values.

The writer must convince readers that the organization has a history of success and has adequate staff and resources to carry out the proposed project. Note the question about mission: if the project does not fit the mission of the organization, this may raise a red flag that the organization is chasing grant money. If, for instance, an applicant is a church offering computer training in the basement on Wednesday afternoons, the proposal writer must explain how the project fits into the overall church mission

The writer must demonstrate that there is reason beyond the wishes of the organization to propose this project—either the literature says that this sort of project is successful in similar circumstances or members of the target population have indicated a strong need and desire for the service.

The writer must identify similar projects and tell how this organization's project will be different. After identifying other technology projects, the writer will have to explain how this project rounds out the offerings in the community.

Is the project replicable elsewhere? Can others learn from your mistakes and successes?

Should this proposal be funded?   __Yes   __ No

Presentation

Completeness

Your grant application must be complete with all required attachments. If the RFP or guidelines do not provide a checklist of application components, create one of your own and check against it as you collate your grant package to ensure that everything is in order. The following is a grant application package checklist from a national foundation. Many others require the same or similar attachments:

Sample: Grant Application Checklist

**Private Foundation
Grant Request Checklist**

Please remember to include all the following with your grant request and refer to the proposal guidelines for more details. Consideration of your proposal will be delayed if you do not follow these guidelines.

PROPOSAL

1. Executive summary must include:
   - amount requested;
   - duration (the first day of the month through the last day of the month ex. June 1, 2000–May 31, 2001)
   - up to 3 proposed grant activities (Briefly list major activities that will support your strategic objectives.) and up to 3 grant products (List expected tangible results of foundation support, e.g., printed material, video, CD-ROM, and Internet publication.)

2. Full proposal as per guidelines

ADMINISTRATIVE INFORMATION

Include:
   - head of organization (President or Executive Director) not department head
   - project director's name and title
   - financial officer's name and title
   - payment information—wire transfer OR check, not both
   - organization's EIN number

> An Employer Identification Number (EIN) is similar to a social security number for an individual.

BUDGET

   - use foundation's budget format—summary and narrative
   - budget signed by **both** project director and financial officer
   - list project total per year and amount requested from foundation
   - explain carry-over funds, if a renewal

ALSO INCLUDE IN PACKAGE

   - tax-exempt IRS letter
   - most recent annual report
   - current operating budget
   - most recent financial report

> Federal grants ask for your Employer Identification Number (EIN) rather than this letter, which they use to verify your IRS 501(c)(3) status. This funder wants both.

Universities and organizations that have received a grant in the past two years do not need to send these materials

Letter of endorsement signed by head of institution or someone with fiscal responsibility. Letter must include:
   - name and purpose of project
   - project director
   - amount requested (must match amount on budget and in executive summary)
   - duration for foundation's part of project (the first day of the month through the last day of the month ex. June 1, 2000–May 31, 2001)

> The cover letter for this funder must include the specific information listed.

4. CVs for key project staff

5. Four hard copies of final proposal. (Note: for requests of $50,000 or less only two copies are required)

If you fax or email additional materials, you must also send us a hard copy for our files. Requests will not be considered if your institution has any outstanding reports due to the foundation.

Please contact staff with questions
BE SURE TO RESPOND FULLY TO THIS CHECKLIST.

Typography

Always follow the outline exactly as provided in the grantmaker's guidelines or RFP. Number or letter your sections as they appear (e.g., 1, 2, 3, I, II, III, A, B, C, etc.). Number subheadings exactly as they appear. If instructions appear in bullet form under a heading, identify them with callouts in bold and/or italic type so the reader is sure that you are responding to every question.

Shorten the instructions into identifiable headings and subheadings. For instance, the instructions might say, "Identify the need in your community for a technology center." You can shorten the heading to "Statement of Need" or "Need for Project." Pull the salient information from the question. "How have you involved constituents in the development of your project?" becomes the subheading "Constituent Involvement."

Unless you are instructed otherwise, use the typeface considered most readable: twelve point size in a simple serif font such as Times or Palatino for the body of the narrative. You may use sans serif typeface for headings and subheadings as a way to help clarify and call out section changes.

Page margins are often prescribed by the grantmaker; when they are not, a standard is one inch on all sides. If you are allowed to bind a document in a three-ring binder or folder, expand the left-side margin by half an inch to accommodate the paper punch.

RFPs from the government will instruct you whether to use single or double spacing between lines. If there are no instructions regarding line spacing, you may single space. Try to leave a line space between paragraphs rather than indenting each paragraph, and definitely add a line space between the end of one subheading and the beginning of another within the document.

Page Counts Often Count

Again, you must follow instructions. Most foundations take the position that your high school English teacher may have had: the proposal needs to be as long as it takes to make your points well. Even so, be courteous. Foundation staff and trustees are no more eager than you are to read a voluminous, highly technical tome. Try to limit your concept paper to ten or fewer pages. Grant proposals are not the most exciting reading experience anyway, so make them succinct.

RFPs, on the other hand, often have hard and fast rules for page counts and, increasingly, since the advent of eGrants (the electronic submission process established by the government), even word or character counts. If you do not adhere to the page counts, they may throw away your entire application. At the very least, if they require ten pages and you send twelve, they'll take two off and throw them away. You'll lose points for the sections that are missing, and even if your earlier sections score 100 percent, it will likely not be enough to achieve a strong score against the competition.

Paper Selection

Once upon a time grants were always submitted on stationery-quality paper. When you submit on paper today, however, copy stock is perfectly acceptable except when you are writing about environmental protection. In those instances, be sure to select and print on paper that has a recycled symbol. The use of recycled paper in other instances, though not mandated, says something about the organization's values, so you might consider using environmental standards for all your office supplies.

Use 8½ x 11-inch paper stock. If more than half your narrative is composed of lengthy charts that must be printed landscape to capture the information (such as a logic model) consider creating your entire document in landscape. Though the length of the lines on the page may annoy a reader, it's possible that continually shifting the grant package to read different pages will be equally or more so.

Pagination

Always include a header or, more preferable, a footer, with the page number of the narrative. When requested for longer grant applications, you may even have to number appendix documents successively, so run copies of existing documents such as the audit through your printer in order to print just the footer on them. This also enables a table of contents for longer grant applications.

Include the name of the organization, the project name, and the location of the nonprofit applicant in the footer. Here's a horror story: years ago, two nonprofits in two different states applied for the same federal grant. Both nonprofits were called "The Bridge." One of the organizations scored high on its application and was awarded funding; the other was not. Someone made a mistake, however, and sent a grant agreement and first check to the wrong Bridge. When the successful applicant learned of the error, its staff were told that it was too late. The government had no appeal process and had expended its grant funds for the program. Your lesson: be sure that every page of your narrative contains identifying information so your project, nonprofit, and location are easy to find.

Binders and Dividers

Unless you are instructed otherwise, do not use binders, tabs for sections, or any other presentation material simply to make your proposal look better. Binder clips or staples are best. If you are sending to a foundation, use a paper clip so the staff can easily take apart your proposal to make additional copies if they need them. The federal government prefers staples to keep grant proposals whole and separate from others sent to the same reviewers. If your project is too long to be captured by a desk stapler, take it to a shipping or copy center and ask to use their power stapler. These tools will securely bind fifty or more pages into one document.

Color, Photos, and Graphics

In general, avoid beautifying your proposal. Beautification items are any photos, color type, bindery materials, or any other thing that is not necessary to present the proposal content clearly and concisely. If an organizational structure or a process plan is more understandable in a graphic, absolutely use a graph or illustration. When you do, reduce the content of your narrative, both to make space for the graphic and to justify the use of an illustration over a narrative explanation.

Color type is an unnecessary expense in toner or copying. Even lines in graphs can be printed as grayscale or patterns to separate one from another and make a chart more readable. If you are attaching an existing color document, such as a four-color program brochure or annual report, be sure to attach one to every copy of the proposal unless otherwise instructed. (Sometimes a foundation will request one set of attachments and several copies of the proposal.)

Do use charts to create timelines, goal and objective lists, or other items that are made more readable and understandable by their use. Leave them in black and white and use bold, italics, and underscoring to separate information. A few notes about charts:

- Sometimes a table does not transfer into an online submission. Be sure to save your document with charts in Adobe PDF format to preserve the chart parameters.
- If the RFP says the document must be double-spaced, you must also double-space information in all charts unless additional instructions indicate this is unnecessary.

Copies

Most grantmakers will instruct you on the number of copies to deliver. Federal grants require one original and various numbers of copies. Follow the instructions. Be sure that your original is clearly the original: support letters are on original stationery (often color) from the organizations, cover letters are submitted on original stationery, and all attachments are off the press. Use blue ink for all signatures on original cover sheets and assurances and support letters. The blue will copy as black and set the original apart from the copies. Finally, just to be sure, attach a sticky note or sticker to the front page or cover letter of the document, taking care not to cover essential information, indicating "original." If you do so, use the word "copy" on all copies in the same place that you marked the original.

If you do not have the tools at your office to make collated copies, you will save time by going to a copy center and running them on a machine that will. Collating is time consuming and susceptible to human error. Don't trust copy machines either. Check through all your copies to be sure that all pages are included and in order. Send the number of copies requested in the RFP.

Some foundations state the number of copies they would like in their guidelines, but many do not. Call the foundation and ask before you deliver the original submission. Many only want one, but a lack of information is not an excuse for assuming.

Filling out Forms

Completion of requisite forms always seems to be the last thing a grantwriter does before submitting the proposal. Don't make this mistake. While there are many forms that require only a signature (after reading, of course) by the director and/or board chair of the applicant organization, many others require detailed information. Although some information may have to wait until the last minute (i.e., final budget totals), you should at least be familiar with the information you will need to complete the form. Trying to gather such things as the Employer Identification Number at the last minute can make you crazy and maybe even cause you to miss your deadline.

Style Tips

- Do not use the word "feel," as in "we feel this is the right approach." Replace it with "believe."
- Do not use "hope," as in "the outcomes we hope to accomplish..." Replace it with "plan."
- In third person, an organization or business is an "it." The possessive form of "it" has no apostrophe.
- Cut the fat from your sentences. Replace "due to the fact that," with "because."
- Avoid old fashioned sounding prepositions such as "upon," as in "upon request." Use "on." Also avoid strings of redundant prepositions such as "inside of."
- Go "which" hunting in your document. Replace "which" with "that" in restrictive clauses.

Cover Sheets

Most grantmakers require, at minimum, a cover sheet that contains important information about the applicant organization. Foundations generally have their own formats, though some will use the form from the regional association of grantmakers' common grant application.

The following is a sample cover sheet from a family foundation with instructions for its completion:

Sample: Foundation Cover Sheet

FAMILY FOUNDATION APPLICATION
PROPOSAL COVER SHEET

Date of Application:_____

ORGANIZATION INFORMATION
Legal Name of Organization Applying: _____
(Should be the same as on IRS determination letter and as supplied on IRS Form 990)

> Enter the legal name and the dba (doing business as) if the organization is known by another name.

Year Founded: _____   Current Year Operating Budget: $_____

> This is the operating budget of the entire organization.

CONTACT INFORMATION
Executive Director/Chief Operating Officer: _____

Address (principal administrative office):   _____

_____

Phone and Facsimile Numbers: (_____)_____ (_____)_____

E-mail Address and Web Site: _____

> In some instances you will enter the name of the project coordinator if relevant.

Project Contact Person, Title, and Contact Information (if different from above): _____
_____
_____

> It is a good idea to name the project with a memorable title or acronym.

PROJECT INFORMATION
Project Name (if appropriate) and Brief Description of Project: _____
_____
_____

> Divide the amount of the request by the total project cost.

Total Project Cost: $_____   Amount Requested and Percentage of Total Project: $_____* _____%
If the amount requested exceeds $30,000, applicant must also provide additional items listed under "Family Foundation Proposal Requirements."

> This grantmaker has a shorter application process for small grants.

Dates of the Project: _____ - _____   Geographic Area Served: _____

Diversity Information (by percentage, as appropriate):

> The request for this data on the organization and its beneficiaries indicates that diversity is valued by this foundation.

	0-6 yrs.	7-18 yrs.	19+ yrs.	Male	Female	Ethnic Minority
Board	--	--	--			
Staff	--	--	--			
Project Beneficiaries						

Previous Support: Have you previously received support from the Family Foundation? YES* ___ NO ___
If yes, please attach detail of when, how much, and for what purpose(s) the Foundation provided support.

AUTHORIZATION

_____   _____   _____
Signature, Chairperson, Board of Directors   Date   Printed Name and Title

_____   _____   _____
Signature, Executive Director   Date   Printed Name and Title

The federal government's cover sheet is called a standard form 424 or "SF424." The request for information on SF424 may vary with department and occasionally for different grant programs from the same department, but is always accompanied by several pages of instructions for its completion.

SF424s come with an RFP package or are downloadable at www.grants.gov. Following is a sample 424:

Sample: SF424 Cover Sheet

APPLICATION FOR FEDERAL ASSISTANCE

Version

Complete only one of these two boxes. Programs are usually non-construction.

1. TYPE OF SUBMISSION:
Application
☐ Construction
☐ Non-Construction

Pre-application
☐ Construction
☐ Non-Construction

2. DATE SUBMITTED — Applicant Identifier

Enter date application is mailed.

3. DATE RECEIVED BY STATE — State Application Identifier

4. DATE RECEIVED BY FEDERAL AGENCY — Federal Identifier

Leave blank.

5. APPLICANT INFORMATION

Legal Name:

Organizational Unit:
Department:

Organizational DUNS:

Division:

Dun and Bradstreet number is entered here. (Apply for one, if needed, at www.dnb.com.)

Address:
Street:

Name and telephone number of person to be contacted on mat involving this application (give area code)

Prefix: First Name:

Mr./Mrs./Ms., etc.

Middle Name

This number is assigned by the IRS and is proof of the organization's nonprofit designation.

Last Name

State: Zip Code

Suffix:

Country:

Email:

6. EMPLOYER IDENTIFICATION NUMBER *(EIN):*
☐☐-☐☐☐☐☐☐☐

Phone Number (give area code)   Fax Number (give area code)

Check this box for second- or third-year renewals.

8. TYPE OF APPLICATION:
☐ New   ☐ Continuation   ☐ Revision

If Revision, enter appropriate letter(s) in box(es)
(See back of form for description of letters.)
☐   ☐

7. TYPE OF APPLICANT: (See back of form for Application Types)

Other (specify)

CFDA number from RFP

9. NAME OF FEDERAL AGENCY:

Revisions are allowed in rare cases such as invention development. Six months must pass between applications.

10. CATALOG OF FEDERAL DOMESTIC ASSISTANCE NUMBER:
☐☐-☐☐☐

TITLE (Name of Program):

11. DESCRIPTIVE TITLE OF APPLICANT'S PROJECT:

A list provides code letters for universities, public entities, and types of nonprofit organizations.

12. AREAS AFFECTED BY PROJECT *(Cities, Counties, States, etc.):*

From RFP

PROPOSED PROJECT

Start Date: Ending Date:

14. CONGRESSIONAL DISTRICTS OF:
a. Applicant   b. Project

e.g. Department of Justice, Department of Health and Human Services, etc.

15. ESTIMATED FUNDING:

The project name goes here.

a. Federal	$	.00
b. Applicant	$	.00
c. State	$	.00
d. Local	$	.00
e. Other	$	.00
f. Program Income	$	.00
g. TOTAL	$	.00

16. IS APPLICATION SUBJECT TO REVIEW BY STATE EXECUTI ORDER 12372 PROCESS?

a. Yes. ☐ THIS PREAPPLICATION/APPLICATION WAS MADE AVAILABLE TO THE STATE EXECUTIVE ORDER 1237 PROCESS FOR REVIEW ON

DATE:

b. No. ☐ PROGRAM IS NOT COVERED BY E. O. 12372

☐ OR PROGRAM HAS NOT BEEN SELECTED BY STATI FOR REVIEW

Call your representative's office to find out in which district the organization and project are located.

17. IS THE APPLICANT DELINQUENT ON ANY FEDERAL DEBT?

☐ Yes If "Yes" attach an explanation.   ☐ No

Insert budget totals below.

18. TO THE BEST OF MY KNOWLEDGE AND BELIEF, ALL DATA IN THIS APPLICATION/PREAPPLICATION ARE TRUE AND CORRECT. THE ... EN DULY AUTHORIZED BY THE GOVERNING BODY OF THE APPLICANT AND THE APPLICANT WILL COMPLY WITH THE ...NCES IF THE ASSISTANCE IS AWARDED.

...ntative

Prefix   First Name

Middle Name

Last Name

Suffix

State single point of contact information.

c. Telephone Number (give area code)

...ed Representative

e. Date Signed

Previous Edition Usable
Authorized for Local Reproduction

Standard Form 424 (Rev.9-2003)
Prescribed by OMB Circular A-102

Budget Forms

Budget forms vary by funder. The federal government provides two such forms—one for construction projects (SF424B) and one for all other projects (SF424A). Grant proposals use SF424A; the proper use of SF424B is very narrow as the federal government does not send RFPs for construction projects. A sample SF424A budget form follows.

Sample: SF424 Budget Form

Complete both pages before summarizing here.

See instructions for code numbers.

CFDA number from RFP

Often totals are automatic, but check to be sure.

Total columns above.

Percentage allowed may be predetermined.

BUDGET INFORMATION - Non-Construction Programs

OMB Approval No. 0348-0044

SECTION A - BUDGET SUMMARY

Grant Program Function or Activity (a)	Catalog of Federal Domestic Assistance Number (b)	Estimated Unobligated Funds		New or Revised Budget		
		Federal (c)	Non-Federal (d)	Federal (e)	Non-Federal (f)	Total (g)
.		$	$	$	$	$
.						
3.						
. Totals		$	$	$	$	$

SECTION B - BUDGET CATEGORIES

6. Object Class Categories	GRANT PROGRAM, FUNCTION OR ACTIVITY				Total
	(1)	(2)	(3)	(4)	(5)
a. Personnel	$	$	$	$	$
b. Fringe Benefits					
c. Travel					
d. Equipment					
e. Supplies					
f. Contractual					
g. Construction					
h. Other					
i. Total Direct Charges (sum of 6a-6h)					
j. Indirect Charges					
k. TOTALS (sum of 6i and 6j)	$	$	$	$	$
7. Program Income	$	$	$	$	$

Authorized for Local Reproduction

Previous Edition Usable

Standard Form 424A (Rev. 7-97)
Prescribed by OMB Circular A-102

All other sources of income are listed here.

SECTION C - NON-FEDERAL RESOURCES				
(a) Grant Program	(b) Applicant	(c) State	(d) Other Sources	(e) TOTALS
8.	$	$	$	$
9.				
10.				
11.				
12. TOTAL (sum of lines 8-11)	$	$	$	$

Divide grant award into appropriate payments. If purchasing necessary equipment, your first-quarter payment may be higher than the others.

SECTION D - FORECASTED CASH NEEDS					
	Total for 1st Year	1st Quarter	2nd Quarter	3rd Quarter	4th Quarter
13. Federal	$	$	$	$	$
14. Non-Federal					
15. TOTAL (sum of lines 13 and 14)	$	$	$	$	$

SECTION E - BUDGET ESTIMATES OF FEDERAL FUNDS NEEDED FOR BALANCE OF THE PROJECT				
(a) Grant Program	FUTURE FUNDING PERIODS (Years)			
	(b) First	(c) Second	(d) Third	(e) Fourth
16.	$	$	$	$
17.				
18.				
19.				
20. TOTAL (sum of lines 16-19)	$	$	$	$

For projects lasting two years or more.

SECTION F - OTHER BUDGET INFORMATION	
21. Direct Charges:	22. Indirect Charges:
23. Remarks:	

Authorized for Local Reproduction   Standard Form 424A (Rev. 7-97) Page 2

Leave blank if a twelve-month project.

Assurances

Assurances are necessary in all federal grants. They are narrative documents citing laws, guidelines, and other rules for doing business with the federal government. In other words, they are the preface to contracts you will sign if you are successful in grantseeking. Assurances are part of the application package or can be downloaded at www.grants.gov. Print the assurances and have the director of the applicant organization sign them. There is usually nothing to complete except the name of the organization and date of signature. In a few cases, you must attach a short narrative. For example, school districts must assure that the project proposed will be available to all students and attach a document stating efforts they will making to provide access, for instance, to students who are blind.

Attachments

Foundations require a few attachments and allow a few others. Most often, foundations require:

- A copy of the current IRS determination letter indicating 501(c)(3) tax-exempt status. Nonprofit organizations keep this letter and copy it dozens of times. It must be kept in a safe but convenient place. Never send your original letter.

> **Fitting Information into the Spaces Provided**
>
> Until recently, forms that accompanied grant applications were only available as hard copies or noninteractive Adobe PDF files that had to be printed and completed by hand. Many grantwriters retained typewriters so the forms would look professional when they were submitted. Most forms are now available as interactive PDFs or Microsoft Word documents, so they can be completed, changed, and reprinted from your computer. When you do encounter one that requires printout before completion, you may have to print legibly by hand or locate a typewriter at your local library. Be sure to take several copies of each form to allow for errors.

- List of Board of Directors with affiliations. Affiliations of board members are important. Do you have a board with known fundraisers or civic leaders? Does the composition of the board include representatives of the target population? Is the board diverse?
- Organization's current annual operating budget, including expenses and revenue. This is different from the project budget and can be several pages long.
- Most recent annual financial statement (independently audited, if available; if not available, attach Form 990). If the most recent audit is more than three years old, attach it with a more recent Form 990 tax statement. Do not assume, however, that a 990 can be substituted for an audited financial statement in all cases. Call your program officer to clarify.
- Letters of support should verify project need and collaboration with other organizations, but are optional attachments except in the case of letters from collaborating agencies.

Though not mandated, you may also attach annual reports of the organization, program brochures, organizational charts, or other pertinent information. If you mention a report (such as an evaluation of a past project) or other document in the narrative, but choose not to attach it, be sure that you can provide it if it is requested by the grants officer.

Submitting Your Proposal

The federal government has established eGrants, which allows you to complete and upload all forms and narrative sections of your proposal. It also affords you one more day to finalize the proposal because you do not need to ship the document the day before the deadline. Regardless of how well you plan, you will likely encounter proposal projects that push against the deadline, and you'll be grateful for another few hours. With eGrants, you still must pay the cost of shipping or mailing all original and signed forms, but after the deadline date. When you submit by eGrants you will be assigned an application number. Put the number on the mailing envelope and ship the documentation within a week of the deadline for application. The day after you submit to eGrants, you may elect to download your application back from eGrants and will receive the entire collated document with all forms (minus signatures).

Many foundations now also accept (and some mandate) e-applications. Check their websites and guidelines for specific information concerning instructions, deadlines, and troubleshooting.

If you are submitting a paper application, you can deliver it in person, select an overnight shipping service, or use the United States Postal Service (USPS). Choose the option that ensures your proposal will arrive before the deadline date and time. Some applications provide a "submit by" date, others provide a "received by" date. If you are to submit by a certain date, you must retain proof of the date through a USPS date stamp or computerized shipping receipt. If the application must be received by a certain date, you should probably select an overnight shipping service that provides a tracking number so you have proof that the proposal arrived by the deadline. Though it's good advice to ship two or three days before the deadline, it's more likely that you will be shipping proposals the night before they are due and, therefore, will require a guarantee of overnight delivery.

If you are submitting a grant to a local foundation, deliver it in person or mail it through the postal system.

A note on delivery: the federal government checks incoming mail for contaminants and other dangerous items. If you use the USPS, be sure to send it a few days in advance of the deadline to allow for this process.

> ***TIP***
>
> Sometimes you pay extra for a "by 10 a.m." delivery guarantee from an overnight service. Use your tracking number online to see if it was delivered by 10 a.m. You will often find that the proposal arrives much later. It sometimes even bumps up against the 5:00 p.m. EST deadline. Be sure to take your receipt and proof from the website to the shipper if you choose to ask them for a refund of overpayment or for a plan for backing up their guarantee next time. The dollars spent for an early delivery are peanuts compared with the lost opportunity for grant funding on a proposal that arrives late.

Summary Tips for Writing Grant Proposals

No uninspired or ineffective program was ever funded because the proposal was well written; however, good programs have an extra edge if the proposal is clear, concise, and easy to read. Remember, reviewers often read dozens of proposals in a day. You can make yours more memorable if you:

1. **Use the Active Voice:** Passive voice gives readers the impression that service magically occurs (e.g., services were received by forty individuals"). Avoid a tendency to be modest or self-effacing on behalf of the organization, and use active voice construction (e.g., "xyz nonprofit organization served forty people last year.)

2. **Explain Acronyms and Terms:** Never assume that the reader knows the same acronyms or buzzwords that are common to your organization or field of interest. (e.g., HUD, R&D).

3. **Form Alliances with Others:** Collaboration is key, but it must be based on the best and most cost-effective way to address the issue. Never collaborate simply for the sake of seeking funding.

4. **Keep Your Research and Data Up-to-date:** Statistics can inform the proposal reader, but may be deadly when the reader knows more than you do or when your idea is based on decade-old information about your population. The same is true about your research—perhaps your idea has already been put to the test.

5. **Follow Instructions and/or Format:** If the funder has "need" as the first point, he or she wants you to address need first. Also read questions and instructions carefully. Often the funder mandates spacing (single/double), font, type size, and margin and page limits. Any deviation from the instructions may result in your proposal being tossed out before review.

6. **Develop Strong Goals, Objectives, Outcomes, Action Steps, and Timelines:** Be sure to frame objectives and outcomes as measurable. Be realistic in what you expect the program to do and in what period of time.

7. **Write Your Abstract or Summary Last:** Use the narrative to identify key points you want to bring out in the abstract.

8. **Check Your Budget:** Does everything add up? Are costs realistic and reasonable?

9. **Plan for Letters of Support:** Educate your supporters on how to write a letter of support, or write their letters yourself and ask for their signatures. Plan well in advance of your deadline to gather these letters.

10. **Know Your Audience:** Will the grant proposal be reviewed by peers? If so, what would you want to know if you were reading? Will it be reviewed by government officials or foundation trustees? Learn everything you can about foundations and their trustees, and, if possible, about government departments or readers. Read annual reports from foundations to learn more about the staff and trustees. Meet with potential funders whenever you can.

11. **Watch Trends in Funding:** For several years, collaboration has been a mandatory eligibility criterion. They still are valued, but emerging issues, like a recent focus by many funders on professional development, can take you by surprise. Also watch for trends in funding particular types of programs or organizations (e.g., "Audience Engagement" strategies for arts organizations) and be first to develop programs that meet your local need and fill the requirement.

12. **Enlist Draft Reviewers:** Hand off the final draft with the criteria or rubric the decision makers will use to evaluate your proposal. Ask your own reviewers to make suggestions for strengthening the proposal. The writer is too close to the work to evaluate the program in the same critical manner a reviewer will.

13. **Be Proactive:** Rather than solely responding to RFPs, plan strong programs, identify what works, whose help you need, and what it will take to implement your plan. Then go seek funding for your program. If it's likely to work, there's likely to be a funder out there just waiting to hear your solution.

CHAPTER 9

Individualizing Your Proposals
by Type of Project

When you undertake proactive grantseeking, you will find that different foundations are interested not just in different program areas, but in different types of support. For instance, many foundations will not fund operations or debt retirement. Some funders may fund faith-based initiatives but will not fund projects that include religious conversion activities. These limitations and preferences must shape your approach to the individual funders: if one does not provide capital funding, perhaps it would consider funding a new project you are planning in your new building; if another isn't interested in seed funding for a new project, perhaps it would entertain a sustainability effort later.

Each of the following types of projects includes a definition, a description of potential funding sources, some strategies for presenting the proposal, and a sample grant proposal (or partial proposal):
- Capital grant
- Challenge grant
- Capacity-building grant
- Sustainability grant
- Demonstration project
- Operations
- Special populations project

Capital Grants

What Is It?

Capital refers to tangible goods—equipment or buildings. In a capital grant proposal, nonprofit organizations may request funding to purchase computers for all staff, to erect a broadcast tower or a new office building, to buy transportation vans or buses, or to purchase a suite of dialysis machines. Remember, however, that many foundations do not fund the purchase of equipment, like computers, unless the equipment is necessary to implement a program. In other words, they are interested in funding what you will do with the computers.

When a nonprofit organization is purchasing, constructing, or renovating a building, or when it must make large and costly purchases of equipment, it often will undertake a "capital campaign." A capital campaign is an organized attempt to raise a large sum of money (often multimillions) from hundreds of donors.

Generally, a grant writer will not run a capital campaign but will write grants for the foundation division of the campaign. There are fund-raising consultant organizations that specialize in managing large capital campaigns.

Appropriate Funding Sources

Capital campaigns are often organized by size of donation and type of donor, with foundations generally accounting for approximately half to two-thirds of the overall budget. They are often staged so that a number of donors have committed a significant amount toward the goal before the campaign goes public for broader support. At some point after you raise funds from foundations and major donors, the campaign fund-raising targets will include board members and staff of the organizations and the general public when there is broad public benefit from the construction project (for example, an arena, hospital, or art museum). The federal government rarely funds capital construction projects and allows capital purchases only when they are necessary to implement a project plan. State government will sometimes fund civic improvement projects, but this is something that is negotiated between legislators, governors, and civic leaders and does not require a grant proposal.

There is at least one large, national foundation that funds capital campaigns throughout the U.S.; however, like others, it requires that most capital funding first come from the city or region in which the project will be based or constructed.

Strategies

Strategies for raising capital vary by the size of the goal. For instance, if a nonprofit is raising a few thousand dollars to purchase computers and accessories, it may be able to raise the money with just a few well-placed requests of local foundations or supportive wealthy individuals.

Large capital campaigns, however, can run the course of several years—both to complete the project and to raise all the necessary funding. Often, a nonprofit organization hires a consulting firm or a project manager to plan and oversee the campaign and to keep up the staff's spirits during the long fund-raising process.

Writing grant proposals for capital projects around which there will be a campaign is somewhat easier than writing project proposals because several things are completed already: a case statement that can be modified to complete the need section of the proposal, as well as goals and outcomes for the capital project itself. The evaluation, too, is relatively simple. A capital construction project would be considered successful if the project were completed on time and within budget. You should note, however, that foundations are increasingly reluctant to fund capital campaigns that do not also have objectives and planned outcomes for enhanced projects or expanded services that will be enabled by a construction project. The "if we build it they will come" method of capital planning has a long list of failures. Sustainability matters! Funders are also looking more closely at building needs assessments and utility plans that include adequate revenue to sustain increased services in a new space.

Most foundations do not fund endowments; however, they may want to see that your organization is planning for the future and expect you to have an endowment or restricted fund to support maintenance as a line item in your capital budget. While that foundation may not earmark its donation for the endowment, perhaps a wealthy local individual will, and it sends the message that you are planning ahead so you can maintain and operate a new facility. When funds are raised for an endowment, the nonprofit can establish an operations or maintenance endowment (often held in perpetuity by a community foundation) and draw from the fund's income to help defray annual operating costs.

Another foundation hot button in capital campaigns is planning for access by people with disabilities. If you are constructing a two-story building, you must budget for an elevator and include railings in restrooms or aisles, not only because this is often required by law, but because foundations want to see that you are available to everyone who might need your services.

Sample: Capital Grant Proposal

This capital campaign will attract foundation funding and funding from area manufacturers and business leaders who have a special interest in training future employees and strengthening the local economy.

Write out the name of the organization on first reference; thereafter, use the acronym, but also write out the name occasionally.

Neighborhood improvement is a focus for a community foundation, the audience for this proposal.

A Renaissance Zone is a neighborhood targeted for improvement that is offering tax abatements or incentives to new developments or commercial improvements.

Urban Center Community College

A. NARRATIVE

1. Executive Summary

Urban Center Community College (UCCC) is requesting a $250,000 grant toward a $10.9 million capital project—the Southwest Technical Education Center (S-TEC), which will be constructed in an urban center Renaissance Zone on Godfrey and Rumsey Streets. Fifteen community colleges in the state received state funding for an S-TEC. UCCC received two such grants: one for the urban center that is the object of this proposal, and another for a center in a more rural location. The sixteen statewide S-TECs are required to offer training and education for high-wage, high-demand careers as defined by workers and employers in their respective communities. In the Urban Center area, those jobs have been identified as automotive service, construction trades, and manufacturing.

Once developed on an 11-acre vacant lot in the Black Hills neighborhood, within walking distance from residents of the Central neighborhood, the S-TEC is expected to be a catalyst for further development, revitalization, and improvement in these neighborhoods. Residents of the area will benefit from nearby job training and ancillary services designed to improve the economic status of their families. Businesses in Urban Center will benefit from a new source of trained, skilled workers.

2. Purpose of Grant

Needs Statement

In the past ten years, the Urban Center Metropolitan Statistical Area has experienced a population increase of 13 percent. Wage and salary employment by place of work has increased more than 39 percent. With current unemployment levels at record lows, employers are scrambling to find qualified workers and are focusing on maximizing existing worker skill levels. Unprecedented growth in manufacturing has increased the need for skilled building trades workers to construct, renovate, and maintain the factories, commercial buildings, and residences that have resulted from this economic development. Skilled automotive technicians are necessary to service the personal and commercial vehicles for the ever-increasing population.

Currently, workforce development programs in high-paying, high-demand career positions (e.g., automotive service, building/construction trades, and manufacturing) are housed in a facility leased from the Urban Center Public Schools (UCPS). The current facility on Leon Street is no longer adequate to the need of current and potential UCCC students in these programs as it is in poor repair and is shared with a UCPS alternative high school.

The proposed site of the UCCC S-TEC Center is eleven acres in a near-downtown Renaissance Zone on Godfrey and Rumsey Streets Southwest. Residents of the area (Central and Great Neighborhoods) are, according to 1990 census figures provided by the Urban Center Planning Department, approximately 38.6 percent white, 29.14 percent African-American, 33.25 percent Hispanic, and 2.04 percent Asian, Native American, and other. The median household income of neighboring residents is approximately $17,304, with approximately 29.45 percent of nearby households living below the federal poverty level. Unemployment rates are 20.9 percent in the

Central Neighborhood and 12.6 percent in the Great Neighborhood. These community members report being hampered from full-time employment by several factors, including but not limited to language barriers (nearly 25 percent of residents of both neighborhoods report not speaking English well), lack of reliable transportation, lack of public transportation for second or third shifts, and/or lack of education/training necessary to qualify for well-paying jobs.

Goals, Objectives, and Action Plans

Urban Center Community College proposes to construct a 74,000 square foot technical educati center on the corner of Godfrey and Rumsey S.W., on an 11-acre site donated by StateCon Gas Company. The new building will house the Automotive Technology, Building Trades Apprentice, Furniture Manufacturing, and Welding programs currently housed at the center leased from the Urban Center Public Schools. In addition, the facility will house Occupational Training offices, classrooms, distance learning technology, and a State Works! Service Center.

The goal of the capital campaign is to construct a state-of-the-art technical training center that will achieve several community development and workforce development outcomes, as described below:

> The need statement provides several reasons for selecting the site because the neighborhood is a focus of this funder. When the applicant goes to another potential funder with a stronger interest in job training or economic development, it would strengthen this need section with more evidence of the need for targeted skills and use research on local economic trends to emphasize those funders' interests.

Community Development/Neighborhood Improvement Outcomes:

- Be a catalyst for nearby revitalization, development, and change. In collaboration with other community agencies/services developing programs in the neighborhood (e.g., potential Town Center/Community Police Precinct in Franklin School; City Media Center neighborhood communications studio; Central Neighborhood Arts Center; Urban Center Public Schools; Hispanic Community Center; Hispanic Health Clinic, and others) to improve the quality of life for area residents.

- Strengthen the Renaissance Zone neighborhood surrounding the S-TEC Center by reclaiming and remediating a large, currently vacant piece of land. (Along with its land donation, StateCon has provided necessary financing for environmental clean-up of the property.)

- Provide "walk to work" opportunities for neighbors; provide space for other services for students and neighbors, including but not limited to a library, technology access, and a State Works! intake office.

- Provide all classes in both English and Spanish; provide translation services and/or bilingual tutoring programs for individuals for whom English is a second language.

Workforce Development/Neighborhood Economic Growth Outcomes

- Provide job training in high-wage, high-skill, high-demand occupations, thereby meeting the need of area employers for skilled workers and the needs of individuals for high-wage jobs.

- Establish a network between and among UC, AC, and BC Counties; State Virtual Automotive College, and State Community College Virtual Learning College to provide instruction, counseling, advising, financial aid, library services, registration services, and job placement to students off campus.

> In a grant proposal to a funder that emphasizes environmental issues, the entire proposal would be restructured to emphasize these outcomes.

- Provide new or improved training programs in targeted industries.

Timetable for Implementation

The timeline for the construction project is as follows:

January 2000	Cabinet meeting and public campaign kick-off
February 2000	Community presentations, campaign information sessions with community constituents
March 2000	Campaign volunteers to complete solicitation calls and necessary follow up
April 2000	Phase two solicitation and pledge confirmations
May 2000	Final follow-up and celebration. Cabinet dismissed
June-July 2000	Official ground breaking
August-Sept. 2000	Construction begins
Fall 2001	Facility opens

Planning for collaborative relationships and initiatives designed to improve the quality of life for neighbors in the surrounding area will be ongoing throughout the capital campaign and beyond.

Partners and Roles

An advisory board composed of approximately 80 percent private business representatives from the three occupational training areas and 20 percent community residents and leaders will provide direction, leadership, and oversight of planning, implementation, and evaluation of all programs and services at the Center. Area partners in the center include Lonnie Tuff, StateCon, Major Manufacturing, Urban Center Spring and Stamping, Associated Builders and Contractors, The Manufacturers Council, Chemical Coaters Association, and others. The S-TEC center will be linked to the State and with the other fifteen S-TEC centers being established across the State for sharing problem-solving efforts and results.

Similar Projects/Agencies

Urban Center Community College is the only community college in the State to have been awarded two State grants for construction of S-TEC centers. (The other is being built in Nearby County in partnership with the Nearby Area Intermediate School District.)

Urban Center Community College and the State University are partners in the Applied Technology Center, a part of the downtown campus. This partnership allows students from our community to further their educational and career goals by completing a Bachelor's degree program without traveling to the State University. With the expansion of another State University in downtown Urban Center, individuals will have even more opportunity to continue to advance their education, careers, and earning potential.

The S-TEC facility will house the only college-level programs in automotive servicing, welding, metal stamping, building trades, and apprentice programs in Urban Center. These are all high-skill, high-wage occupational areas with solid career path opportunities in engineering, management, quality control and many other areas.

The applicant provides a simple timeline indicating major events and benchmarks of the campaign.

Again, the proposal emphasizes an area of interest to the community foundation.

Note that neighborhood residents are not included on the advisory group, but they are included in the constituent involvement section of the proposal.

While there are other educational programs in the area, the applicant sets this project apart by pointing out how it differs from others, and where it doesn't, by claiming collaboration rather than competition with those programs.

Constituent Involvement

The State requires that each S-TEC have a private sector governing board to decide the types of training to be offered and the services available in the Center. This Board will be composed of representatives from area businesses, neighbors of the Center, and community leaders. Before it finalizes construction and floor plans, UCCC plans to hold focus groups among neighbors to discuss the Center and what it can mean to the neighborhood and to hear neighbors' requests for additional services in the building. Finally, in response to the wishes of neighbors and the Urban Center Public Schools, S-TEC will offer K-12 exposure to occupations, outreach to girls about nontraditional career choices for women, and shared staff and facilities with UCPS.

Qualifications of Key Project Staff

Urban Center Community College has more than twenty-five years of experience in the operation of employment and job-training programs serving dislocated workers, the economically disadvantaged, unemployed, and under-employed individuals, as well as providing customized training programs for current employees at hundreds of employers throughout west State. Throughout the years, management staff, project coordinators, and instructional staff have developed and maintained linkages with FIA, SUA, State Rehabilitation Services (SRS), County government and its services, Urban Center Housing Commission, Women's Resource Center, Urban Center Public Schools, County Intermediate School District, The Business Attraction Program, United Way, and numerous other educational providers.

> In the case of very large institutions, most staff are key personnel, so the writer focuses instead on the institutional history and capacity rather than any one individual.

Instructional staff in all occupational programs are respected practitioners in their field, have demonstrated work experience in their occupational area, and hold all appropriate certifications.

Long-term strategies for funding

> Long-term strategies for funding is another way of asking for a sustainability plan.

Once the Southwest S-TEC is completed, UCCC will move programs currently housed at the Occupational Training Center and apprentice programs currently housed in a variety of makeshift training labs into the Center. These programs and the additional opportunities at the Center will result in a project student population of more than 2,500 students per year. Tuition generated from these programs and the annual general fund transfers are expected to cover operational costs. Numerous business leaders have also committed to assisting with establishing a "technology endowment" to assist with ongoing equipment needs and technology upgrades.

> This discussion provides some evidence that the college will not rely on grant funds.

3. Evaluation
Evaluation Plans

Like other capital projects, the construction of the S-TEC will be judged successful if it is constructed according to timeline and within budget. In addition, UCCC plans to further develop an evaluation plan during construction that will be used to judge the success of long-range objectives, including but not limited to the number of neighborhood youth or adults using the Center, the number of neighborhood students who become employed as a result of their training, and the duration of their employment. The final evaluation will also provide data and observation on the Center's effect on the surrounding neighborhood to determine whether constructing the Center in a Renaissance Zone did, in fact, serve as a catalyst for improvement and change.

> The applicant provides a second evaluation of the planned outcomes for the construction project. This evaluation will help the applicant judge how well this project meets the specific goals of the community foundation funder.

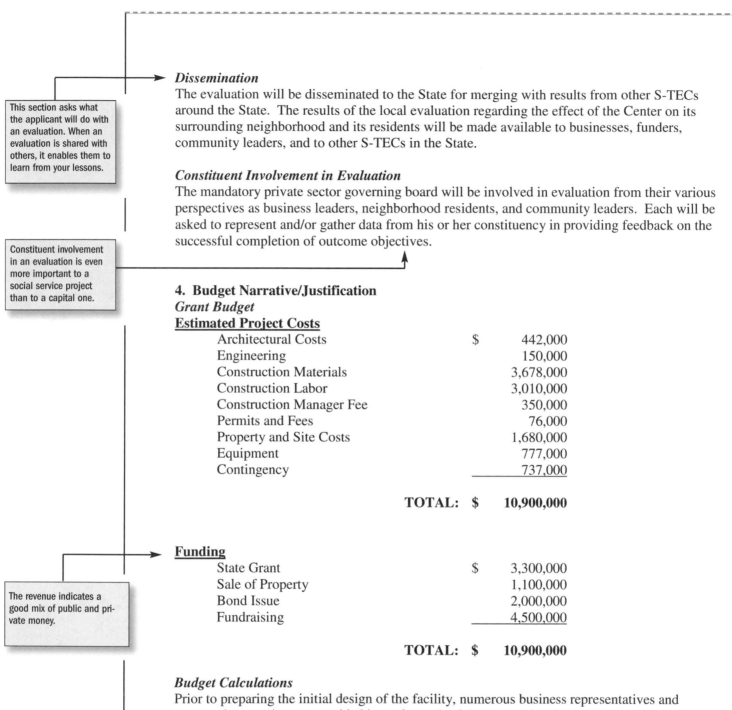

This section asks what the applicant will do with an evaluation. When an evaluation is shared with others, it enables them to learn from your lessons.

Dissemination

The evaluation will be disseminated to the State for merging with results from other S-TECs around the State. The results of the local evaluation regarding the effect of the Center on its surrounding neighborhood and its residents will be made available to businesses, funders, community leaders, and to other S-TECs in the State.

Constituent Involvement in Evaluation

The mandatory private sector governing board will be involved in evaluation from their various perspectives as business leaders, neighborhood residents, and community leaders. Each will be asked to represent and/or gather data from his or her constituency in providing feedback on the successful completion of outcome objectives.

Constituent involvement in an evaluation is even more important to a social service project than to a capital one.

4. Budget Narrative/Justification
Grant Budget
Estimated Project Costs

Architectural Costs	$	442,000
Engineering		150,000
Construction Materials		3,678,000
Construction Labor		3,010,000
Construction Manager Fee		350,000
Permits and Fees		76,000
Property and Site Costs		1,680,000
Equipment		777,000
Contingency		737,000
TOTAL:	**$**	**10,900,000**

Funding

State Grant	$	3,300,000
Sale of Property		1,100,000
Bond Issue		2,000,000
Fundraising		4,500,000
TOTAL:	**$**	**10,900,000**

The revenue indicates a good mix of public and private money.

Budget Calculations

Prior to preparing the initial design of the facility, numerous business representatives and community constituents provided input for each of the occupational areas to be housed in the Center. This information was then forwarded to architect JM from Design Associates who developed the initial renderings, program statement, and project budget. The project will be put out for bid and verification of cost estimates.

This statement indicates that budgets are rounded estimates. Applicants try to estimate slightly high so they are not caught having to raise additional money for cost overruns.

Funding Sources

Through early January 2000, UCCC has received the following financial commitments for the construction project:

State	$3.3 million S-TEC grant
Lonny Tuff	$1.5 million lead donor gift
StateCon	$1 million, land value
StateCon	$250,000 cash
Major Manuf., Inc.	$100,000 in products
Associated Builders & Contractors	$50,000

> The building will likely be named for the lead gift donor.

UCCC must raise $4.5 million from the community to complete the project. It is requesting $250,000 each from The Major Manufacturing Foundation, The Urban Center Community Foundation, Family Foundation, and Major Donor Foundation, and is currently in discussion with civic leaders and smaller foundations concerning grants of as-yet undetermined amounts. The campaign cabinet is divided into categories with cochairs representing the appropriate industries for further fund-raising within the three categories: manufacturing, auto service, and trades and construction. Leadership gifts from the three sectors started to arrive at UCCC during the second week of January 2000.

Priority Items for Funding

The Urban Center Community Foundation grant will be applied toward the $10.9 million capital cost for construction.

> This section of the proposal asks, "if you do not receive the full amount of your request, which aspect of the project would you prioritize for funding?" The response in this case indicates that whatever the amount of the gift, it will go to the overall fund. There are not priority funding requests; a less-than gift would simply mean that the college must ask another funder to increase its gift or find additional funders to make up the difference between the planned income and that granted.

5. Organization Information

Organizational History

Urban Center Junior College was established in 1914 by the Urban Center Board of Education and is located in the Central High School Building of the Urban Center Public Schools. Its first graduating class numbered forty-nine students.

Through a 1991 vote of the people of County Intermediate School District, the school was renamed "Urban Center Community College," and benefited from countywide support and a dedicated Board of Trustees.

The college has grown in the past eighty-five years to serve more than 25,000 students annually (full- and part-time) and issues approximately 1,100 degrees or certificates each year. The campus includes classroom buildings, a learning center and library, a music building, field house with natatorium, student center, theater, occupational and technical education centers, and parking ramps. The newest addition to the campus, Science Center, opened in January 2000.

Mission and Goals

Urban Center Community College is a vibrant institution of higher education dedicated to enriching people's lives and contributing to the vitality of the community. Its mission is to provide the community with learning opportunities that enable people to achieve their goals.

> Once written, the history can be revised slightly for use with other grantmaking audiences for this project.

Current Programs, Activities, and Accomplishments
UCCC has had a number of recent accomplishments, but the most relevant to this request is its successful job training program. The program currently enrolls more than 450 people annually. Final performance data for open-entry, open-exit programs at UCCC reflect a completion rate of 83 percent, a placement rate of 87 percent, and an average starting wage of $9.22 per hour. Eighty percent of job training graduates are still working after ninety days. Locally, more than 153 different employers hire repeatedly from among UCCC job training participants.

The Urban Center Community College Foundation will be the fiduciary agent for all grants to S-TEC. The Foundation (list of board members is attached) is responsible for administering more than $10.9 million in contributions annually.

Organizational Chart
The composition of the governance board for the Southwest S-TEC is not yet finalized. This board, which is mandated by the State to have 80 percent private sector representation, will include business leaders from the three target occupations, community leaders, and neighbors from the Central/Great community.

> Rather than attaching an organizational chart for the entire college, the applicant provides information relevant only to this project.

Challenge Grants

What Is It?

Though the two terms are often used interchangeably, there are subtle differences between challenge and matching grants. A challenge grant is made by a foundation to assist the nonprofit in raising funds from other sources. Challenges are often made either at the beginning or the end of capital campaigns to help launch or close out the effort. A challenge grant is given most often in a 1:1 or 2:1 ratio. Before the non-profit can receive its grant award, it must demonstrate that it has donations from the other funding sources in the amounts mandated.

In the case of a match grant, the foundation agrees to meet what you raise within a given time and up to a specific amount.

A match requirement is entirely different from a matching grant. Federal grants often have a match requirement, meaning, for instance, that if the nonprofit must provide a 10 percent match, it can ask for $200,000 in grant funds only with the guaranteed offer of $20,000 of its own funds or those of its partners. Sometimes a match can be made of in-kind donations, which include space, equipment, etc., but most often, grants require cash matches.

Appropriate Funding Sources

Some national foundations issue challenge grants to stimulate giving from local sources to projects that address their goals. For instance, one major national funder makes a multimillion grant for teen centers in urban areas provided that local donors grant several million among them for an operating endowment. Another example is a national foundation that focuses on health issues. It often offers challenge grants to launch a health initiative designed to raise local money and, more importantly, local awareness about an important issue such as smoking, lead-based paint, or HIV/AIDS.

Many of your local foundations will consider challenge grant requests. There is little risk on their part, since if the applicant does not raise the challenge, the foundation does not pay out the grant funds.

The federal government has match requirements on many of its grant opportunities, but generally does not offer challenge grants.

Strategies

A challenge grant can either be requested or assigned. Because some funders are extremely reluctant to be the only funder for a project, they may push the applicant organization to find other funders by offering a challenge grant. When and if other funders come to the project, you will get your award. It's a better strategy, if you think this may be the case, to simply request a challenge grant. In this way, you demonstrate to the first potential funder that you understand that more funding sources are necessary and you are willing to do the work needed to educate and excite potential funders about your project.

In the following sample challenge grant application, the public access station is located in a blue-collar suburb (a bedroom community) that has few major donors and a population that has not historically supported large capital campaigns. The foundation is located near the suburb. The staff of the foundation know the composition and giving history of the bedroom community and the struggle the nonprofit will face in raising necessary funds.

Sample: Challenge Grant Proposal

SECTION II

This project is also a capital one, but, in this case, the organization took out a loan to fund construction and is asking the community to fund only the interior layout and design. The local foundation may be the only major donor to the project; therefore, the necessity to stimulate giving by the public.

Project Introduction

WYKY seeks to expand service to the communities of Wy, Ky and Lye Township by completing the interior of a brand-new and permanent home for the station. Ready for occupancy on August 2, 2002, the new 10,000 square-foot community television facility will be the largest in the United States, and for good reason: WYKY is one of the most heavily used community television stations in the country.

Since WYKY's mission is to promote community communication, the most appropriate theme for the interior design of the facility is "community." The capital campaign, therefore, seeks to create a "community within a community," a place where the hundreds of community volunteers who speak several languages and come from a variety of backgrounds and classes can work together in a representation of the neighborhoods where they grew up, live, work, and communicate.

This introduction does not summarize the major sections of the proposal or state up front what the applicant is requesting. A cover sheet required by the donor requests summary information, so the grantwriter is free to introduce the project and applicant rather than creating an introductory abstract.

Project Name

"Look Inside WYKY," capital campaign

Project Description

WYKY has constructed an $800,000, 10,000 square-foot broadcast center on Center Park near Gizzard Parkway and 52nd Streets. The interior construction is designed to honor local (Wy/Ky) history with friezes, storefronts, cafes, a brick walkway and other architectural and artistic details. Various wall murals will record the history of growth in the cities and honor the diverse ethnic heritages now residing in the area. The cost for the interior construction is $500,000, which WYKY is seeking from the community.

Features of the interior include:

- The Drive In-ternet (modeled after the Historic Drive In and offering high-speed Internet access)
- Friezes and facades depicting the industrial and agricultural growth of the area
- Master-control cafe where people may watch and learn the broadcast industry or meet informally for coffee and discussions
- Permanent offices for the Wy Jaycees (and other nonprofit organizations as requested)
- Two studios and three edit bays
- Free meeting space for the Jaycees, Wy-Ky Area Chamber of Commerce, District 9 Little League Association, Rotary Clubs and other nonprofit organizations and associations
- Indoor brick walkways, outdoor furnished patio, and kitchen facilities

Because the community is not composed of traditional major donors, WYKY is requesting a challenge grant to be used during a December 2002 telethon to announce the campaign publicly, provide a status report of funding to that date, and encourage financial commitments to the Center from community members.

The applicant requests a challenge grant to spur giving from a community that historically has not been composed of philanthropists.

Audience

An estimated 80 percent of residents of Ky and Wy are aware that they have a public access community television station and have watched the station at some time. Of viewers:

- 30 percent are between the ages of 18 and 30
- 40 percent are between the ages of 31 and 50
- 25 percent are between the ages of 51 and 65
- 5 percent are over age 65

> This grantor asks for the audience for all projects. It's another way of asking about the target population, stakeholders, or constituency.

In addition, the channel reaches an estimated 3,200 Vietnamese individuals with the only programming available in their native language. An Asian New Year Celebration held by WYKY drew more than 2,000 people. WYKY also provides special Spanish language programming for the estimated 9,400 individuals in the viewing area who are of Latin heritage.

> The organization makes a point of addressing the needs and interests of various ethnic groups that comprise the community.

More than 260 volunteers—from teens to seniors—help produce, host, and broadcast WYKY programs and annually donate more than 13,000 hours. WYKY specializes in family-oriented programming, educational (school readiness and reading) programs, and programs for non-English-speaking populations.

Need

In 2000, for the third time in twenty-eight years, WYKY was asked to move from its leased space. Since this effort disrupts broadcasting and requires cost and labor not ordinarily budgeted, the Board of WYKY encouraged staff to explore construction of a permanent facility.

At the same time, with four full-time and three part-time staff, more than 250 volunteers, and a growing demand from community members for quality programming, WYKY has outgrown its current facility, which is composed of one studio, one editing room, and two offices. The new facility is 10,000 square feet and affords the station two studios, three private edit bays, a graphics and animation station, and ample office and meeting space for staff, volunteers, and community members. WYKY also plans to provide free meeting space for local nonprofit organizations and will house the offices of the Wy-Ky Jaycees on site. The Jaycees have signed a two-year lease, revenues from which will offset increased operating costs.

The expanded facility will also provide space for new programs such as family-centered high-speed Internet access and computer training for children through seniors. On-site training in community television production will offer classes tailored to the specific needs of the more than three hundred individuals who take classes annually, and address identified needs for improved organizational and communication skills. Ongoing classes include organizing production, editing, scriptwriting, studio and mobile production, hosting, and computer/Internet use. A central master control site is being designed specifically to recruit additional volunteers and act as an introductory training site.

> The applicant makes a point of telling how it will sustain operations in the larger facility. This also demonstrates its willingness to work with other local nonprofit organizations.

Outcomes

The planned outcomes for the project include:

- Increase availability of free and reduced-cost meeting site for area nonprofit organizations and affiliations and for the general public.
- Increase volunteerism in the communities.

- Improve communication and organizational skills of local citizens who participate in WYKY production classes.
- Create a family-centered environment that highlights the history of Wy and Ky and is equipped with the current television and computer equipment available for public access.
- Provide the Wy-Ky community with an asset that will increase in value due to its location and value to community members.

Collaborations

The capital project includes office space for the Wy-Ky Jaycees and will be offered rent-free for meetings of the Jaycees, the Wy-Ky Area Chamber of Commerce, the District 9 Little League Association, Rotary Clubs, and other nonprofit organizations and associations in the area on request. Any member of the Wy-Ky public may use the facility for a reduced rate.

> The writer makes a negative (no collaboration on the construction project) into a positive (ongoing relationships with area nonprofit organizations).

While there are no collaborators to the construction project, WYKY supports the following organizations with programs and exchanges: Wy Public Library. Wy-Ky Area Chamber of Commerce, Wy Park High School, East Ky High School, Ly High School, Fry High School, Guy High School, Wy Christian High School, Ky Historical Commission, Wy Cultural Commission, Wy and Ky Police and Fire Departments, Wy and Ky Parks and Recreation Departments, AARP, and Retired Senior Volunteer Patrol.

Similar Projects

WYKY is similar to other public access television stations like FLTV and WKIT. No similar construction projects are competing for donations at this time.

Budget and Funding

Construction costs for the facility ($800,000) were financed on a twenty-year loan from Bank & Trust. This funding will enable WYKY to build and occupy the building. Interior design costs are sought from the public. A budget of line-item expenses for the construction project is attached, as is a list of project components with naming opportunities for local businesses and individual donors.

> This section does not speak to consumer involvement in the design of the building because there wasn't any. If there had been community input, the grantwriter could make a stronger case for funding.

Sustainability

The capital project is a one-time expense. Operations are sustained annually by a government-allotted portion of cable revenues, private donations, and small fees for classes. Volunteers operate the station, reducing ongoing operating costs.

Evaluation

The project will be judged successful when constructed on time and within budget.

Consumer Involvement

Nearly five hundred people volunteered to work on at least one community television production in 2001. In addition, approximately 250 volunteers regularly use the broadcast center annually and commit more than 13,000 hours of service. Last year, the one WYKY studio was used for local productions more than seven hundred times, editing facilities were used 283 times, the remote television truck was used 105 times, and volunteers checked out portable cameras 264 times.

Organization Background
History, Mission, and Goals
The Wy Cable TV Commission was appointed and launched in November 1974 in response to Wy resident's desire to have their own television channel to broadcast local events and news and to provide an opportunity for educational volunteerism. The company was joined by Ky in 1995 and named "WYKY." In 1997, the broadcast area expanded again to cover Lye Township. Now in existence for 28 years, WYKY is the second oldest community television station in the U.S.

WYKY's mission is to maximize television communication opportunities for cities of Wy, Ky, and Lye Township and to promote civic involvement through volunteer participation in televised community events coverage. Toward that end, WYKY offers family-oriented programming and news coverage, classes in television production, diverse volunteer opportunities, and equipment lending.

Capacity-building Grants

What Is It?

A capacity-building grant expands the ability of a nonprofit to provide its services. Nonprofit applicants usually have to convince a funder that they have the expertise and capacity to be successful at implementing their grant-funded project. However, in some cases, it makes sense to look for ways to build capacity of the nonprofit: when demand for services exceeds the ability of the organization to provide those services; when a new project requires a skill or expertise that the organization doesn't have; or when the nonprofit has an opportunity to grow but is held back for lack of human, financial, or capital resources.

Sometimes a foundation will add capacity building (and often the funding for it) into a project grant to help ensure its success.

Appropriate Funding Sources

Capacity-building grants are usually provided by local foundations who know the need of the community and the strength of the nonprofit organizations that serve the community. Sometimes, national foundations launch an initiative to build capacity among several organizations in different locations. For instance, one foundation strengthened community foundations by providing funding to encourage trustees to do site visits with staff. Another selected a city that was economically decimated and racially divided and provided minigrants to help sustain and strengthen the city's smallest nonprofit organizations, and a third provided research on building audiences for arts and cultural programs, which it shared with those organizations through the use of reports and consultants.

Though they are not called so, many federal grants could be classified as capacity-building grants in that they often enable nonprofit or public services to do more or do better.

Strategies

You can approach capacity-building fund-raising proactively or reactively, though you must sift through RFPs to find the one that is right for the organization and community it serves. It's best to discuss with local foundations a new, emerging need or a growing need and your organization's plan to expand to meet the need. They will likely invite you to submit a proposal. Most are more interested in strengthening existing nonprofits than in starting additional ones.

Sample: Capacity-Building Grant Proposal

Description

Craterville, Midwest is a small, unincorporated city (population 22,000) located south of Green River in Gye and Bye Townships, Kanton County. The Craterville Fire Department (CFD) last year responded or coresponded with adjacent departments to more than 1,300 calls with a team of fourteen paid/on-call and three full-time firefighters. CFD cotrains, coresponds, and shares equipment with six adjacent semirural communities in southwest Midwest: Dyes (Gye Township), Cyes Township, Dress Township, Middleton (Thy Township), Bye Center (Bye Township) and Leighvillle Township. All seven share common borders and are adjacent to or along established flight paths of the Kanton County Airport. ◄

> Departments in small communities usually share resources and usually go out together on calls. It's their way of building their own capacities, so it is a strong case to make for this department.

Because none of the seven communities is adequately equipped with sufficient staff, volunteers, or equipment, increasingly, all seven fire departments respond together to emergency calls in the region, and leadership from all seven meet regularly to discuss shared problems and solutions. This inter-reliance among the departments forms a stronger response team than would otherwise be available in smaller communities, and all departments and communities realize an economy of scale in purchases, maintenance, and training.

CFD seeks with this FEMA grant to accomplish two primary goals: improving firefighter safety and providing vital equipment needed and shared by the consortium. ◄

> Goals are selected from those provided in the FEMA RFP.

Goal A: Improve firefighter safety. Toward this end, CFD plans to purchase a replacement base station, ten portable radios, one set of five headsets, and seventeen pagers to facilitate and improve field communications. As learned from the events of September 11, 2001, many of the rescue workers died directly as a result of communications device failure. It also plans purchase of a fixed generator to ensure normal central-command operations and communications in the event of power failures. The community experienced six such failures last year from tornadoes, ice, and other weather damage or from damage to high-tension power lines and power supply stations from accidents or age. The generator would fill another need in the community, as well, in that the fire department could become a shelter for residents in crisis.

> The enabling legislation for the FEMA grants referenced 9/11. Fire departments that understand what went wrong on that day when so many rescuers were lost should reference the date to justify their selection of equipment.

CFD also plans the purchase of equipment never owned by the department, but necessary to protect firefighters during aerial firefighting and rescue. Calls for this type of service have increased annually and now include approximately three annual calls. This purchase will include six sets of fall-arrester harnesses, safety ropes and bags, carabiners, and pulleys to protect firefighters engaged in aerial work. Other necessary equipment not currently owned by the department includes ten life vests, which CFD would purchase to protect firefighters engaged in water rescue with an inflatable boat also requested and described later in this narrative.

> The generator is important to this community and is on a FEMA list of approved purchases.

Critically important to the safety of CFD firefighters is replacement of obsolete and damaged personal protective equipment, including seventeen flashlights, ten complete sets of turnout gear, and seven thirty-minute SCBAs. The flashlights are issued to all firefighters and are necessary equipment both for finding a way to rescue in dark or smoky places and for signaling location when a firefighter needs rescue or support. The turnout gear is more than ten years old. The need for replacing turnout gear is urgent. They have consistently failed vapor tests and, consequently, no longer meet National Fire Protection Agency (NFPA) standards and no longer protect firefighters performing their duties. CFD, therefore, plans the immediate purchase of seven sets

> After 9/11 FEMA found that many fire departments, especially those in smaller communities, had out-of-date and damaged equipment and had not purchased with tax dollars equipment that would help them perform rescues or protect their lives at the response site.

of turnout gear as afforded by its annual budget, and requests the remaining ten from FEMA. Also urgent is replacement of the department's SCBAs. CFD has for several years rebuilt its SCBAs by taking apart failed units and reusing functioning parts or purchasing parts they did not have. The existing SCBAs are more than nineteen years old; consequently, parts are no longer available. The department has purchased ten new units from its annual budget and requires seven additional units to bring all firefighters into compliance with applicable NFPA and OSHA standards.

Goal B: Provide vital equipment needed for coresponding and cotraining among the consortium fire departments. CFD plans a critical purchase of a fixed compressor/cascade fill station both to ensure the safety of its own firefighters and to share with adjacent departments requiring centrally located SCBA filling. Currently no member of the training consortium owns a fill station and all must seek refill and service at departments in the larger cities of Kyle or Wick.

CFD also plans the purchase of a 35 mm camera for use in fire investigations. CFD's captain will soon complete training for certification as a fire investigator, making him the only certified fire investigator in the consortium. CFD currently uses a digital camera, which facilitates sharing information and findings with other departments; however, the digital photos cannot be used as evidence in courts. The CFD last year investigated twelve suspicious fires in Craterville alone. Consortium departments indicate that they have similar numbers of requests for investigation.

The community has changed, but the firefighters' equipment has not.

Changes in the surrounding landscape force the purchase of two additional pieces of equipment that were not previously needed and/or are not available from members of the consortium. The I-6 highway is under construction and slated for opening in fall 2007. The project, referred to as "southbelt" by area residents, will run through the heart of Craterville, within 1/2 mile of the CFD, and is expected to deflect traffic from the primary east-west corridors now bisecting commercial and residential areas. The cloverleaf exit to the only north-south corridor at US-xxx is in Craterville and will be the second largest interchange in the State of Midwest. Both this intersection and the new highway are expected to increase traffic dramatically and, consequently, to increase the number of accidents to which CFD will respond. All of the consortium members will be affected by the new highway but none more than CFD; therefore, all have agreed that CFD is the most appropriate department to purchase and house a portable extraction tool for use in highway or industrial accidents and particularly for use in carrying up the hills created to support the new I-6 highway and interchange. All members of the consortium have generator-powered extraction tools, but CFDs purchase would be the first battery-powered, lightweight and portable unit available for their use.

A second environmental change is the creation of new manmade lakes and ponds within housing developments and natural creeks that bisect the community. Less than ten years ago, a child from a Craterville mobile home park drowned in the creek despite CFD rescue attempts, and last year, a new development resulted in construction of a 40-acre lake in Craterville and near residents of Dyes and Byes Center. To assist in water rescues expected to increase as the number of water facilities does, and to share with consortium members that are experiencing similar growth, CFD seeks to purchase an inflatable rescue raft. The raft will hold up to two rescue workers and one victim at a time and is easily transportable.

CFD's final request is for a portable computer and projector to be used for cotraining exercises with consortium members. CFD is the consortium member most qualified, in that it employs two trained paramedics, to deliver the fifteen credit hour medical-rescue training required of fire, police, and sheriff department personnel for recertification as Medical First Responders (MFR). While the equipment itself would not be shared with consortium members in this case, the training is offered free at CFD to all affected municipal personnel in and outside of the consortium.

Financial Need

> FEMA grants were available regardless of financial need, but went first to the communities with the greatest need. It was important to emphasize that this department's needs were urgent.

The CFD's annual $470,000 budget is supported 100 percent from local taxes. The composition of the community, however, places financial strains on both the department and city residents. The median household income of Craterville taxpayers according to 2000 census is slightly more than $40,000, while the median income in Kanton County (including the core city of Green River) is nearly $46,000, and the median income in the State of Midwest exceeds $53,000. Craterville includes thirteen mobile home parks with a combined population of at least 1,800 households. On average the mobile homes generate an estimated six hundred calls annually while providing only an average $12 each in annual taxes. The community includes five large apartment complexes, one of which is designated rent subsidized for low-income residents. In addition, a State-operated mental health facility houses approximately 275 residents who, last year, generated 104 calls (8 percent of calls) for assistance at a cost of $12,000 to CFD and its community. The facility pays no taxes in support of fire department services.

CFD's budget is used to pay firefighter salaries and to maintain vehicles and the fire station. Equipment had not been upgraded for several years prior to September 11, 2001. At that time, residents and civic leaders prioritized allocations of funding to the extent possible to improve firefighter capabilities and safety. As a result, CFD has recently purchased ten SCBAs and plans to purchase seven urgently needed sets of turnout gear. The community clearly cares about its firefighters/rescue workers' safety; however it lacks, by itself, the financial resources necessary to bring the department's equipment into compliance with NFPA and OSHA standards for firefighter safety.

> In this section, the grantwriter justifies the expense of equipment by pointing out that it will be shared with six other departments and that the benefits to those communities would outweigh the cost of the investment.

Cost-Benefit

CFD seeks four expensive purchases that would be shared minimally with its six consortium partners: a fill station, inflatable raft, extractor, and camera, and a fifth that would be used to train consortium members and other medical rescue workers throughout the region. Total cost of these five items is $42,850 (approximately 35 percent of the grant request). Use of the requested equipment will benefit more than 150 firefighters currently employed by a member of the consortium. The number of individual residents or visitors who will benefit—who are likely to be saved from injury or death—as a result of life-saving equipment purchases or training cannot be calculated.

The remainder of the grant requested is allocated for the purchase of critically needed firefighter safety and communications equipment. The total cost of these items ($80,740) is approximately $4,750 investment in each CFD firefighter.

> After 2002 when FEMA first offered these funding opportunities, it began offering any department additional funding so they could hire a professional grantwriter for their narrative applications. The reimbursement was available even to fire departments that did not receive grant funding. This situation is extremely rare.

Sustainability Grants

What Is It?

Most grant applications ask how you will sustain a project after funding ends. To reply to this, you need a plan for raising revenues from memberships, fees for service, partnerships, and fund-raising efforts to continue the project without grant funds. On rare occasions, you can apply for a grant to carry you over the period between start-up funds and self-sufficiency—to develop and carry out the sustainability plan you should have developed prior to receiving the start-up grant.

Appropriate Funding Sources

Local foundations are the most likely sources for sustainability grants as they are most aware of a project's success and most invested in seeing it continue. If your community does not have local foundations, seek grants from smaller state or regional foundations that have similar goals and have previously made grants in your community.

Strategies

Of course you would never try to get start-up funding for a project that will require grant funds forever. (Nor would you be successful if you did try.) Often, however, start-up funding is not enough to implement a project and get it to the point that it can support itself. If the project has proved very successful during its start up and pilot, you can develop a list of new funders (try not to return to the start-up funders) and make the case for why they should help you sustain the project for a few more years. You must, as a part of the grant, develop a strong plan that demonstrates how you will spend that time weaning the project from grant funding.

Sample: Sustainability Grant Proposal

City Media Center
MoLLIE Project

A. NARRATIVE

1. Executive Summary
The City Media Center launched its Mobile Learning Lab for Information Education (MoLLIE) in Fall 2004. Currently MoLLIE is equipped with twenty Apple iBook wireless laptops and sixteen digital cameras for use in K-12 public and parochial schools. MoLLIE staff and interns teach students to use the equipment to produce films at the close of a unit of instruction. For instance, students studying environmental protection might develop films about the watershed, ozone layers, the Great Lakes, or any number of other topics. Teachers use MoLLIE projects as a replacement for term papers, dioramas, and other traditional means of demonstrating learning.

MoLLIE has demonstrated remarkable learning outcomes since its inception, but struggles now with maintaining the service to the schools. To date, schools have had to pay little or nothing to have MoLLIE and training in the classroom. Now, CMC has developed a process for teacher application and school administrative review of those applications. In this way, we can highlight learning outcomes to the administrators and ask for their approval for an incremental copay requirement for school projects. Ultimately, through this and other negotiations and small project grants, we hope to make MoLLIE sustainable by those it serves at the end of three years.

> MoLLIE has been in the schools without cost to the schools. In other words, the nonprofit CMC has made an error in judgment in thinking that the schools would subsequently find the money to pay a fee for service. It is now asking a local foundation to overlook that error and help keep the program going while it implements a process that helps schools take over increased costs of paying for the service.

2. Purpose of Grant
Needs Statement
In fall 2004, City Media Center (CMC) received a federal grant to launch the Mobile Learning Lab for Information Education (MoLLIE). A van equipped with twenty Apple iBook wireless laptops and sixteen digital video cameras, MoLLIE brings technology tools and education to K-12 classrooms and to other areas of the community that lack access, equipment, software, and/or training. Students are taught digital film and editing skills, Internet skills, and website design to improve educational outcomes for their own and other classes in their schools.

> This is a request for a three-year grant with different amounts of funding each year. If it is awarded, year two and three funding will be contingent on the organization having met and reported on year one and two objectives.

MoLLIE has helped CMC close the digital divide in the City. Students of MoLLIE do not need transportation to attend a technology center for instruction or computer use. Instead, MoLLIE goes to them. Its after-school programs and evening stops cover more territory than could seven or eight site-based centers, and its programs fully engage children, teens, and adults in technology learning and application. It also addresses a bias, particularly among African Americans, that computer technology is for geeks. Working on a MoLLIE project—with video cameras, laptops, and a group of friends—then watching your work air on CityTV, according to participants, is "very cool."

Since January 2005 MoLLIE has provided technology and training services to more than twenty-five area schools and educational agencies, and its educational services go beyond mere enrichment. The MoLLIE team, in partnership with area teachers, provides technical assistance and equipment to facilitate the teaching of state-mandated curricular outcomes and objectives.

The nature of the MoLLIE program is inherently cross curricular, matching the computer and digital technology lexicon and training with the classroom teacher's subject-specific lesson planning. MoLLIE engages students at a multi-sensory level. Students use video technology to write, shoot, edit, and telecast their own curriculum-linked, self-produced presentations. MoLLIE has been used by area educators to teach a broad range of subjects including Science, Language Arts, English as a Second Language, History, Social Studies, Careers/Employability, and Health.

Its original plan was submitted to the federal government, which provided money to launch the project.

MoLLIE's original plan for sustainability called for increasing fees for service after the initial one-year grant, but unfortunately, CMC has found that those most in need of its services; i.e., K-12 public schools, are those that are unable to pay to sustain the program. It also found that it required additional time to demonstrate MoLLIE's effectiveness, which it has now done. In fact, the outcomes of the MoLLIE project have surpassed our most optimistic projections—in terms of numbers of children served, the quality of student work, and the enthusiasm and creativity of the many committed teachers with whom we've worked. Though we've served 50 percent more students than originally projected, the real story of MoLLIE's success lies in the learning outcomes among those school children. Assigned video projects after a unit of instruction, students learn at the highest levels of the rubric scale and of Bloom's taxonomy—and they learn lessons that will be with them for the rest of their lives.

A project requesting sustainability funding must have exceeded expectations and be highly valued by participants.

To sustain these learning outcomes, we must sustain the MoLLIE project in schools. The City Media Center (CMC), therefore, is seeking funding for the coming three years while it transitions services to fee-based. During the transition, CMC plans to work with school administrators and school teachers to help them understand the cost and benefits of MoLLIE and to work to cut overhead costs of the project. CMC has determined that it costs approximately $1,500 to provide three half-day hands-on video training and production experiences. CMC plans to require teacher applications for MoLLIE services with a small, but increasing annually, copay requirement. CMC would identify a team of volunteer school administrators and community members to review the applications, to approve the learning goals for proposed MoLLIE projects, and to determine the ability to copay for services. We will provide some guidance to teacher applicants on raising their copay funds (SACUL grants*, parent support, school foundations, school's corporate partners, events and event allowances, etc.). (*The State Association of Computer Users and Learners offers $2,000 grants to teachers to provide creative computer instruction.)

The applicant has a broader plan in place to build up the schools' abilities to pay for services.

We already know that MoLLIE works to improve academic outcomes for school children. Now we need to impress on school officials and parents that MoLLIE will not always be free. Adequate funding would enable CMC to continue the project during the three-year transition to a fee-for-service MoLLIE. We will encourage copay, but will not limit project fund awards during year one based on ability to copay. At the end of three years, we should have a strong mix of fee-for-service projects that supplement those that cannot pay. We will also have a portfolio of instructional units, crossing all academic disciplines and grades, that incorporate video production as a final project, and that have demonstrated achievement of academic outcomes and standards.

Many of the schools where MoLLIE is needed most are those facing severe budget constraints.

Goals, Objectives, and Action Plans

CMC holds the following goals and objectives for MoLLIE during the three-year transition period from free to fee-based services:

- Sustain MoLLIE services for the next three years while transitioning to fee-based services.
  Obj. 1A: Apply for grants from various community sources
  Obj. 1B: Continue building partnerships with County Intermediate School District, City and other Public Schools, parochial schools, Nonprofit Incubator, and others to support MoLLIE services or reduce costs.

- Highlight MoLLIE products so community and school officials understand the learning value.
  Obj. 2A: Enlist school district administrators to serve on committee to review teacher applications for MoLLIE services
  Obj. 2B: Continue weekly CityTV show of MoLLIE products. Expand effort by promoting upcoming shows in various schools.
  Obj. 2C: Continue negotiations to add MoLLIE segments to City Educational Access Television station.

- Develop portfolio of instructional units (all academic disciplines and grades) that use MoLLIE and that have demonstrated achievement of academic outcomes/standards.
  Obj. 3A: Develop application process that highlights teachers' academic goals for projects; assist teachers in raising copay fees for MoLLIE services.
  Obj. 3B: Evaluate learning outcomes against teacher goals after projects are completed.
  Obj. 3C: Share curriculum across academic disciplines and grades to encourage more teachers to participate in MoLLIE

- Develop and implement schedule for upgrading MoLLIE equipment.
  Obj. 4A: Determine capabilities of existing equipment and of newly available equipment.
  Obj. 4B: Continuously review upcoming technologies to determine best time to buy.
  Obj. 4C: Recycle used equipment into other CMC or school programs as it is replaced.
  Obj. 4D: Seek community resources for donated or low-cost vehicle replacement.

Timetable for Implementation

> A three-year request merits a three-year timeline.

CMC plans the following timetable for transitioning MoLLIE to a fee-based service:

Year One (2006-07)

- Apply for grants from community sources.
- Develop teacher application form.
- Enlist school district administrators' participation in review committee.
- Promote MoLLIE services in schools through the use of television and print media.
- Achieve, by end of year, a mix of at least 10 percent copay for services.
- Reduce overhead costs by moving MoLLIE staff to Steepletown and implementing labor-for-rent exchange program.
- Continue building partnerships with school officials and CISD.
- Begin equipment upgrade cycle.
- Evaluate cost effectiveness of MoLLIE and learning outcomes of MoLLIE projects.

Year Two (2007-08)
- Apply for year two support from existing funding sources; identify other supporters.
- Develop and promote portfolio of learning outcomes from past projects.
- Achieve, by end of year, a mix of at least 25 percent copay for services.
- Develop arrangement with CISD that may channel some school technology funding to MoLLIE.
- Continue equipment upgrade cycle.
- Negotiate with community car dealer for low cost or donated vehicle to replace or upgrade MoLLIE van.
- Evaluate cost effectiveness of MoLLIE and learning outcomes of MoLLIE projects.

Year Three (2008-09)
- Apply for year three support from existing funding sources; identify other supporters.
- Explore potential for raising fees through consulting in other communities to establish their MoLLIE programs.
- Achieve, by end of year, a mix of at least 50 percent copay for services.
- Continue equipment upgrade cycle.
- Evaluate cost effectiveness of MoLLIE and learning outcomes of MoLLIE projects.

3. Evaluation

Defining and Measuring Success:

The project will be judged successful according to the following measures:

- It raises copay levels from schools meeting or exceeding the objective (i.e., 10 percent year one, 25 percent year two, and 50 percent year three).
- By the end of year three, The MoLLIE educational portfolio contains lesson plans and learning outcomes for grade levels 2 through 12 in every subject.
- MoLLIE services (or potential expanded services) are 80 percent or more sustainable within three years through copay, pass-through technology funding from potential sources, consulting fees, and small project grants.
- At least three school administrators (from different districts) serve on the MoLLIE educational program review committee.
- Students meet or exceed learning outcomes and objectives stated in teacher applications.

Evaluation is linked to the goals and objectives of the grant.

4. Budget Narrative/Justification

Budget: MoLLIE: Three Year Operations

A. Organizational fiscal year: July 1 to June 30

B. Time period this budget covers: July 1, 2006 to June 30, 2009

For a CAPITAL request, substitute your format for listing expenses. These will likely include: architectural fees, land/building purchase, construction costs, and campaign expenses.

Expenses: include a description and the total amount for each of the budget categories, in this order:

	Amount Requested of CCF	Other Funding Sources	CMC/CityTV and In-Kind	Total
Salaries, taxes and fringe benefits	$ 90,000	$180,000	$ 90,000	$360,000
Consultants & professional fees			$ 15,000	$ 15,000
Travel/Mileage		$ 3,000	$ 3,600	$ 6,600
Equipment (computers and camcorders)	$ 25,000	$ 95,000	$ 50,000	$170,000
Supplies		$ 15,000	$ 3,000	$ 18,000
Marketing/Promotions		$ 10,000	$ 22,500	$ 32,500
Rent & utilities			$ 10,500	$ 10,500
Evaluation		$ 5,000	$ 10,000	$ 15,000
Van and equipment maintenance and/or replacement		$ 30,000	$ 5,000	$ 35,000
TOTALS:	$115,000	$338,000	$209,600	$662,600

Revenue: Include a description and the total amount for each of the following budget categories in this order. Please indicate which sources of revenue are committed and which are pending.

	Committed	Pending
1. Grants/Contracts/Contributions		
Local government	$127,500	
State government		
Federal Government	$ 27,825	
Foundations (itemize) City Community Foundation		$115,000
Corporate Foundation		$ 90,000
Mr. & Mrs. Wealthy Foundation		$100,000
All Girl Foundation (special project)	$ 10,650	
Other (not yet identified or approached)		
Individuals		
2. Earned Income		
Events (teacher training at CISD)	$ 15,000	
Publications and Products	$ 750	
3. Membership income		
4. In-Kind support		
5. Other (specify)		
School co-pay for MoLLIE services		$170,000
Art Organization contract	$ 6,000	
CISD		
6. TOTAL REVENUE	$187,725	$475,000

> The organization has applied to several other local funders and potential partners but has few commitments prior to making this application

> Note the budget justification explaining each line item in both the expenses and revenues.

Budget Calculations:

Expenses:

Salaries, taxes, and fringe benefits are calculated at approximately $10,000 per month for thirty six months. CMC provides $90,000 as in-kind services of staff; those costs are allocated under revenues as local government donation since they derive from franchise fees. Consulting and professional fees include fund-raising and marketing consulting and are provided from CMC's annual budget.

Equipment costs include upgrading all computers and cameras during the course of the five years, recycling existing computers, and expanding the number of computers available. In each funding request to date and subsequent to this one, CMC has requested a portion of the requested grant for equipment upgrade. Existing equipment is currently valued at $50,000 and is offered in kind for its use to recycle in schools and other CMC programs.

> A strength in this proposal is that the applicant is investing its own resources into sustaining the MoLLIE project.

Supplies are provided by CMC and through a line item in several existing project grants (e.g., portion of the Women's Foundation, Arts Organization, and Department of Justice grants/contracts noted in revenues). The remaining portion of necessary supplies will be allocated from publications and products earnings (which cover costs of some tapes and DVDs) and from school copays. Marketing and promotions are allocated similarly, with the Arts Organization contract and Youth Film Festival proceeds providing some sources of funding.

Rent and utilities for MoLLIE staff to be housed at Nonprofit Incubator is $4,500 cash provided by CMC/CityTV through cable franchise revenues and $6,000 in labor exchange over three years.

Evaluation will be internal and will require a minimum investment for consultation and staff time of $5,000 annually in each of three years.

CMC currently spends approximately $5,000 annually on van maintenance, insurance, etc., which comes from cable franchise fees (local government). Thirty thousand dollars are allocated for the purchase of a new vehicle with four seats and ample cargo room for equipment (currently only two staff may ride in the MoLLIE van; others go in their own cars). CMC hopes to negotiate a donation or greatly reduced cost for the new vehicle from a local dealership.

Revenues:
Much of MoLLIE's ongoing funding listed as CMC/CityTV and in-kind comes from cable revenues to CityTV and is allocated as a part of CityTV's annual budget. These expense items include salary and fringe benefits for staff, consulting fees, supplies, marketing and promotions, evaluation, and van maintenance and insurance.

Other revenues include special MoLLIE project grants and contracts that are described below and can be used to offset the cost of MoLLIE in schools.

Earned revenues derive from teacher training sessions at CISD, which generate $1,250 per training session. CMC expects to provide four sessions annually. Also included in earned income is a small cost charged to students when CMC makes a duplicate DVD or VHS tape of their school project for them to keep and share with their families.

> Earned revenues will be applied directly to the project and will not go into the CMC's general budget.

Pending revenues include three grants currently being requested of the City Community, Corporate, and Wealthy Foundations. Also included is the amount of copay (calculated as 10 percent, 25 percent, and 50 percent of total program costs each year) that CMC expects to generate from schools in its effort to become self-sustaining.

Demonstration Projects

What Is It?

A demonstration project proves or disproves a theory held by the nonprofit applicant and/or the grantmaker. Demonstration projects are funded to enable new types of services and corresponding research and evaluation needed to prove the theory. They are sought by applicants eager to attempt something new.

Appropriate Funding Sources

Most demonstration project grant opportunities come in the form of requests for proposals from government departments or government agencies and from some large foundations that have launched initiatives they are testing in different communities. A nonprofit organization seeking demonstration project funding proactively would look first to the larger foundations that see themselves as learning organizations and have demonstrated through past grantmaking their willingness to take risks.

Strategies

Perhaps no other type of RFP generates more responses that are simply chasing grant dollars than demonstration opportunities. Too often, small nonprofit organizations don't really understand what they are getting in to and see an RFP as an opportunity to build their funding base. For instance, the sample grant that follows is a response to an RFP requiring communities to establish a roundtable of juvenile justice and other social service programs for girl offenders, to have the members discuss the issues surrounding girls at risk of offending, and to develop a community plan for addressing those issues. The originator, in this case, the state Family Independence Agency (FIA), received numerous proposals to launch actual programs for girls and only a few that focused on the research and convening aspects of the program.

The best strategy to write a successful demonstration project is to carefully analyze the RFP or guidelines and to discuss with staff and other organizational leaders the match between the project described in the RFP and the organization's mission and goals.

Sample: Demonstration Project Grant Proposal

PROGRAM NARRATIVE

One of the primary purposes of the project, once funded, will be to gather data that will define the problem. This section of the grant seeks information that will provide a case for funding research in this particular community and a baseline against which to measure programs that arise after the study period.

1. **PROBLEM STATEMENT. Describe the problem exactly as it exists in your community. Define the nature and magnitude of the problem to be addressed through your proposal. Analyze the causes of the problem. Document statements with valid, current statistical data to clearly demonstrate why the problem exists. Identify the source and date of your information.**

Studies show that girls do not get as much individual attention when programs are for both genders.

The grantwriter requested specific data from the county juvenile justice department.

Such data will prove helpful to the study and subsequent program design.

The data were provided by the agency offering the grant.

Although there are several nonprofit organizations in greater Green River, Midwest, that provide crime prevention or intervention services for young people, these programs, with some exceptions such as Planned Parenthood and other programs for pregnant/parenting teens, have historically focused on the needs of urban and near-suburban boys. In a few instances, some of the organizations that serve boys have attempted to adapt their programs or to include girls in existing programs to address the following data indicators:

- Court referrals (data for actual arrests is unavailable at this time) for girls in Green River totaled 1,376 in 2005—nearly one quarter of court referrals for all juveniles in 1998. To date in 2006, court referrals of girls totals 660—again, one quarter of court referrals for all juveniles (Kenton County Juvenile Justice).
- Predominant crimes among girls referred to Juvenile Justice so far in 2006 include, in order of highest rates: retail fraud, minors in possession, running away, curfew violation, assault and battery, and assault with a dangerous weapon. These were also the top violation categories last year, but running away was the second most prevalent violation for which girls were referred in 2005 (Kenton County Juvenile Justice).
- Last year, rates of second degree retail fraud among girls exceeded that of boys, and runaway rates totaled the same for boys and girls. To date in 2006, the rate of runaway girls referred to the court is the only case in which the incidence among girls is higher than that among boys; in fact the rate of girls referred for running away is double that of boys in 2006 (Kenton County Juvenile Justice).
- In the ten years between 1994 and 2004, pregnancy among girls ages fifteen to seventeen rose nearly 40 percent: from an estimated 531 pregnancies in 1994 to an estimated 1,370 in 2004 (Kenton County Health Department).
- Minority girls are more likely than white girls to be incarcerated (in Kenton County, six per 100,000 incarcerated girls are majority; thirty-four per 100,000 are minority) (State of Midwest).
- Females are committed to institutions at younger ages than males on the average. African American females are committed at an average age one year younger than Anglo American females (fifteen vs. sixteen years) (Midwest Family Independence Agency, 1987-2003).
- Female juvenile offenders most often enter the juvenile justice system at a time of family crisis (Midwest Family Independence Agency, 1987-2003).
- More than one quarter (27 percent) of delinquent girls in Midwest report at least one suicide attempt. Many are found to be clinically depressed, particularly those who are pregnant or parenting (Midwest Family Independence Agency, 1987-2003).
- Forty percent of female juvenile offenders have neglect charges; 40 percent have abuse charges on their records (Midwest Family Independence Agency, 1987-2003).

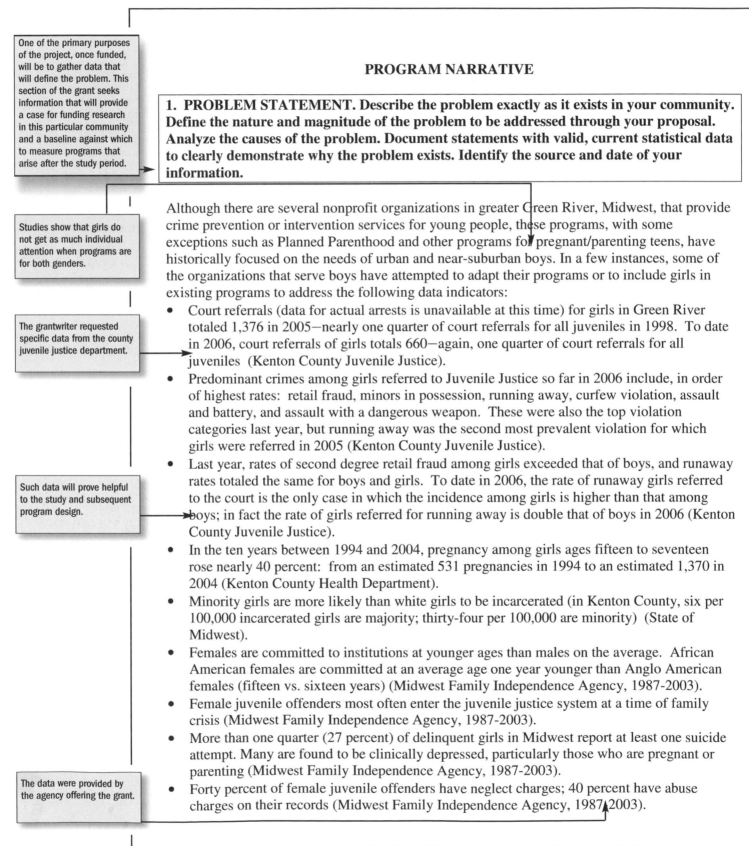

- Female offenders have a high incidence of sexually transmitted diseases; most report that their sexual partners are five or more years older than they (Midwest Family Independence Agency, 1987-2003).

- Types of crimes for juvenile female offenders have not changed except for dramatic increases in cases of assault, particularly domestic abuse (Midwest Family Independence Agency, 1987-2003).

> Although the grantor probably knows this, it helps to have the applicant state it. If you don't acknowledge a problem, it's difficult to correct.

Adaptations to boys' programs or the inclusion of girls in boys' programs simply does not work. Research shows that boys receive more attention in mixed-gender programs, which could exacerbate girls' feelings of inferiority. Adapting existing boys' programs does not address the range of needs among girls at risk, and often, the programs are delivered by personnel who have worked successfully with boys and have little incentive or understanding to revise their approaches when working with teen girls.

> Grantwriter cites research to support the premise that girls' programs should be developed separately from those for boys.

Indeed, adapted boys' programs seem to run counter to fulfilling the most basic of girls' needs: "to be understood, to be encouraged, and to be given positive direction in a world which, for many of them, is all too often confusing, threatening, and uncaring" (Bilchik, Girls, Inc.). Even the local data necessary to analyze the full scope of the problems of girls at risk for juvenile offending is sparse or disjointed. Girls have not been the focus of any previous systemic initiative in the greater Green River community.

Family Dialog, Inc., a nonprofit counseling service for youth at risk and their families, seeks to convene several community leaders of programs for youth with the intention of breaking the mold—laying aside all current programming and, together, gathering and analyzing local, state, and national data on the issue of young female juvenile offenders, and—armed with this education—developing a systemic approach to addressing the range of causes and problems experienced by girls in greater Green River.

> The nonprofit volunteers are to develop a system response.

The forum, "Girl Talk," will be composed of community leaders to include (but likely not be limited to) representatives from Green River Youth Commonwealth, a recreational program (summer camp and two urban centers) supervised by Green River police officers for at-risk urban youth; Boone Services, a residence for teen mothers who cannot remain in their homes during and after pregnancy; Alternate Directions or a similar school program for pregnant and parenting teens; Wildwood, a residential program for youth who have offended; Kenton County Juvenile Justice Department; Family Dialog, Inc., a mentoring and training program for at-risk youth and their families; Archer Circle, which includes Advice Center for Teens, a mental health provider for youth; urban and contiguous-suburban school districts; Kenton County Health Department; Girls Scouts of America, Kenton County; Green Valley State University Office of Community Research; City and contiguous-suburb police departments; Family Independence Agency (FIA) and Child Protective Services (CPS); Planned Parenthood; and Project Rehab, an alcohol and drug abuse prevention organization. Family Dialog, Inc. will also recruit at least five adolescent girls from various socio-economic strata and life circumstances and at least two parents of teenage girls to participate on the planning team.

Family Dialog, Inc. staff believe that this mix of team members can assist in gathering data necessary to analyze the problem and to measure results of later program design and implementation, and to plan an effective, system-wide response that includes prevention, intervention, and treatment for the problems of female juvenile offenders and those at risk for offending.

> **II. PROJECT DESCRIPTION. Outline clearly, and in detail, your overall project. Include a chronological plan of your goals (what the project will achieve). Include a description of project activities and job descriptions of all positions to be funded by federal funds.**

The goal of the community-wide planning initiative, "Girl Talk," is to develop a systemic approach to preventing, intervening in, and treating the problems of female juvenile offenders and girls at risk for becoming offenders.

A project coordinator will be hired to convene team members, facilitate meetings of the team, ensure information exchange among team members, develop and maintain communications among and between team members, and attend all local, state, and national workshops on the problems of female juvenile offenders. The coordinator will be a contract position for the duration of the planning period. The coordinator will work closely with the Office of Community Research at Green Valley State University to coordinate data gathering regarding girls in the juvenile justice system and other girls at risk in the community, and to scan other communities for successful programs for girls.

Once data is gathered and analyzed, the team will work with a professional social worker (likely also from the Office of Community Research) to develop a risk-indicator scale, which would be used by various community institutions (schools, religious organizations, clubs, mental health or healthcare providers, etc.) to determine girls' levels of risk for offending. Data gathered on the status of girls in the community, on early responses to the risk indicator scale, and from an analysis of successful girls' programs in other communities, will be used to inform the design of the community-wide approach to addressing girls' problems.

Based on the data, the team will design a program to prevent, intervene in, and treat the problems of at-risk girls in greater Green River. A professional writer will develop and write this comprehensive plan. The writer will also develop subsequent grant proposals for submission to local foundations, the State of Midwest, or other appropriate sources, to generate the support necessary to implement the girls' program in its entirety. (It will be agreed among the partners at the outset of the planning process that no agency should attempt to seek funding to "play its part" in the solution; rather, the solution should be systemic—greater than the sum of its parts— and thus, be funded as a community initiative.)

| Though program funding is a later question, it makes sense to write about it earlier in the proposal. |

The planning process will be evaluated based on the completeness and clarity of the objectives for the completed program plan, its ability to be replicated in other communities, and simultaneously, its relevance to the status of girls in greater Green River. The source of the evaluation is not yet determined, but is likely to be a social work Ph.D. from a local university.

Additional costs required to complete the systemic plan for girls' programming include travel and accommodations, clerical support for team meeting minutes and reproduction and distribution of the program plan; office supplies, and postage.

A timeline for completing all components of the project is as follows:

10/06-12/06: Contact all potential team members to discuss the planning initiative and obtain commitments to participate for the duration of the planning period. Develop contracts for services of project coordinator, clerical staff hours, and writing services.

10/06-12/06: Identify and contract with an evaluator.

1/07-12/07: Monthly (or more frequent) team meetings.

1/07-3/07: Data gathering from all local community sources regarding the status of local girls to be performed by Green Valley State University Office of Community Research. Scan and analysis of other programs in the nation that successfully address the problems of girls in their communities.

3/07: Use data to develop and disseminate risk analysis indicator to local institutions.

5/07: Analyze risk analysis indicators for problems of girls and extent/range of problems in local community.

6/07-8/07: Develop and write comprehensive, holistic plan for addressing the identified problems of girls who have offended or are at risk for juvenile offense.

8/07: Evaluate plan for completeness, responsiveness to data, and potential for success.

9/07: Finalize timeline and budget for implementing program plan across the system.

10/07-12/07: Devise plan for funding and develop list of potential local, state, and national funding sources. Develop and submit grant proposals to comply with funding-source deadlines.

III. PROGRAM OBJECTIVE. Objectives are specific, quantified statements of expected results of the project. The objective must be described in terms of measurable events that can be realistically expected under time constraints and available resources. Objectives must be related to the problems. Describe who will do what, by when, and why.

The goal of the community-wide planning initiative is to develop a systemic approach to preventing, intervening in, and treating the problems of female juvenile offenders and girls at risk for becoming offenders. Toward this end, Family Dialog, Inc. holds the following objectives:

1. To convene a group of representatives from various systems and organizations in the local community who have an interest in providing services for at-risk teenagers. Expand the group as advised by members to include organizations or systems that represent all aspects (including those discovered during study) that affect the lives of girls (Project Coordinator; Family Dialog, Inc.). ◄─────

   The grantwriter assigns responsibility for each objective. It is critically important that everyone involved read and approve these objectives.

2. To conduct surveys (risk analysis indicators), gather data (local, state, and national), and review girls' programs in other communities to inform the group on the needs of girls and form the basis for a new systemic approach to resolving girls' issues (Project Coordinator; Office of Community Research at Green Valley State University).

3. To draft a program design that is responsive to the needs of local girls and replicable at least in part for addressing the needs of girls anywhere (Team and writer).

4. To evaluate the program design for completeness, responsiveness, and potential for success (outside evaluator).

5. To prepare a funding plan and submit requests for funding regarding systemic implementation of the plan (writer; project coordinator; Family Dialog, Inc.).

> The planned report will serve a broader purpose than simply reporting the fact finding of the community team.

6. To disseminate the program plan to community members, funders, other communities, and others in the local community who have an interest in improving girls' status.

7. To be fully prepared to implement a system-wide plan for addressing the needs of girls involved in the juvenile justice system or at-risk for involvement.

IV. PERFORMANCE INDICATORS AND EVALUATION. State exactly how each objective will be measured. Performance indicators (activities which evaluate and document your program's effectiveness) should be matched to your specific objectives. Specify the criteria and procedures to be used. Identify the person responsible for the evaluation of this project.

> The writer need not state how the evaluation will be done, but can leave that to a professional evaluator. Instead, the writer identifies the questions that an evaluation should answer to prove that the organization has achieved its project objectives.

The following questions will be used as performance indicators and as the basis for evaluation:

1. Was the community team representative of all sectors that deal with or should deal with the problems of adolescent girls? If some organizations were deemed appropriate but chose not to attend, what reasons were cited?

2. Did the compiled data (quantitative and qualitative) help team members form a clearer picture of the needs of and risks faced by adolescent girls?

3. Were the data referred to and addressed in forming a systemic plan for addressing the problems of adolescent girls?

4. Is the completed draft program design based on available data (qualitative and quantitative)? Is the program replicable? Does it address the priority needs of adolescent girls at risk in Kenton County? What is the expected potential of the program's success?

5. Has the writer developed a comprehensive plan for funding program implementation? Does the plan include a broad mix of funding sources? Have at least four grant applications been prepared and submitted by December 2007?

6. Have all members of the team received complete copies of the final program plan and additional copies for distribution within their organizations? Have at least 250 copies of the plan been distributed to community decision makers?

Operations Grants

7. Have all team members endorsed the plan and promoted it with their Boards of Directors, if appropriate? Are all identified individuals or organizations that will participate in the plan in agreement with the proposal? Have all questions from participants or readers been addressed satisfactorily (i.e., is there broad "buy in")?

What Is It?

V. PLANS FOR PROJECT PICK UP WITH LOCAL FUNDS. Please describe the effort that will be made for local assumption/retention of the project after federal funding has expired.

The cost of the cross-sector problem solving team and development of a systemic plan for addressing the needs of at-risk teenage girls is a one-time expense. Costs for implementing the plan developed under this grant will be sought primarily from local sources, which will include but not be limited to: The Family Foundation, The Green River Foundation, Corporate Foundation, Independent Foundation, and Women & Girls Foundation. Businesses, such as Major Manufacturing, Inc., Major Engineering, Hamburgers of West Midwest, Jacks Enterprises, etc., will also be asked to provide funding for implementation depending on the case to be made for their involvement. Family Dialog, on behalf of the consortium of organizations that participate, will also seek funding for implementation from Midwest United Way and other state and federal funding sources as applicable.

> This is what this grant, if successful, will fund. It will not provide funding for programs that arise from the study.

Operational funding supports the general purposes of an organization including it: rent, utilities, salaries, supplies, and similar budgetary items. It is also called general support and core funding.

Use of these funds can be broader than that of program funding. Use of funds is unrestricted so the grantee can use funding strategically in the way they think best. Though operations funding is often used to support the operations of the organization, it can also be used for emergency program funding, strategic planning, or for a quick response to a new opportunity.

Appropriate Funding Sources

Federal government grants do not fund operations. Similarly, large or remote foundations do not fund operations of nonprofits unless they are located in the same community as the foundation and that foundation has a financial stake in the community, or the foundation has a stake in the nonprofit as a cornerstone organization needed to achieve its program objectives.

Most often, the only source for operational funding is a local foundation that sees your nonprofit as providing essential and valued services.

Strategies

For years, operational funding was the most difficult to get from grants. Nonprofit organizations had to devise new projects in order to appeal to grantmakers' interests in innovation. These new projects were difficult to sustain regardless of their outcomes. In recent years, many foundations have reconsidered their position and now look at a community's nonprofit infrastructure and have determined to keep key components of that structure strong. As grantwriter, it is your job to determine which funders in your community are willing to provide operations grants and under what circumstances.

The following sample is written by a public-broadcast station to a corporate foundation:

Sample: Operations Grant Proposal

Project Narrative

Summary

CGVN is west Midwest's only source of public television programming (PBS) and the state's only source of Instructional Television (ITV) for schools. The station seeks a continued operational grant ($69,000 over three years).

Project Description

CGVN is public-broadcast television serving West Midwest through funding from viewers, government, and its host, Green Valley University. The station airs quality television programs from the Public Broadcasting Service (PBS), National Public Radio (NPR), and other local and national radio and television producers.

CGVN provides the state's only full-service instructional television service (ITV), serving nearly 206,000 school children and 11,000 teachers from more than one hundred school districts in Midwest. ITV is an integral part of the curriculum for hundreds of thousands of students in Kenton County. Even preschool age children benefit from educational television in their homes because CGVN broadcasts PBS' award-winning programs like Sesame Street, Dragon Tales, Clifford, Arthur, Sagwa, Caillou, and Barney and Friends. Adults are informed with how-to programs, news, documentaries, events coverage, and health and family issues series. And everyone in the viewing area enjoys nationally produced programs such as Antiques Roadshow, NOVA, Frontier House, Exxonmobile Masterpiece Theatre, Great Performances, and Mystery!

> The foundation values education, so the writer sets this channel apart from others with information about its educational shows.

Audience

CGVN's range is 1.5 million people in western lower Midwest and northwestern Midwest, and extending east to Jackstone, Midwest.

> The writer has skipped over the need section. The need should never be about the organization, but about the audience or target population.

Goals and Objectives

CGVN's goal is to continue to support and air quality programming for adults and children. To that end it holds the following objectives:

Objective A1: Hold annual fund-raising events to garner community financial support.

Objective A2: Seek ongoing relationships with area funders who are committed to quality cultural and educational programming.

Objective A3: Continue contractual arrangements with PBS to secure award-winning programming for west Midwest.

Collaborations

CGVN is supported by Green Valley State University and the viewing public. CGVN raises most of its annual operating budget from viewers and members, but seeks annually approximately 11 percent of underwriting for specific programs from area foundations and corporations.

> The writer indicates that the station asks local foundations for a small percentage of annual support. The community demonstrates its value for the station with ongoing funds.

Similar Projects

CGVN is the only public broadcast station in West Midwest and the only full service Instructional Television Station in the State of Midwest.

Budget and Funding

CGVN's annual operating budget derives from the following sources:

Budget and Funding (Approximate):

Viewer Members:	68 percent
Federal	12 percent
Corporate & Foundation	11 percent
Green Valley State University	9 percent
	100 percent

Consumer Involvement

Viewership of PBS programs has increased each year since 1989. Similarly, ITV service has increased the number of teachers and students it reaches and the number of programs provided to schools.

Organization Background

> The grantwriter focuses on the organizational background to convince the grantmakers that this is one of the important pieces of the nonprofit infrastructure in this region.

CGVN's mission is to educate, inform, and entertain the West Midwest community through quality programming and community events. CGVN also serves national and international audiences with quality locally produced programming including Fly Fishing with Glen Blackwood, Habitat Earth, The Deadly Fuse, and others.

CGVN's broadcast stations are licensed to Green Valley State University as public radio and television facilities operating from the Major Public Broadcast Center, as part of the University's downtown city campus.

Further:

- CGVN provides the Midwest's only full-service Instructional Television Service serving nearly 200,000 school children and more than four hundred schools in eleven counties throughout West Midwest.

- In addition, in 1989 CGVN initiated the establishment of M-ITV Consortium—a partnership with the state's twenty-two REMCs. M-ITV meets monthly in Capital City and acts as the screening, evaluation, and buying group for video and print materials for every school district in the state. CGVN acts as the buying agent and keeps track of legal use rights and distributes programming to the statewide distribution center and to individual REMCs. By pooling resources and money, CGVN is able to purchase the latest in video materials for the state's 1.5 million students.

- Preschool and K-5-age children benefit from educational television in their homes from award-winning programs like Sesame Street, Dragon Tales, Clifford, Arthur, Sagwa, Caillou, and Barney and Friends. Home schooling programs often incorporate the educational programming into their curriculum as well.

- The FCC mandates all network stations to broadcast three hours per week of children's programming. While most stations broadcast cartoons and sitcoms, CGVN broadcasts forty-four hours of quality children's educational programming per week, and during the school year an additional twenty hours.

- Through its participation in Ready to Learn, a national program with a goal that all American children start school "ready to learn," CGVN has trained more than 5,000 parents, teachers, and caregivers, distributed 30,000 books, and reached 30,000 kids since launching the program in April 2000.

- Adults are informed with how-to, news, documentaries, event coverage, and health and family issues series.

- Nationally produced programs are available such as Antiques Roadshow, Frontier House, Exxon-Mobil Masterpiece Theatre, Great Performances, and Mystery!

- Local programming is offered such as Ask the Expert, Outdoors, West Midwest Week, and much more.

- CGVN offers several public-service features, many of which are not found anywhere else in West Midwest. For the hearing impaired, closed-captioning of programs displays the program's dialogue and sound effects in text over the picture for easy reading. CGVN also has a Telecommunication Device for the Deaf (TDD) so it can receive messages about its programming from hearing impaired viewers. For the visually impaired, Descriptive Video Services (DVS) is also offered and can be obtained through the Secondary Audio Program (SAP) channel on newer model stereo TVs and VCRs. This service is also provided for those who speak foreign languages so that they may receive certain programs in languages other than English.

Special Populations

What Is It?

Some grantmaker programs (and sometimes, an entire foundation) focus funding on programs that address the needs of specific population segments: people with physical or mental disabilities or with a certain illness or condition, women and girls, gay and lesbian people, exoffenders, the recently unemployed, senior citizens, or teenagers.

Appropriate Funding Sources

There are a handful of RFPs issued annually from governments and foundations that seek to fund projects for segments of the population that have a great unmet need for services.

There are also a handful of foundations in the nation that are established to address the needs of a population segment: primarily women and girls. If your organization is also focused on one specific population segment, you need to identify the funders in that subset of foundations. If you have just one program (rather than an entire organization) focusing on the population segment, you may apply to one of these special population funders if their goals and eligibility criteria fit that of your program.

Strategies

Communities that have existing collaborations centered around the needs of population segments (e.g., exoffenders), are best positioned to be successful in responding to an RFP. It rarely works to establish such a collaboration simply to respond to the request. If the commitment and need exists, there are probably local organizations talking together to find ways to respond.

Do not adjust a program simply to fit into a foundation's or RFP's focus for funding, but only to respond to an existing need. For example, if you operate a recreation center for teens, you might have established a program or hours of operation for teens in wheelchairs, or a special night of the week in which only girls attend and work with a woman trainer or coach. These programs may be fundable by a special population funder for people with disabilities or for women and girls. Be aware, however, that if you mix together your populations (e.g., boys and girls) a special populations funder is not likely to fund your project because it's not specific to the needs of their target population.

The following sample focuses on the need to improve the representation of women in journalism and was submitted to a foundation focused exclusively on funding projects for women and girls:

Sample: Special Populations Grant Proposal

Grassroots Journalism

Problem to be addressed

In Laura Flanders book Real Majority, Media Minority, the author makes the point that women not only continue to be a minority in the journalism profession, but as news sources, they are limited to "gender-specific" stories.

In the News Media Leadership lists for 2005, men outnumber women almost two to one in media positions. Within those positions, women are still disproportionately in news areas of lesser importance such as the advice column, nutrition, interior decorating, family tips, and entertainment. Women tend to be missing or in small numbers on editorial staffs, as feature writers, and beat reporters for government, economics, and foreign affairs.

In our own studies, local news continues to have women's voices at a rate of about a third of men's in all news stories. In addition, women appear as news sources when the focus is on consumerism, parenting, and gender issues, such as domestic violence. Women rarely are used as sources in economics, government (except with the case of a woman governor), and general civic affairs.

Targeted population

Young women in the County between the ages of thirteen to twenty-four

Goals & Objectives

To encourage young women in the county to consider journalism as a profession, the Institute for Information Democracy (IID) proposes a summer training program in journalism. This training will include components such as:

- How to do investigative and grassroots journalism
- Incorporating a gendered critique in news
- Developing written and on-air reporting skills
- Video camera and editing
- Producing news stories

Participants will take classes in grassroots journalism. These classes will help participants develop skills in communication, research, writing, and community assessment.

A second portion of the training will focus on video camera use and editing. Participants will learn the technical skills needed to film and edit news stories, as well as perform on-air narrative and develop interviewing skills.

Participants will also have an opportunity to meet with local women in journalism. This will be a roundtable discussion on the challenges and opportunities the female journalists face, as well as an opportunity for participants to engage these women on their profession.

Margin notes:

The applicant has done research on where women are underrepresented in one field of work and shares the findings of the research with the funder.

The grantwriter should have given a specific number of participants. The funder will likely ask during the due diligence process.

The program will be available only to young women, which is a criteria of the foundation.

The project involves the community.

Each participant will be required to produce a minimum of five news stories for the local public access station. The stories will be evaluated by the staff of IID both for content and style before approval for airing on the station. Stories will also be submitted to local and state news outlets in TV, radio, print, and online sources. IID will post these news stories on its own website under the IDD Media News section. ◄

> Though the grantseeker doesn't (and need not) say, it's likely that having your own news stories air on television locally, and possibly elsewhere, will build self-esteem, addressing a prevalent problem among young women.

Timeline

Journalism classes will begin the week of June 7th
Filming and video editing classes the week of June 21st
Meeting with local women journalists the week of July 5th
Production of news stories between July 12-August 27
Evaluation, selection, and dissemination of stories the week of Sept. 6th

Budget

Project coordination & Journalism classes (IID)	$3,000.00
Training in video filming & editing	$1,050.00
Cost of tapes/distribution of news stories	$100.00
Refreshments for classes	$100.00
Total	$4,250.00 ◄

> The budget is reasonable for a three- or four-month project. Only in a minigrant such as this one is it acceptable to present only the cost side of a budget.

CHAPTER 10

Grantwriting in Different Fields of Nonprofit Practice

The nonprofit field includes diverse organizations from arts and cultural practices to services for people who are homeless or hungry. There are nuances within each discipline that require slightly different approaches and/or focus. This chapter provides sample grants as learning tools from the following fields:

- Arts organizations
- Medical service organizations
- Educational institutions
- Technology organizations
- Social/human services
- Local government and services
- Faith-based organizations
- Environmental organizations
- Economic development

We purposely provide a range of sample grants: some were successfully funded, some were not. All are, like the humans who wrote them, flawed in some way. For your edification, comments will point out both the strengths and weaknesses of these proposals.

Arts Organizations

Whether they focus on visual or performing arts, arts organizations combine to make up the cultural fabric of a community—the museums, dance, theatre, and music programs that educate, entertain, and enrich people's lives.

Strategies

Most arts organizations are not self-sustaining solely through admissions or contracts, and therefore require grants to continue their annual programs, educational programs, and to support new shows. Often arts organizations, especially those in urban areas, seek and receive both operational and special funding from local foundations. The National Endowment for the Arts and state agencies dedicated to the arts are also sources of funding for special projects.

Sample: Arts Organization Grant Proposal

Goals/Vision

As is apparent in the attached performance lists and the description of its programs, Crescent Theatre has historically worked successfully to develop and nurture children and family audiences. It has this past year, however, adopted a new vision and work plan for the immediate future: developing an enthusiasm for the arts among uninclined adults in the community. Staff have attended "Learning Audiences" workshops to learn more about the continuum of participation in the arts and to identify ways to reach uninclined audiences "where they are," and bring them into the continuum of arts engagement. Staff and the Board of Crescent Theatre embrace this new direction as both a means to ensure Crescent Theatre's continued success and support and to strengthen community arts as a whole. Crescent Theatre is one of the first organizations in the region to work with the Family Foundation in establishing a local adult-audience-development process and is a recent recipient of a Family Foundation grant enabling the hiring of a full-time staff person who will be committed to this effort.

> There is a relatively recent movement among arts organizations and funders to engage new audiences. Classic arts events had been losing audience (and, thus, revenue) and needed to develop plans for better reaching new attendees.

Community Crescent Theatre in Green River, State is a forty-six-year-old arts organization composed of three distinct programs, which serve the organization's mission "to enrich, challenge, and entertain by producing and presenting quality theatre." Programs include:

- Crescent Presents (formerly "Council of Performing Arts for Children," a part of the community for the past thirty-four years), which will present sixty-four performances of thirteen productions in schools and community performance venues between October 2005 and May 2006.
- Crescent Theatre in the Park, which will produce five main-stage shows in the 2005 season.
- Magic Crescent, a summer season of three children's productions.

The Convenor is a community-improvement process advised by nearly thirty traditional and nontraditional civic leaders. Following an adapted Continuous Quality Improvement model, the Convenor process seeks to create the conditions for sustainable community change by gathering and sharing information, building networks and communication linkages, developing a community-based shared vision and indicators, developing competencies (such as leadership, problem-solving, systems thinking, and other skills) among community members, and identifying and developing tools and resources necessary to continue the effort for the long term. Put simply, those who are participating in the Convenor effort believe that this community can solve its problems and improve the quality of living for all if we first decide where we want to direct our collective skills and resources.

> The grant reviewer will likely wonder why the "Goals/Vision" section focuses on detail about the partners rather than simply focusing on Crescent Theatre.

Currently, Crescent Theatre is working as a member of a Convenor planning team to develop and produce a live, interactive performance consisting of dramatic monologues based on stories taken from real community members, live dance that expresses a vision for the improvement of the local quality of life, and other media components. The performance will be a special part of a Convenor community gathering planned for October 30 and 31, 2005. The focus of this community event will be to gather input on a community vision statement, develop objectives for the next steps in community learning and improvement, and define data and indicators needed to mark the community's progress. The performance will include human stories that illustrate data and indicators about the current condition of the community and will be a means of engaging the audience at this event in the Convenor community improvement process.

> The reason for the detail about Crescent Theatre's collaborators is becoming clearer here.

Crescent Theatre sees its role as being an integral part of the larger community building and improvement process, and the Convenor as being a means to gather evidence of need and interest in the arts among the local adult population. The two share similar, complementary goals for their respective project efforts, as follows:

Crescent Theatre (Adult Audience Engagement Process)	The Convenor (Community Improvement Process)
Develop relationships among arts and other organizations to reach uninclined potential adult audiences	Develop cross-sector relationships to further community problem solving
Identify needs/interests among adult audiences	Identify shared vision for the community
Gather evidence that audience development efforts result in less reliance on traditional donors and improved environment for the arts*	Gather data and indicators to express the "health" of the community and to track progress of the Convenor initiatives
Nurture uninclined audiences by assisting understanding of the relevance of art in their daily lives	Nurture emerging nontraditional leaders and citizens' engagement in community improvement activities
Assist community members in identifying issues and expressing them creatively through establishing artist residencies in neighborhoods	Design a cross-sector community-improvement process that addresses priority issues identified by the community.

> The grantwriter lists no objectives, nor is it clear what the grantmaker is being asked to fund.

*These goals will not be addressed during the planning process.

Planning Process

The planning process will culminate in a contract with a resident artist who will be selected because his or her performance responds to the needs and interests of uninclined adult audiences and to the identified priorities and issues of the larger community.

After the October community meeting, at which the Convenor will present data (including Crescent's interactive presentation), collect visions for the future, and assist community members in identifying common priorities and critical issues, the Convenor's design and indicator teams will analyze the issues and priorities to determine what data should be systematically collected and reported to gauge progress toward improvement on critical issues and will design a process for improvement that crosses sectors and systems in the community.

Crescent Theatre will join in the post-meeting planning to add and share the perspective of the arts, and will develop, in conjunction with the Convenor, an audience-engagement effort that complements the community-improvement process and that responds to identified priorities and issues in the community. For instance, if the community indicates a need for improved relationships between ethnicities, the Convenor will take a cross-sector approach to the problem (one in which the arts will be represented by Crescent Theatre), while Crescent Theatre would likely establish an artist residency program that would work with diverse populations in their neighborhoods to develop cultural presentations for mutual sharing.

Representatives from Crescent Theatre and the Convenor will meet at least biweekly to assist each other in planning and in establishing objectives for the artist residency program. In January all partners in the planning process will have access to the Arts Council's Arts Market Consulting Inc. comprehensive community cultural assessment, which is anticipated to inform further planning and help identify focus group participants. Also in January, the Crescent Theatre director will attend the APAP Showcase to identify up to three potential artists for residency. These artists will be invited to present to the entire planning team in early 2006.

This audience is likely familiar with APAP, but the grantwriter should have spelled it out on first reference.

Focus groups facilitated by the Convenor will also be called on to address issues raised in the Arts Council's report, identify and clarify their needs and interests about the arts, and interact with visiting artists if schedules permit.

By March, the planning team will identify an artist for a residency that responds to the needs and interests of uninclined adult audiences and the identified priorities of the larger community. He or she will be asked to return at least twice to Green River to join in the planning process.

The plan's narrative timeline is rather difficult to follow. A chart in addition to the narrative would have aided the grant reviewer.

Partners

The partners in the audience development process are members of the Convenor design team named above and staff of Crescent Theatre. The Convenor also includes a communications team, an indicator team, a data team, and convening team, and an advisory committee, which, between them, consist of nearly 150 local business, civic, and educational leaders. Some of these individuals will likely participate in planning the audience-engagement effort from their areas of expertise and interest. For instance, the communications team can be called on to aid Crescent Theatre in generating interest in and publicity for the residency program; the indicator team will establish measures of the effectiveness of the residency program.

The examples help the reader understand the rather complex relationship between the arts and community improvement organizations.

The planning partnership is entirely collaborative. The Convenor will benefit by Crescent Theatre's efforts to use the arts to engage community members in the larger community improvement process. Crescent Theatre will benefit from the Convenor's map of the community's issues, priorities, and vision. In addition, Crescent Theatre and the audience-engagement process will benefit from a professional, continuous evaluation and documentation process that allows all participants and leaders to learn from the process as it unfolds and to revise plans quickly should the need arise.

Funders who focus grantmaking in the arts have a section on artistry that is not found in more general grant application outlines.

Artistry

Crescent Theatre has not yet selected an artist or discipline for the audience-development project; rather, selection will be a part of the planning process. The artist will be selected based on his or her experience in working with small community groups and diverse audiences. Special consideration will be given for artists that have previously worked on audience-development projects so that all the partners can continue to learn as the process unfolds.

Planned outcomes should have been set forth clearly in the planning process section of the grant.

Crescent Theatre will contract with the artist and be responsible for successful outcomes. The Convenor will assist this process by identifying and framing objectives for the audience-engagement effort, facilitating focus groups of uninclined adult audience members, and continuing a learning history documentation project throughout the residency. The artist will assist in framing the objectives and, in planning with Crescent Theatre, the sites and programming for the residency.

Organizational Capacity

After the large community engagement meeting in October, the partners will meet biweekly to plan an artist residency that responds to identified priority issues and that furthers both Crescent Theatre's and the Convenor's goals. Meeting discussions will be documented as part of the learning history.

Meetings will include various members of The Convenor's design team and one or two members of Crescent Theatre staff (the director and the audience-engagement specialist to be hired in October 2005 under a three-year grant from the Family Foundation). When the artist is selected and available, he or she will be asked to join one or two meetings to continue planning the residency.

> Clearly, the grant RFP or guidelines focus on planning for an artist in residence project. This proposal would not be a strong response to an RFP seeking to fund the actual artist in residence because neither that person nor a critical staff member, the audience-engagement specialist, have yet been identified.

This effort will be the first project for the audience-engagement specialist and will require his or her focus between meetings of the planning group. He or she will be hired based on arts and community development experience and understanding or desire to learn about the process for engaging uninclined adult audiences.

The adult audience-engagement process is still new to this community; however, the Arts Council is currently working on a comprehensive community cultural assessment with Arts Consulting, Inc. This report will assess the perceptions, attendance patterns, and influence of venues among regular, infrequent, and nonattendees and will be completed by January 2006. The planning team will cooperate and assist this effort and believes that the final report will inform the planning process and ensure the success of the subsequent artist residency.

> There is little comment on the capacity of the collaborating organization to fulfill its roles in this project. The grantwriter has assumed that because this is a local funder, it would be familiar with all the organizations mentioned. In doing so, he or she has lost the opportunity to market the distinctive qualities of the collaborating organizations.

Documentation and Evaluation

The evaluation of this project will be completed in two levels. Level one measures progress on the specific goals of the audience-engagement process. Level two focuses on using the components of "Learning History" to document and strengthen the broad areas of community and organizational learning.

> A learning history is a specific type of evaluation used by organizations that are attempting a new effort in which learning is equally, if not more, important than outcomes.

Level 1: Evaluation of Audience-Engagement Strategy

Using both quantitative and qualitative methods, Crescent Theatre and the Convenor will collect data to answer the following questions:

- Were we able to identify uninclined adult audiences?
- Have we identified the needs and interests of the uninclined audiences?
- Does the planned artist residency respond to priority issues identified by the community and the identified needs of the uninclined audiences?
- Have unanticipated partners joined the planning effort? What has been their contribution?
- Were the benefits derived from the October arts presentation balanced for the Convenor and Crescent Theatre?

> The statement "using both qualitative and quantitative methods" is very vague about the evaluation methodology. However, the questions that follow form a framework for developing the methodology.

Level 2: Using Learning Histories to Document the Planning Process
A second evaluation measure, which will be particularly useful for honing and improving both the community improvement and audience-engagement efforts and for sharing with other communities that wish to learn from our experiences, will be Learning Histories. Staff of the Convenor will join with others to document the effects of project activities, ask critical questions about the learning as it occurs, determine the implications of the learning on future project direction, and empower all participants to take action based on new learning.

As part of the Learning History evaluation, Convenor staff will gather data from several different sources including documents such as white papers, proposals, meeting minutes, assessments and surveys, interviews, and other records. Individually and with other participants, they will record their own and the groups' reflections and responses to data and events. Finally, staff will organize, synthesize, and chart the data and reflections for use in "Interactive Learning Sessions," which involve planning participants in interpreting and validating the data and finding points of agreement for improvements to the planning and implementation processes.

Data gathering and organization into the Convenor's Learning History will be ongoing and continuous throughout the planning and implementation of the audience-engagement process. Interactive Learning Sessions will be held at the end of the planning process and will culminate in a synthesized report of the process's history and blueprints for future activities.

Medical Service Organizations

Hospitals, clinics, health departments, and a number of healthcare and health-related programs all require funding to purchase expensive equipment, to perform research, to operate programs for the under- and uninsured, and to deploy special initiatives focused on specific health concerns.

Strategies

Grantwriting for the medical community can be highly specialized, especially when the writer needs to become an expert in the science of medicine in order to write a response to an RFP. Medical programs receive funding from local foundations and from the government. A few large, national foundations fund demonstration projects in various communities that are focused on major national health concerns such as smoking, lead paint hazards, asthma, HIV/AIDS, and many others.

In the following sample, the grantseeker met with the trustees of this non-staffed foundation prior to submitting. In the meeting, the grantseekers learned more about the grantmaker's interests and highlighted those findings in the grantseeking letter.

Sample: Medical Service Grant Proposal

September 15, 2004

The Robert and Virginia Wealthy Foundation
700 Bank Building
Any Street
Anytown, USA

Dear Rob and Virginia,

Thank you for this opportunity to write on behalf of the Kyleton County Pediatric Asthma Network (PAN), a consortium of individuals from area healthcare institutions and related agencies (including Green River Children's Hospital and Major Health, the American Lung Association of State, Catholic Health Services, and the Green River Public Schools), who, since 2002, have collaborated to improve pediatric asthma management among children from low-income families. With pilot funding from 2002 to 2004, PAN provided education for more than 4,000 physicians, nurses, school personnel, parents, and others who care for children with asthma, and intensively case managed fifty children from low-income families.

Some of our findings in the pilot were startling. On the broader, national view, we learned that prevalence of pediatric asthma is increasing—a 56 percent rise in cases between 1988 and 1997. Costs are escalating as asthma is the most frequent reason for chronic-illness hospitalization among children and teens and costs the U.S. more than $712 million annually or $1.3 billion when costs include parents' missed work days, outpatient visits, and medication. Asthma disproportionately affects minorities: minority individuals are 22 percent more likely to have asthma than whites and, worse, African American children are three times more likely to die from asthma-related illness.

Locally, The Green River Children's Hospital—one of four area hospitals that admit children—admitted 404 children with asthma in 2002. More than 50 percent of these children received Medicaid assistance with the average $3,161 per child cost of care; nearly 30 percent of those for whom ethnicity data were available were minority children.

On a very personal level, our case management workers have encountered families where, despite cleanliness, asthma education, and motivation, low income prevents some of the most basic safeguards against asthma in the home, such as new bedding, mattress covers, and appropriate pillows.

Kyleton County Pediatric Asthma Network, with its mission "to improve the lives of all infants, children, and adolescents with asthma by providing educational and professional expertise," can make a profound difference for these children, improving not only the quality of their lives, but the quantity.

To do so, we need your help to expand comprehensive case management services, develop and provide certification standards for educators and healthcare professionals, build community

---

This is an acceptable form of address because of the writer's personal relationship with the funder.

The letter reminds the funder that this proposal is not unexpected.

The first paragraph of the letter corresponds to the first section of a grant and focuses on the need for service.

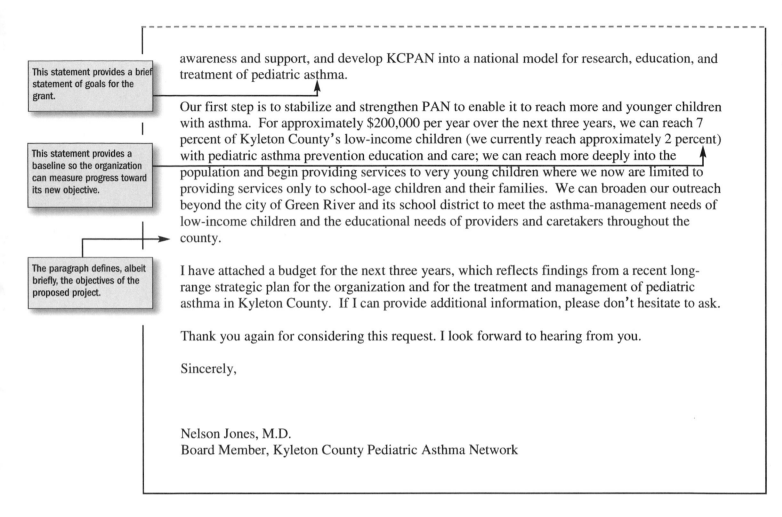

This statement provides a brief statement of goals for the grant.

This statement provides a baseline so the organization can measure progress toward its new objective.

The paragraph defines, albeit briefly, the objectives of the proposed project.

awareness and support, and develop KCPAN into a national model for research, education, and treatment of pediatric asthma.

Our first step is to stabilize and strengthen PAN to enable it to reach more and younger children with asthma. For approximately $200,000 per year over the next three years, we can reach 7 percent of Kyleton County's low-income children (we currently reach approximately 2 percent) with pediatric asthma prevention education and care; we can reach more deeply into the population and begin providing services to very young children where we now are limited to providing services only to school-age children and their families. We can broaden our outreach beyond the city of Green River and its school district to meet the asthma-management needs of low-income children and the educational needs of providers and caretakers throughout the county.

I have attached a budget for the next three years, which reflects findings from a recent long-range strategic plan for the organization and for the treatment and management of pediatric asthma in Kyleton County. If I can provide additional information, please don't hesitate to ask.

Thank you again for considering this request. I look forward to hearing from you.

Sincerely,

Nelson Jones, M.D.
Board Member, Kyleton County Pediatric Asthma Network

Educational Institutions

Educational institutions include public and private K-12 school districts, intermediate school districts (ISDs), college and universities, charter schools, and special educational programs and institutions. (Note: When examining eligibility, both school districts and ISDs are defined by government funders as Local Educational Associations or LEAs.)

Strategies

State and federal governments make grants to schools, though the amount and the programs can change dramatically with government administrations. Some states offer formula grants, meaning that they expend money based on enrollment, level of poverty, etc. to all districts in the state. Formula grants do not require an application, but are listed in grant opportunities on state websites. To be considered for non-formula, competitive grants, districts must submit a proposal.

Many foundations are reluctant to fund public schools because they see that as the role of government and taxpayers. Educational organizations need to be highly strategic to approach foundations.

Sample: Education Grant Proposal

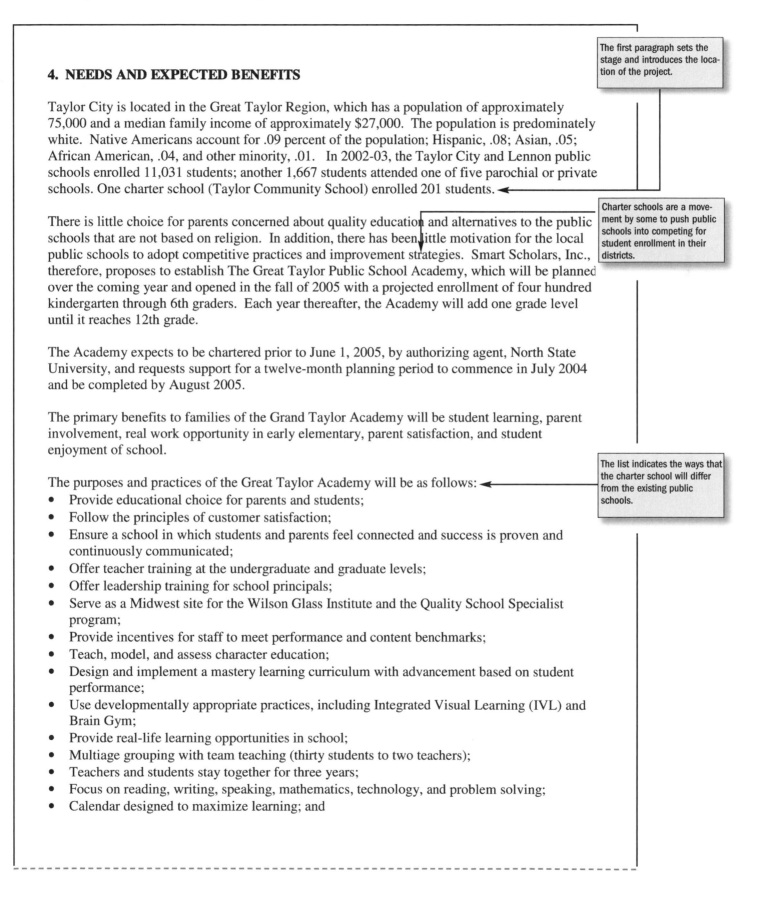

4. NEEDS AND EXPECTED BENEFITS

Taylor City is located in the Great Taylor Region, which has a population of approximately 75,000 and a median family income of approximately $27,000. The population is predominately white. Native Americans account for .09 percent of the population; Hispanic, .08; Asian, .05; African American, .04, and other minority, .01. In 2002-03, the Taylor City and Lennon public schools enrolled 11,031 students; another 1,667 students attended one of five parochial or private schools. One charter school (Taylor Community School) enrolled 201 students.

> The first paragraph sets the stage and introduces the location of the project.

There is little choice for parents concerned about quality education and alternatives to the public schools that are not based on religion. In addition, there has been little motivation for the local public schools to adopt competitive practices and improvement strategies. Smart Scholars, Inc., therefore, proposes to establish The Great Taylor Public School Academy, which will be planned over the coming year and opened in the fall of 2005 with a projected enrollment of four hundred kindergarten through 6th graders. Each year thereafter, the Academy will add one grade level until it reaches 12th grade.

> Charter schools are a movement by some to push public schools into competing for student enrollment in their districts.

The Academy expects to be chartered prior to June 1, 2005, by authorizing agent, North State University, and requests support for a twelve-month planning period to commence in July 2004 and be completed by August 2005.

The primary benefits to families of the Grand Taylor Academy will be student learning, parent involvement, real work opportunity in early elementary, parent satisfaction, and student enjoyment of school.

The purposes and practices of the Great Taylor Academy will be as follows:

> The list indicates the ways that the charter school will differ from the existing public schools.

- Provide educational choice for parents and students;
- Follow the principles of customer satisfaction;
- Ensure a school in which students and parents feel connected and success is proven and continuously communicated;
- Offer teacher training at the undergraduate and graduate levels;
- Offer leadership training for school principals;
- Serve as a Midwest site for the Wilson Glass Institute and the Quality School Specialist program;
- Provide incentives for staff to meet performance and content benchmarks;
- Teach, model, and assess character education;
- Design and implement a mastery learning curriculum with advancement based on student performance;
- Use developmentally appropriate practices, including Integrated Visual Learning (IVL) and Brain Gym;
- Provide real-life learning opportunities in school;
- Multiage grouping with team teaching (thirty students to two teachers);
- Teachers and students stay together for three years;
- Focus on reading, writing, speaking, mathematics, technology, and problem solving;
- Calendar designed to maximize learning; and

- Numerous involvement opportunities for parents, including but not limited to a seat on the board, input on practices and policies, classroom volunteerism, and participation in teacher training.

5. PROPOSED ACTIVITIES, OBJECTIVES AND TIMELINE

Planning will begin in <u>July 2004</u> when the principal moves to the Great Taylor region and begins establishing relationships with other educational professionals, parents, business leaders, and other community members. These relationships are at the core of the Quality School philosophy and many of the planned activities for the school, which will likely include a drive-up coffee shop for parents who drop their children off in the morning and contracted relationships with area businesses that provide dry cleaning pick-up, meals to go, and other amenities that ensure, first that parents are not inconvenienced by driving their children to school each morning and evening, and second that families have more quality time together after school since they haven't a complex series of errands to run. Other amenities that may be established during the planning period include a small student-staffed convenience store with grocery staples such as bread and milk, and contracted individual activities such as music lessons, karate, gymnastics, or other activities that parents want their children to participate in, but require additional driving and time away from the family. With these alternatives in place, children may stay after school until 5:00 p.m. for enrichment activities or work in the stores and be picked up at a time more convenient for parents' work schedules.

Beginning <u>July 1</u>, the principal will seek a site, design, and contractor for the school building, which will be designed to support learning and be flexible for future growth. Also in <u>July</u>, the principal will begin recruiting clerical support staff to assist in the planning and to work at the school when it opens.

<u>Throughout the planning period</u> and with assistance from the board of directors and the advisory panel, the principal will finalize the curriculum, based on the State framework, which will have a comprehensive focus on useful learning. All student-run businesses within the school will be tied to the curriculum objectives. The panel, board, and principal will establish assessment criteria, which will include opportunities for each individual student to perform learning demonstrations for teachers and parents to certify his or her comprehension of learning content. The principal will also develop and write a plan for building relationships that encourage parent involvement, which will be shared with all staff for implementation.

<u>By January 2005</u>, the principal will have developed and launched a public relations campaign to inform community members about their new educational choice. Student recruitment will begin in January and continue throughout the spring and summer with a lottery to ensure fair and equitable access slated for <u>April 2005</u>. Once students are enrolled, the Academy will convene a group of parents to define and select traits to be modeled and taught through character education. The Academy will then purchase materials and develop training necessary to further parents' character education goals.

In <u>March and April 2005</u>, the principal, board of directors, and advisory panel will begin recruiting teaching staff according to established criteria, including but not limited to: state

---

Side annotations:

One of the barriers to charter school enrollment is the necessity for parents to drive their children to school rather than use school buses.

The school will be designed to appeal to parents as well as their children.

Since the timeline is written into the narrative, the writer has underscored dates to help the reader navigate.

Traditional education shies away from character education, leaving it to parents. It is necessary to have parent involvement in the design of this component.

certification, interest in the quality school philosophy, and ownership for student performance regardless of ability. Teacher training in Brain Gym, Integrated Visual Learning, Quality School, and the curriculum will be scheduled on various days throughout June and August 2005. Because the Great Taylor region is a recreational and tourist attraction, school will begin shortly after Labor Day 2005.

6.   EVALUATION

The planning period will be evaluated and judged successful according to the following criteria:
- School will open with an enrollment of at least 350 in the fall of 2005.
- All student applicants will have participated in a lottery to ensure equitable access to the school.
- Teachers will be competent in Quality School principles, IVL, Brain Gym, brain-based research related teaching strategies, and all curricular subjects.
- Relationships with parents, community, and public schools will be established, positive, and continually nurtured under an organized plan for developing relationships and parental involvement.
- Curriculum will be based on the State framework; assessment and reporting procedures will be documented and ready to implement.

In addition, the school program itself will be evaluated after its first year according to the following criteria, and additional criteria that arises from the planning period: ◄———

> This criteria answers the state's need for data on student performance.

- Student performance on SEAP reading, math, writing and science tests (Spring 2007)
- Exit demonstrations by students to evidence reading, writing, speaking, and problem-solving competency
- Student attendance figures
- Parent involvement statistics (attendance at conferences; volunteerism)
- Parent surveys
- Student surveys
- Continued enrollment

> See chapter 7 for guidance in writing the staff qualifications portion of a grant proposal.

7.   STAFF QUALIFICATIONS ◄

8.   EQUITABLE ACCESS ◄

> Though there is an assurance form to sign, the grantseeker must also write a narrative about policies that protect equality.

The Great Taylor Academy will be an equal opportunity employer, which plans to hire all staff (teaching, support, and administration) based on their qualifications and agreement with school policy, regardless of their ethnicity, color, sexual orientation, gender, age, disability, or other discrimination.

Although every effort will be made to mirror the ethnic composition of the community, students will be selected for the school by lottery. All students will have an equal opportunity to submit their names for lottery, regardless of their educational ability/disability, ethnicity, color, gender, or physical disability. ◄———

> The community is not ethnically diverse, so the lottery system should have no significant impact on the ethnic composition of the student body.

The Academy will accept all students as selected by lottery regardless of their ability to pay for amenities or after-school activities and will endeavor to provide assistance to families in need.

All learning activities will be geared to the individual student. Those requiring additional assistance in any subject matter, or those with diagnosed learning disabilities, will receive assistance to remediate indicated problems and achieve their greatest learning potential.

The grantseeker claims that most of the population, lacking choice, are already educationally disadvantaged.

9.   SERVICE FOR EDUCATIONALLY DISADVANTAGED STUDENTS

Research supports the concept that students in schools that do not adopt quality school practices are educationally disadvantaged. The Great Taylor Academy will, therefore, establish its school based on best practices and research indicators for quality education, including ensuring small class size, which has been demonstrated to support learning, particularly in cases of children who come from low-income families. Another demonstrated quality practice is keeping children with the same teacher for three years, which is also planned for the Academy.

Each child will be individually assessed at the time of lottery selection. Educationally disadvantaged children will have an equal opportunity to be selected in the lottery. Staff will develop an individual learning plan for each child and continuously assess and monitor progress and communicate with parents or guardians.

This is a rare request for information asking the respondent to describe the way that schools and families will work together to educate students.

10.   COLLEGIAL INVOLVEMENT

Quality schools are based on strong relationships that link administrators, teachers, support staff, students, families, and communities in symbiotic support centered on the child and his or her learning. Brain-based research and effective schools research support the idea that children, youth, and adults learn best in a relationship that is free from fear. Therefore, the Academy will focus on building and nurturing positive relationships—from greeting children and families each morning at the front door, to providing coffee and conveniences to parents, to communicating regularly with family members, to ensuring after-school activities and guidance.

All staff and board meetings will be conducted in the same manner as the educational programs. Individuals will be greeted, acknowledged, and welcomed at all meetings. Staff will be afforded collaborative paid planning time and be encouraged to engage in a wide variety of social activities with and without their students.

Parents will have input and involvement in the development of the character education curriculum and in the development of many school policies. They will be invited to participate in learning demonstrations rather than tests, which are culminating events following segments of learning. The school will host numerous family events including but not limited to picnics, game nights, multicultural events, music presentations, plays, and festivals, as well as learning demonstrations.

At parents' request, the school will establish contracts with area instructors and offer such after-school enrichment activities as karate, music lessons, voice lessons, gymnastics, or others.

Students will run an in-school coffee house with a drive-up window for parents dropping off their students in the morning. In addition, other possible in-school real-life facilities and services, such as a convenience store, dry cleaning pick up, meal pick up, or other family amenities will not only reduce the need for families to run errands after picking up their children, but will also support relevant learning experiences for children. Parents will be sent monthly bills for after-school activities and other amenities, further reducing the need for errands such as running to the bank. ◄—

> One of the philosophies of the school principal is that homework erodes family time and can sometimes reduce the quality of family time if it creates arguments. Her school, then, wants to afford as much family togetherness time as possible.

11. QUALITY ASSURANCE

a) Current plans and ideas will be more fully explored during the planning process. However, the Academy will base its curriculum on the State framework for language arts, mathematics and science. As a part of the planning, the principal and Advisory Panel will develop and write content and performance standards and assessment criteria that correlate with the State core curriculum.

b) LL, a nationally recognized expert on research-based instructional design, is on the Advisory Panel to ensure that all instruction is built on sound research and best practices.

c) The Academy will be an alternative to the public and parochial schools currently available in the Great Taylor region. All Academy professional development courses will be available to public and parochial teachers and administrators. Children in the public schools may attend a fee-based summer school at the Academy and, once relationships are established with the schools, students in other schools will be afforded an opportunity to receive Integrated Visual Learning Therapy, which will only be available at the Academy.

d) The Academy will begin demonstrating effectiveness by scores on the SEAP in the spring of 2007 as well as through performance demonstrations, culminations of learning activities that will be open to parents and community members.

> The grantwriter should indicate how the school will get a building—do they have money to purchase or construct? If not, where will the funds come from?

e) Though it does not yet have a site or building, the Academy has a web page (www.TaylorAcademy.com) and an 800 number with voice mail. The principal and Advisory Panel hold a goal for providing a high level of access to technology and computer-aided instruction for all students, but this awaits further planning to determine best selections and use of funding. All teachers will have access to technology and communications devices and will receive training in their use.

f) As a renowned expert in Continuous Quality Improvement for schools, LL will assist in the development of a continuous improvement plan for the Academy and provide for parent input on policies, procedures, and offerings. Parents and students will be surveyed regularly about the Academy, and their feedback will be incorporated into continuous improvement plans.

Charter schools are often founded to follow a specific approach to education. The grantmaker, therefore, wants to know which school of thought the charter will follow.

12. EDUCATIONAL MODEL AND REPLICATION

In developing the school and curriculum, the Advisory Panel and principal will use two schools as resources: Jones Elementary, which was cited by NEA Today as possibly the best elementary school in the nation and has been the subject of four videotapes, two books, and several journal articles; and Smith Developmental Academy, a successful charter school that integrates several established models and programs of developmental education.

Both models have demonstrated parent satisfaction as evidenced by waiting lists for student applications. Both have practiced Integrated Visual Learning and have implemented the Glass model school principles, such as brain-based research learning activities, choice theory, and continuous improvement for quality.

A part of the assessment process will include a plan, developed with LL, for continuous quality improvement. The principal and all members of the Advisory Panel have authored several books each on their respective areas of expertise and will document the establishment of the Great Taylor Academy for replication in other communities.

13. BUDGET NARRATIVE

This number indicates a state cost-center code

110   Instruction - Basic Programs
$9,680 is requested to purchase staff training in Quality Schools, a four-day course that will be provided to twenty-two teachers in August 2005 at a cost of $440 per teacher. $5,000 is requested for curriculum training, also to begin in August 2005, for twenty-two teachers. The Academy requests $6,600 to train twenty-two teachers in Brain Gym at a cost of $330 per teacher for the five-day workshop.

120   Instruction - Added Needs
$12,500 is requested to purchase curriculum materials such as Literacy readers, mathematics manipulation tools, and science materials. All materials will be used in training and in the classroom.

240   School Administration
        $40,000 is requested as follows:
        -   $30,000 toward the principal's first-year salary to enable planning, relationship building, school design and construction, and curriculum and assessment development.
        -   $10,000 toward first-year salary for one clerical support staff to assist the principal in planning activities.

250   Business Services
        $19,400 is requested to purchase advertising and to recruit staff and students as follows:
        -   $5,400 billboard space at $900 per month for six months

- $3,000 local newspaper and Taylor Magazine advertisements targeted to parents and students at $500 per month for six months
- $5,000 for teacher recruitment and reference checks
- $6,000 for mailers and postcards for direct mail campaign to inform public about educational choice offered at the Academy

280   Central Support Services
$4,000 is requested for telephone fees, including voicemail charges and long-distance conferences between Advisory Panel members.

Technology Organizations

Technology organizations focus on providing equitable access to equipment and training in a community, or "closing the digital divide." They include media centers, Internet providers, computer services, and others.

Strategies

Under the Clinton administration, federal and state grants were available for efforts to improve access to technology in rural and central urban areas because, historically, for-profit providers had supplied infrastructure such as Internet cabling first (and sometimes only) in areas that would produce revenues and profits for the company. These grant opportunities have been phased out as more and more people now have access to technology.

Without specific technology grants, organizations that are not technology providers and that need computers and other high-tech equipment often must include funds for such purchases as part of a project grant request and indicate the necessity of the purchase to achieving the project objectives. Technology organizations often collaborate with other nonprofit organizations, enhancing their efforts and sharing responsibilities for creative programs.

Sample: Technology Grant Proposal

1. Approach
a. Goals and Objectives

[Though there is no problem statement section, the grantseeker indicates the need for choosing this approach.]

Green River, Midwest has a population of approximately 198,000; 120,000 of those residents are registered voters. On November 7, 2000, national election day, the City of Green River Clerk's office received 7,783 calls on the main line alone—three times the call volume of an average month (2,756). Nearly all of the calls asked one or both of two questions: Am I registered? and/or Where do I go to vote? Calls from voters to the Clerk's office overburdened the lines to the extent that poll workers could not get through. Individuals who dropped in to their nearest precinct with questions about their registration and voting site often left without the necessary information, and many were unable to cast their votes.

[This sentence states the number of program participants.]

The City Media Center (CMC) has the technology, expertise, experience with the target population, and community partners to address this difficult issue for the Clerk's office and citizens, and simultaneously to engage qualified college students in the electoral process.

[This statement explains the acronym on the first reference]

CMC plans to recruit ninety college students from six area colleges and universities, equip them with laptops programmed with the Statewide Voter Registration list or "Qualified Voter Files (QVF)" and mapping software, and deploy them to work in Green River's seventy-seven voting sites. CMC will produce and air Public Service Announcements in the weeks prior to the election to ensure that voters know that they can go to the nearest precinct if they have questions on Election Day.

The students, who will participate in a training program in October, will not duplicate the work of poll workers, but will assist them by looking up registrations and ensuring that each voter has come to the correct polling place. For those who are registered in a different precinct, the college workers will look up electronic maps to that precinct and advise the voter where he or she is to go.

Seventy-seven college students will work the polls, though CMC will recruit ninety to ensure coverage, despite illness or emergency, at each of the seventy-seven polling sites for the one hundred precincts in the City. The college students will interact throughout the day with veteran poll workers in the city and with high-school students who are recruited annually to work in each precinct as part of a community-service project.

CMC holds two overarching goals for the Help America Vote College Project, each of which will be achieved by its measurable objectives and will result in a measurable outcome:

Goal 1. Assist voters in identifying the appropriate precinct in which to vote by providing on-site, immediate responses to questions about registration and voting.
> Objective 1.a.: Program seventy-seven laptop computers with Qualified Voter Files (QVF) and electronic maps and directions for all precincts.
> Objective 1.b.: Train ninety college students to use computers and software and to work as poll assistants.

[This is a measurable outcome.]

Planned Outcome 1: Reduce call volume to City Clerk's office by at least 25 percent less than that of 2000.

Goal 2. Engage college students in the electoral process by putting them "in the thick of things" on Election Day.
> Objective 2.a.: Contact one or two professors at each of six area colleges/universities and request assistance in recruiting students as poll assistants.

Objective 2.b.: Recruit ninety college-student poll assistants and pair them with veteran poll worker to promote discussion of experience and enthusiasm for the work.

Objective 2.c.: Train students to use the technology, to provide friendly, responsive service to citizens on behalf of the City, and on the various responsibilities of poll workers.

Objective 2.d.: Provide college students brief historical perspective about the importance of voting and provide take-away fact sheets to share with their peers.

Objective 2.e.: Survey students about their voting behaviors prior to the application process; survey them about their experience the day after elections; survey students about their voting behaviors one year after their service at the polls.

Planned Outcome 2: Students will report greater interest in election process and issues, and increased voting in subsequent elections. ◄─────────

> There is no way to measure the goal stated in the RFP (to engage college age students in the democratic process) within the timeframe of the grant (October through November 2004), other than to do a longitudinal study of participants' voting behavior. It might have been a mistake, however, to plan an evaluation that fell outside the grant period, as there would not be a way for the grantmaker to hold the grantee accountable for evaluating the project. The grantwriter should have assumed that, given the funding timeframe, "engagement" meant on election day only.

b. Innovation

The City Media Center is an umbrella for four affiliates: CityTV cable television (public access), City radio, GREAT Internet service provision and computer consulting for nonprofit organizations, and Institute for Information Democracy (IID), a media literacy organization. Green River CMC was the first and remains one of only a few full-service community-based and owned telecommunications centers in the nation.

Within, CMC has computer expertise (GREAT), numerous projects involving a network of young adults (CityTV's Youth Channel and Future Kulture, and IID's media literacy projects), a well-publicized position that "information is the currency of democracy" (IID), and the means to develop and air multimedia public service announcements in a timely manner (City radio, CityTV, GREAT websites). It also has a long history of providing information for the electorate, including its Annual Teledemocracy Project, taken at the request of the League of Women Voters, which analyzes media coverage of candidates and issues, hosts candidate forums, and provides a website with information on the records and stands of all candidates in local, state, and national elections.

Each of the CMC affiliates has numerous programs that bring staff in contact with diverse community members—homeless individuals, nonprofit and civic leaders, children, teens, and seniors. From these relationships, CMC has built partnerships with every sector in the City: government, health care, education, human services, housing, and more. This proposed project furthers partnerships with six area colleges/universities, including Green Valley State University, Private College, Catholic College, Christian College, Green River Community College, and Business College, and assists CMC's long-time partner and first supporter, the City of Green River.

College professors will recruit students from their own and from peers' classrooms. For instance, the Mayor of Green River teaches at Catholic College and has been called on to recruit current and past students to the project; Green Valley State University professors have agreed to recruit students from several of its many schools of study. Students will complete online applications developed by GREAT in cooperation with the City Clerk's office. These applications will contain questions similar to those asked of poll workers, with three notable exceptions. First, students will be asked if they are fluent in another language. This information will be used to deploy students with foreign language skills to work in precincts with the highest number of new, non- or limited-English speaking citizens. ◄─────────

> It would fill an important need to put bilingual poll workers in precincts where many people are not fluent in English.

This ensures equitable access by students.

Second, students will not be asked their party affiliation. This question is necessary for other poll workers to ensure that each precinct has, to the extent possible, equal numbers of Democrat and Republican poll workers to assist voters or to coreview damaged ballots. The students will not be involved with this official work, so will not be asked to declare their parties.

Third and finally, students will be asked on their application about past voting records. This information will not be used to select college workers but as a baseline against which CMC and Green Valley State University's Community Research Institute can later measure changes in their voting behavior and interest in the election process.

The State has just completed interactive electronic State Registered Voter Files and has prepared CDs that CMC will copy and provide with laptop computers for each college poll worker. The student poll workers will type the name of the registered voter into the software. The computer will locate the name, and indicate current voter registration status as well as the precinct and polling site for voting. If the potential voter is at the wrong polling site, the laptops will be equipped to provide maps and driving instructions for traveling from one precinct to another.

Green Valley State University, one of the partners to this effort, holds the "Community Research Institute," which will oversee the longitudinal evaluation of the project and its outcomes. Graduate students may assist in the evaluation and reporting only if they have not participated as poll workers.

CMC will provide each student with a t-shirt printed with a City logo and a graphic that identifies them as the person who can answer voters' questions about polling sites. Further it plans to add approximately fifteen minutes of information to the technology and poll worker training on the historic importance of voting and will provide each student a fact sheet about voting to share with their college peers.

One final innovation is effective and immeasurable. CMC has been a part of a local effort to build a "culture of hospitality" to promote tourism and convention business in the City. It will make customer service a part of the training curriculum for college students. Additionally, the City Clerk will add into its poll worker training some tips for welcoming the student workers to the polls.

This is also called "outputs."

c. Products

CMC will generate the following products from the College Poll-Worker Project:

- Online application, plus at least 150 completed applications from students from six area colleges and universities
- Completed day-after surveys of students rating their experience
- Completed longitudinal surveys given one year after Election Day to record changes in opinions, attitudes, and voting behavior and compare with data gathered in the initial application
- Training materials for student poll workers, including information on voting and hospitality
- Enhanced training materials, including information on working with students, for general poll workers
- Network of professors who are willing and able to recruit students to work in polls
- Tapes of Public Service Announcements (radio and television); web page PSA
- Eighty duplicate CD versions of State Registered Voter Files to be housed at the City Clerk's office (all information will be stripped from the laptops after Election Day)

This section asks the respondent to identify potential barriers to implementing its project and describe what it will do if problems arise. It also asks the respondent to provide a rationale for why it selected this approach.

d. Mitigating Factors/Approach Rationale

CMC anticipates little difficulty leasing or locating within its organization enough laptop computers to accomplish the objectives of the project. The City Clerk's office will provide training materials and will deliver training at the CMC on specified dates. The only difficulty CMC staff can foresee is that more students will apply to serve than the project can accommodate. If this is the case, the City Clerk and CMC Project Manager will review applications to ensure a mix of gender and ethnicity among participants, representation of various languages (predominately Spanish and Vietnamese), and a fair share from each college based on its enrollment size.

Although CMC is undertaking this project in large part to assist interested colleges and universities and to assist the City Clerk in addressing what was, in the last election, a difficult volume of calls, the real value in the project is that it ensures that all those who wish to vote in the November 2, 2004 election will be able to do so. This project is in keeping with the CMC's mission to "build community through media," in that it provides technology tools, training, and information for local citizens and fulfills an organizational goal to provide information as "the currency of democracy."

e. Poll Worker Eligibility

All poll workers (excluding high school volunteers who are trained by the City Clerk's office and receive fourteen hours of community service credit for their participation) must be over eighteen years of age and registered to vote in Kyleton County. All college students accepted to the project must meet these requirements. Since the majority of college students enrolled in the six colleges are from the county, this is not anticipated to be a barrier to recruiting eligible workers.

f. Key Stakeholder Involvement

The City Clerk approached CMC about this project and asked that it lead the effort to engage young people in the voting process and to reduce call volumes from "lost" voters on election day. The Clerk has committed training and training materials, state-level contacts at the Secretary of State's Office and with the person who developed the electronic QVF, and enhanced training for veteran poll workers that will include suggestions for ways to welcome and work with the students.

Two area college professors at Catholic College and Green Valley State University have been contacted and have pledged their support and efforts to recruit students. CMC is now in the process of contacting the remaining four colleges to identify and enlist the aid of professors to recruit from their student bodies. Green Valley State University, one of the partners already engaged to recruit students, will develop the longitudinal evaluation and submit reports of findings to the CMC.

2. EXPECTED RESULTS OR BENEFITS
a. Data Collection

The City Clerk's office will log calls and call volume on Election Day and provide a comparison between calls in the 2000 election and those coming in November 2004.

Students will log all requests for assistance at the polls, including the questions asked and the information provided. These logs will be used by the City Clerk's office to evaluate the need for

Although the reviewers of this proposal agreed that the evaluation plan was responsive to the goals it set for this program and that the results would be of interest to the funder, they nonetheless reduced the score for this proposal section and denied the funding request.

continuation in later years or for ensuring that there are workers and technology in the polling sites that have exhibited the greatest need.

Students will complete an application for the project, which will include a question about their voting habits and attitudes. They will be asked to complete a survey regarding their experience the day after the November 2, 2004 election, and will complete a second survey one year later to determine if their attitudes or voting behavior has changed as a result of their experiences. In the coming year, college students will have an opportunity to vote in school board elections (May 3, 2005), the city primary (August 2, 2005) and the City general elections (November 8, 2005). The final online survey (Survey Monkey) will be requested after the November 8, 2005 election and be compared with information from the initial application for the project collected in October 2004.

Green Valley State University's Community Research Institute will develop the evaluation surveys, deploy them to Survey Monkey.com, email and mail students reminders to participate in the surveys, and report findings from the comparative study by early December 2005.

The project will be judged successful if it achieves the following outcomes:

- Reduces Election Day calls to the City Clerk's office by approximately 25 percent as compared with the November 2000 Election Day call volume
- Increases interest in political process and/or voting by at least 50 percent of participating student poll workers

b. Activities and Accomplishments

Following is a timeline of activities that must be accomplished to achieve the planned outcomes of the project:

The timeline clearly identifies tasks and assigns responsibilities for those tasks.

Date	Activity	Responsibility
By 10/1/04	Contact professors at six colleges to recruit students	CMC project manager
By 10/1/04	Develop online application for student poll workers	CMC-GREAT
By 10/10/04	Recruit at least 150 applicants for student poll workers	CMC and local colleges
By 10/12/04	Review applications to ensure eligibility and determine language skills	CMC and City Clerk
By 10/15/04	Contract with GVSU to design evaluation tool for goals	CMC and GVSU Community Research Institute
By 10/15/04	Hold one hour training for 90 student poll workers	CMC and City Clerk
By 10/15/04	Add tips for welcoming students to the polls to general poll worker training	City Clerk
By 10/20/04	Develop PSAs for radio and television broadcast; develop online announcements at CMC web site	CMC-CITYTV, CITY RADIO, GREAT
By 10/25/04	Ensure PSAs airing daily until election	CMC-CITYTV and CITY RADIO

By 10/25/04	Contract for lease of computers	CMC project manager
By 10/25/04	Test CD of QVF for compatibility with all computers; duplicate CDs	CMC project manager and City Clerk; GREAT
By 10/30/04	Develop or identify electronic mapping system and ensure access	CMC – GREAT
11/2/04	Deploy student poll workers to 77 voting sites (100 precincts) throughout Green River	CMC and City Clerk
11/2/04	Provide technical assistance and trouble shooting to student poll workers	CMC
11/3/04	Survey students with evaluation tool	CMC and GVSU
11/3/04	Record call volume at City Clerk's office on 11/2/04	CMC and City Clerk
By 11/6/05	Survey students with longitudinal evaluation tool	CMC and GVSU
By 12/1/05	All evaluation findings complete	CMC and GVSU

c. Best Practices

According to the Center for Information and Research on Civic Learning and Engagement (CIRCLE) only 42 percent of eligible young voters ages eighteen to twenty-four turned out for the last national election (November 7, 2000) compared with 70 percent of those older than twenty-five. From 1972 to 2000, the rate of turnout for voting among young adults declined 13 percent. Efforts that increase young-adult voter turnout include:

- Allowing Election Day registration
- Early voting at convenient locations
- Voter registration at state motor vehicle agencies
- Mailing sample ballots and information about polling places

Of the above, the State provides only voting registration at the Secretary of State's office that also licenses motor vehicles.

CIRCLE also found that the very best way to turn out the youth vote is to have other youths ask their peers to vote. CMC is therefore committed to providing information about the importance of voting and a fact sheet that will make the college poll workers "experts" on voting among their peers. In addition, the students will be able to assist their peers by sharing information about polling sites and can lead them to websites such as that designed by CMC's Institute for Information Democracy for its Teledemocracy project. This website includes nonpartisan, unbiased information on all candidates and issues on every ballot. Young adults who are informed are more likely to vote.

Finally, simply getting the college students to the polls as poll workers is expected to engage them in voting and to provide them with "insider" information they can share with friends to encourage their voting as well. Interim Director of Youth Vote 2000 said, "Members of the younger generation would be the ideal candidates to work as poll inspectors because they are enthusiastic, dedicated, and most importantly intelligent."

3. BUDGET AND JUSTIFICATION
a. Budget Justification

(1) Equipment: CMC will lease eighty laptops for one week to ensure the CDs are compatible and to have the computers available at the polling places. A local provider has quoted $125 per

computer for the rentals. Three laptops will be used by staff to provide troubleshooting or to replace faulty equipment if there are problems during Election Day. CMC is also providing a few cell phones for those students who do not have them. The students will be invited to call an on-staff troubleshooter and will be provided a list of students who can translate if needed and their numbers and locations.

(2) Supplies: Postage and supplies are required to keep in touch with students throughout the project and to notify them of the final evaluation survey.

(3) Contractual: Payment to college-student poll workers will be reimbursed to the City of Green River from the grant. Payment is calculated at $122.50 for each of the ninety students and includes time at the polls and training session. CMC will commission GVSU's Community Research Institute to provide the surveys, questions for the initial application, and to submit findings in December 2005. This cost is estimated by GVSU at $10,000 total.

CMC's project coordinator will commit 120 hours to the project at $50 per hour for a charge to the grant of $6,000. Services provided by the affiliates include:

- $500 to design and deploy the online application for project participation (GREAT)
- $400 to duplicate the CD of the State Registered Voter File (GREAT)
- $1,500 to develop training materials on the importance of voting and hospitality to add to City curriculum; includes materials and handouts (IID)
- $4,500 to develop and deploy Public Service Announcements on television, radio, and Internet and to write and submit media kits for local media (CITYTV, CITY RADIO, GREAT, CMC)
- $500 to download information and develop a mapping system for polling sites (GREAT)
- $1,200 to provide two troubleshooters in each of three wards. CMC staff will be available to respond to technical difficulties throughout the day. Cost is calculated at $200 for each on-call person.

(4) Other: This line item includes purchasing and printing t-shirts and refreshments for training ninety students and staff. Both items are estimated.

(5) Indirect: CMC is mandated by its Board of Directors to charge costs for fiscal management of all grants for CMC and its affiliates. This cost is 7.5 percent of the total project costs.

> This question is frequently asked in government grants; most grant contracts encourage or mandate the use of a separate account for grant funds to ensure that funds are spent on the items listed in the grant budget.

b. Fiscal Controls

CMC employs a full time accountant on staff. The accountant uses QuickBooks accounting software to manage an annual budget of approximately $1.5 million. CMC annually manages grant funds ranging from $1,000 to $500,000 from local, state and federal sources. Grant funds are maintained separately from other income, and charges against grant funds are itemized against the appropriate line items. Spending is reported monthly to the CMC Board of Directors; grant fund spending is reported as requested by funders.

CMC is audited annually by HH Auditors as required by the City of Green River and has had a balanced budget every year since its inception in 1982. Its audits are published online and made available to all interested parties.

Social/Human Services

Social and human service organizations run the gamut from services for homeless or hungry people to mental health counseling services and everything in between. In other words, most nonprofit organizations, in some way or another, deliver human services. The nonprofit infrastructure exists primarily to make people's lives better.

Strategies

Federal and state governments have departments of health and human services; however, a grantseeker should not limit the investigation of grant opportunities to those coming from those departments. Most grantmakers—including many that are public charities themselves—make grants to social/human service organizations that otherwise meet their eligibility requirements and goals.

Sample: Social/Human Services Grant Proposal

Purpose Statement

The purpose of the "Tools, Talents, and Treasures" capital project is to significantly enhance the capacity of Housing Rehab Services (HRS) to equip low-income homeowners to maintain and improve their homes. Achieving this purpose will also have a community-wide benefit by strengthening our most fragile urban neighborhoods from the inside out through empowering and equipping the residents themselves.

Introduction

Housing Rehab Services is a nonprofit organization with almost twenty years' experience assisting low-income Kyleton County families in their efforts to be successful homeowners. Many organizations help low-income renters become homeowners, but HRS is unique in its mission to help existing low-income homeowners maintain and improve their homes.

Housing Rehab Services' mission is "Building value and dignity by equipping low-income homeowners with critical repairs, low-cost supplies, and quality information while advocating for a strong, vibrant community." Five specific HRS programs work in tangent to fulfill this mission:

- Critical repairs to eliminate threats to health, safety, and affordable utilities, using professional HRS staff and qualified volunteers. Since the early 1980s, HRS has performed more than 27,000 such critical repairs, including replacement of six hundred old furnaces and installation of more than 1,300 new entry doors and locks. In 2000 alone, HRS staff and volunteers provided 1,803 critical home repairs.

- Dependable access for people with disabilities. In 2000, Housing Rehab Services built thirty-three wheelchair ramps and made forty other access modifications for individuals referred to HRS by the Center for Independent Living. Since its inception, HRS has built more than two hundred wheelchair ramps for low-income homeowners. Many of the ramps were designed by HRS staff and built by volunteers from community churches and service organizations, such as The Green River Home Builders Association, which is the single largest source for HRS volunteers.

- Affordable material for low-income "do-it-yourselfers." Since 1997, HRS has sought donations of surplus (mismeasured, out-of-date, slightly damaged, or used) building materials from area businesses and individuals. Through the HRS Builders' Warehouse, these materials are made available to low-income homeowners for 70-80 percent below retail value. For instance, in 2000, HRS received material donations valued at $320,000, which were purchased by low-income homeowners at a cost of $88,795. Since 1997, HRS has sold surplus material with a total value of $1.9 million.

- Essential tools to help low-income homeowners make their own home repairs. In 2000, the HRS Tool Library made 5,500 tool loans, bringing the total over the years to more than 55,000 loans.

- Quality information to equip low-income homeowners with the skills and knowledge needed for regular home repair and maintenance. In 2000 alone, HRS provided formal instruction to

---

[Margin note:] Note the differences in this outline beginning with a purpose statement followed by an introduction. Grant guidelines and RFPs all have different outlines that you must follow.

[Margin note:] Because this is a capital grant, this section focuses on introducing the organization and its history of service; if it were a program proposal, it would focus on describing the program and briefly introduce the organization.

173 students averaging eight class hours each and has engaged in numerous informal instructional conversations.

> The grantwriter summarizes the key accomplishments of the organization to illustrate its value within the community.

These programs have combined to assist thousands of families in Kyleton County to survive cold winters, regain their safety and security, attain greater access to their homes, and live with toilets, sinks, tubs, and windows that simply work properly. Using HRS' "self-help" resources (Builders' Warehouse, Tool Library and Fix-it School) has helped hundreds of talented low-income homeowners equip themselves to perform their own home maintenance, which has enhanced their self-esteem, increased their self-sufficiency, and made it possible for them to be successful, responsible homeowners.

Housing Rehab Services was founded as a nonprofit charitable organization in 1979. Its annual operating budget is approximately $1 million and is provided through government CDBG grants and generous individuals, businesses, churches, and foundations.

> This acronym, community development block grants, is a term familiar to the grantor.

Housing Rehab Services currently functions from two buildings: a 6,500 square-foot building purchased in 1979 and renovated in 1995 and a leased warehouse space (13,000 square feet) just west of US Highway. The need for HRS' many services, however, has now outstripped its current capacity in these facilities. HRS is, therefore, seeking $2.8 million from its community to purchase, add to, equip, and restore the former auto dealership at 2020 Main Street and to expand programming and community partnerships.

Needs Statement

> The introduction has explained the need for HRS to launch a capital campaign. This section, then, can be used for the important function of explaining the community need for HRS.

The 2000 census counted 17,000 families in Kyleton County who owned or were buying their own homes and whose annual incomes were classified as less than 50 percent of the area median income. These families included large numbers of senior citizens living on fixed incomes who have paid off their mortgages; one-parent/one-income families struggling in a two-income economy; and many two-parent families working hard to make ends meet on prevailing wages for unskilled workers.

Effective, sustained home ownership is essential to the stability and livability of residential neighborhoods, particularly neighborhoods at risk from poverty and disinvestment. Certainly, no amount of "outside" assistance can preserve or revitalize a residential neighborhood without the commitment of those who live "inside," most often, the homeowners.

Home ownership itself weighs heavily in ensuring or denying a quality of life among low-income families. Owning their own homes:
- produces a financial stake for families living paycheck to paycheck;
- provides stability for children, which helps them succeed in school;
- makes it possible for older adults on limited incomes to continue living in dignity;
- commits residents to neighborhoods and schools; and
- creates an inviting context for employers and merchants.

However, because these 17,000 or more families own their own homes, they have no landlord to call when repairs are needed. And because they typically live in older homes, they do face repairs. Furnaces and water heaters wear out, leaky roofs rot, old electrical systems labor under loads they were never designed to handle. These expensive repairs, together with a host of less expensive minor problems, add up and take their toll. Between 1990 and 2000 (the last years for which U.S. census data is available), our city's poorest neighborhoods lost 2,100 homeowners—a decline of 11 percent!

When owners lack the resources to keep their homes in decent repair, home ownership becomes a source of frustration and despair rather than a catalyst for pride and economic as well as personal growth. As individual homes deteriorate, so does a neighborhood's integrity. And as neighborhoods deteriorate, economic and social problems balloon to affect everyone.

> The potential funder is a local one concerned with the economic prosperity of the entire community. The grantwriter has tied in these interests without stretching beyond credibility.

Objectives

All projects—capital and programmatic—have both measurable and immeasurable benefits to the larger community and their various constituencies. Housing Rehab Services shares the beliefs that metropolitan communities do not thrive if the central city is faltering, that business and residential renaissance must go hand-in-hand to realize economic vitality and reduce urban sprawl, and that manufacturers and merchants need stable workforces, confident customers, and a thriving community in which homeowners have pride in their homes and their neighborhoods.

Although HRS cannot claim that its project can meet these goals for the larger community, staff and volunteers see this project as HRS' contribution to furthering the rebirth of the downtown and central city areas. As that rebirth is mirrored in commercial and residential neighborhoods, they foresee that:

> In addition to a focus on human service issues, this funder also focuses environmental programming on projects that preserve natural lands. The funder understands that improving a city may help reduce the trend of leaving it and, thus, creating a demand for development on natural lands. Again, the grantwriter has tied in other interests of the funder without overly stretching the point.

- Depressed neighborhoods, once the heartbeat of our city, will again become places of healthy interaction and pride as talented people are equipped with the tools to repair and improve their neighborhoods;
- As homeowners repair and maintain their homes, others in their neighborhoods will be encouraged to upgrade their properties;
- Successful homeownership will have a direct impact on reducing crime in some neighborhoods; and
- The link between suburban volunteers and core-city residents will strengthen under a common commitment to the community as a whole.

Quantitative benefits, which will be the subject of a formal evaluation one year after Housing Rehab Services moves into the new facility, will include the following:

> All quantitative objectives must be measurable.

1. The project will be successfully completed (renovation, addition, and fix-it classroom construction), within budget parameters, by September 2002.

2. HRS will combine its programs under one roof by September 2002.

3. HRS will, by September 2003, increase its program staff to include a full-time staff member to solicit product donations for Builders' Warehouse and another full-time specialist in education and homeowner counseling.

> The qualitative vision for the outcomes of this project are not measurable, and over-promising may compromise the credibility of this proposal.

4. HRS will increase the number of students in the Fix-it school from the current number of approximately 175 students annually to four hundred students per year within one year of moving into the new facility.

5. Surplus building material sales will increase by an estimated 75 percent: from approximately $320,000 valuation per year to $560,000 valuation per year within one year of moving into the new facility.

Evaluation Plan

Quantitative evaluation will be completed one year after move in (no later than September 2003) and will address the objectives listed on page four of this request to the Family Foundation.

Qualitative evaluation will be ongoing throughout the course of the capital campaign and will be based on the following questions:

1. Is the capital campaign and the cabinet assisting Housing Rehab Services garnering greater public awareness—from prospective clients, volunteers, and donors—of its programs?

2. Is the construction project continuing to be sensitive to the needs of its neighbors, both commercial and residential, and does it contribute to a sense of rebirth in this block on Main Street? Is the project serving as a catalyst for additional investment in this depressed neighborhood?

Continuation Funding Plan

HRS enjoys relatively stable annual donations for programming from Community Development Block Grants and through church, business, foundation, and individual support.

"Tools, Talents, and Treasures" is the first time since 1995 that HRS has raised dollars for a capital expense. The 1995 campaign raised $90,000 from The Green River Foundation, Manufacturing Foundation, Private Foundation, and individual donors, which allowed HRS to reconfigure its office space, add a three-bay warehouse addition, and provide a small structure similar to a house in which staff could teach up to three people at a time about electrical, plumbing, or window repair. Though the renovation was extensive, HRS staff and volunteers did much of the work themselves, significantly reducing costs for the projects. Five years ago, HRS received $75,000 from The Green River and Manufacturing Foundations to hire a volunteer coordinator. This has been a highly successful effort, which last year increased volunteer hours at HRS to a labor and material value of $110,000.

This capital campaign, which just received a $100,000 donation from Big Company, will generate funds for one-time expenses. The property will be maintained through staff and volunteers; operating expenses are expected to be less than those currently incurred by HRS in its two facilities, as HRS will realize savings on operations when it no longer must rent warehouse space.

> The organization makes the case that it has been almost ten years since it last sought capital funding.

> This reinforces the statements that the organization not only rarely seeks funding, but will be more self-sustaining after the capital campaign.

Local Government and Services

Local governments can be both grantmakers and grantseekers. Many municipal services, such as police, fire, and city sanitation departments and others qualify for federal funding. And specific municipal initiatives can qualify for federal and state grants. Large national foundations may have RFP initiatives that offer grants to cities to launch programs and/or offer a cash award to exemplary efforts on a specific issue such as downtown revitalization.

Strategies

For many years, cities became regrantors through federal Community Development Block Grants (CDBG), enabling those cities to fund projects they believed important to the continued growth and development of the city. Each city developed its own eligibility criteria and goals. Some cities also qualified for a subset of CDBG grants called Local Law Enforcement Block Grants (LLEBG) to fund neighborhood watch programs, crime prevention services, and special efforts by their police department. At this time, there is serious discussion on eliminating CDBG funding from the federal budget.

Few foundations make grants for city services, though some local foundations will fund special initiatives by the departments.

Sample: Government Service Grant Proposal

1. People To Be Served

The Green River Police Department (GRPD) will continue a project begun in 2000, in which it deployed the SARA problem-solving project under the direction of Team Captains assigned in each of six geographical areas (see attached map) in the City of Green River. Within each geographic area, GRPD Team Captains target for service neighborhoods that have a high incidence of law-enforcement problems such as disorderly juveniles, curfew violations, prostitution, speeding or other traffic violations, vandalism, theft, noise complaints, and others.

In each case, police officers and team captains identify problems through officer observations, citizen complaints, community leader or neighborhood organization complaints, neighborhood businesses, surveys, media reports, input from other departments of the police department such as vice or traffic safety, nonprofit agencies, and courts and probation offices. The team captains then gather other information such as the number of incidents, the known perpetrators, and previous police or neighborhood responses before convening the interested parties and sharing the data. Together, the police teams and complainants analyze the problem and develop a goal for their custom-made response. The team captains familiarize officers with the goal and strategies and launch the problem-solving response, which includes frequent assessment of its effectiveness. If found effective, the officers continue the response. If the response does not address the goal of the problem-solving team, the team regroups to discuss alternatives. All residents of the neighborhood—except those perpetrating the crimes—benefit both from participating in the problem-solving process and from resolving their shared problems.

2. Performance Target/Outcome ◄

> CDBG and LLEBG grant proposals must include performance measures so that the city can report outcomes to the federal government in the manner requested.

The goal of the project is to facilitate problem-solving partnerships between GRPD and city neighborhoods, institute innovative responses to crime-related problems, and address chronic problem areas related to social disorder and physical decay. Performance targets developed in support of the goal for Fiscal Year 2003 include:

a. Each of six geographic areas will institute four to six SARA problem-solving cycles and will work with from two to four neighborhood associations in their geographic areas.

b. Leaders of all the neighborhood organizations that participate in the program will self-report enhanced partnerships with the police department.

c. The police department will include qualitative evaluation data such as customer satisfaction, quality of life improvement, problem-solving successes, and levels of community participation in addition to quantitative data (e.g., response time, arrest numbers) in all project reports.

> The city has established program areas, called "strategies," for its LLEBG and CDBG funds.

The program meets the Neighborhood Development Strategy for Safe Neighborhoods (objectives 1 and 2) in that it proposes work between local law enforcement personnel and neighborhoods to prevent or reduce crime and violence, and it uses neighborhood organizing and problem-solving activities to empower residents, build relationships among neighbors, and support housing and other code enforcement efforts.

> Milestones are benchmarks established to gauge progress and gather data for reporting to the federal government.

3. Milestones ◄

Within each geographic designation area, the police officers will work with from two to four neighborhood organizations, depending on the number of problems that are identified. However, while the units of service are based on the number of neighborhood organizations with which the officers work, the performance targets and milestones center on the number of Problem-Oriented Policing (POP) cycles the officers are able to implement. The milestones listed for each target are the steps in a nonlinear problem-solving process. Numbers needed to demonstrate success do not decrease during the process.

Performance target a: Implement four to six SARA problem-solving cycles in each geographic designation (and among two to four neighborhood associations within the designation):
1. Identify priority problems in neighborhood   24-30
2. Gather other data to consider   24-30
3. Convene problem solving team   24-30
4. Implement proposed solutions   24-30
5. Evaluate implementation   24-30

Performance target b: Neighborhood leaders will report improved relationships with police
1. Identify priority problems in neighborhood   12-24
2. Convene problem solving team   12-24
3. Implement proposed solutions   12-24

Performance target c: Inclusion of qualitative data in police evaluations
1. Identify priority problems in neighborhood   24-30
2. Gather other data to consider   24-30
3. Convene problem-solving team   24-30
4. Implement proposed solutions   24-30
5. Evaluate implementation   24-30

> Milestones often decrease in number with each activity rather than stay the same as in this sample. For instance, if the project proposed employment training, "recruitment" (the first step) might be a high number, "completes training" a lower number, and "successfully employed" a still lower number.

4. Staffing
The project will be coordinated by each of the six geographical area captains. The captains were assigned to their respective posts by the Chief of Police based on their professional qualifications. The Problem-Oriented Policing (POP) project money will be divided equally among the six areas: $30,000 to each area, to be used primarily to fund overtime for police officers to work on problem-solving teams and to implement suggested solutions and to provide needed equipment such as portable breath kits, radar units, and other equipment/supplies.

> Because the police department has previously received this grant, it is a good idea to summarize its success in using past grant funds. This summary does not take the place of a formal progress report, which in the case of LLEBG and CDBG grants is due quarterly.

All GRPD officers are trained in the SARA problem-solving model. Last year, the captains were allotted $25,000 each and demonstrated important outcomes for dollars spent. For instance, in the north sector, officers not only stepped up weekend patrols in an effort to reduce driving under the influence, but contacted by letter and visited several area bar and restaurant owners to enlist their cooperation in promoting cabs and designated drivers. On the southwest side, neighbors were concerned about traffic safety issues around six elementary schools. Officers publicized a crack down, increased patrols before and after school, and stopped and ticketed hundreds of drivers, significantly reducing the risk of vehicular injury or death to children in the area.

5. Organizational Summary
The Green River Police Department (GRPD) provides police service to a city of more than 190,000. The department is composed of 493 sworn and civilian employees with an annual operating budget that exceeds $33 million.

The Department is in the third year of implementing a five-year strategic plan aimed toward Community-Oriented government. A key component to that plan is the development of creative strategies to identify and solve problems in neighborhoods and to bring police and city residents in closer proximity—geographically and socially. The project described in this request is an important and integral part of that effort.

6. Collaboration

The Problem-Oriented Policing project will require close collaboration and partnership with neighborhood organizations and neighborhood leaders in each of the geographic sectors. There must be mutual sharing of information between police officers and neighborhood residents; and residents and/or those most affected by crimes or nuisances in the neighborhood should sit on problem-solving teams with the police officers.

Once the problem-solving team identifies solutions they wish to implement, the police officers, in many cases, can provide the solution. Other cases, such as a need for signage, lighting, or neighborhood cleanup, require collaboration between the Department and residents or other community agencies or city departments.

> Neighborhood associations are also qualified to receive Local Law Enforcement Block Grant funds for crime prevention initiatives. The police department must, therefore, indicate a collaborative relationship with these organizations, which might otherwise be seen by the grantmaker as competitors for these grant funds.

> This may raise questions in the grantmaker's mind about how well these collaborative problem-solving responses will work.

Faith-Based Organizations

Faith-based organizations include houses of worship (churches, synagogues, mosques, etc.) and all the programs operated by them. They also include parochial schools and other organizations that exist to promote their religious beliefs and credos.

Strategies

Until the early 2000s, faith-based organizations, especially smaller groups, often did not qualify for federal grants since they lacked the capacity and infrastructure necessary to evaluate their programs and report progress in the manner prescribed by the government. Currently, there is a federal initiative to improve faith-based organizations' access to and qualifications for federal money, though it is often as subawardees under a larger organization that can coordinate their efforts and oversee reporting. Additionally, some federal grant programs award extra scoring points to faith-based organizations.

Some foundations exist with the express purpose of funding like-minded faith-based organizations (e.g., Jewish Relief Fund, Catholic Charities, etc.). Many private and community foundations expressly prohibit funding for religious purposes; that is, while they may, for instance, fund a church to provide daycare for neighborhood children, they will not do so if the children must attend a service or study scripture as a part of the program.

Sample: Faith-Based Grant Proposal Summary

The cover sheet indicates eligibility for this grant and provides contact information.

1. COVER SHEET

Name of Project	Kyleton County Food Stamp Outreach
Name of Organization	All Churches Emergency Supports (**ACES**)
Mission	"Celebrating the activity of God in our midst, the mission of ACES is to provide opportunities for ministry by linking congregational, individual, and community resources with human needs to help eliminate poverty in Kyleton County."
Name of Project Director	Brian Shaffer
Title of Project Director	Executive Director
Phone Number	555.555.5555
E-mail	Brian@aces.org
Grant Amount Requested	$125,000.00
Target Population	Immigrants, seniors, working poor and unemployed
Geographic Target Area	Kyleton County, Midwest
Selected Outreach Strategy	Outstation/Site Visiting

2. EXECUTIVE SUMMARY

Goals and outcomes are provided as a part of the executive summary.

Project Goal: The priority goals of the ACES Food Stamp Outreach Program are to:
• Expand an existing food stamp outreach program by 200 percent, and
• Increase assistance and ACES to families in need.
As an outcome of these goals the ACES Food Stamp Outreach Program will:
• Enroll 1,000 families in the FIA Food Assistance Program; and
• Assist 2,000 families with applications or referral for additional emergency, health, food/clothing, or other assistance.

Target Population: ACES targets immigrants, seniors, the working poor, and unemployed individuals and families.

Selected Strategy: The ACES Food Stamp Outreach Program will deploy five caseworkers at twenty key food pantries and ten community sites to educate and assist clientele in completing paperwork and overcoming barriers to participation in the Food Stamp program.

Grant Amount Requested: The total project cost is $142,602, of which ACES provides $17,602 in cash contributions primarily for staffing and equipment. ACES respectfully requests a federal

The organization offers, as a contribution to the project, the salary of its existing outreach worker.

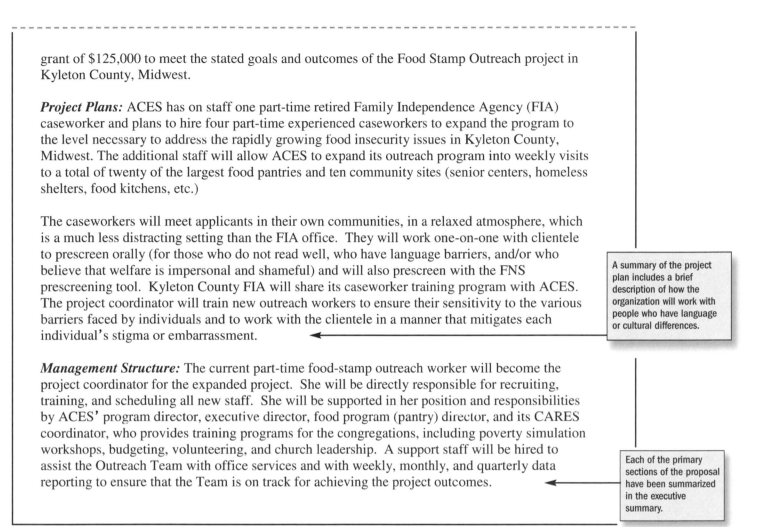

grant of $125,000 to meet the stated goals and outcomes of the Food Stamp Outreach project in Kyleton County, Midwest.

Project Plans: ACES has on staff one part-time retired Family Independence Agency (FIA) caseworker and plans to hire four part-time experienced caseworkers to expand the program to the level necessary to address the rapidly growing food insecurity issues in Kyleton County, Midwest. The additional staff will allow ACES to expand its outreach program into weekly visits to a total of twenty of the largest food pantries and ten community sites (senior centers, homeless shelters, food kitchens, etc.)

The caseworkers will meet applicants in their own communities, in a relaxed atmosphere, which is a much less distracting setting than the FIA office. They will work one-on-one with clientele to prescreen orally (for those who do not read well, who have language barriers, and/or who believe that welfare is impersonal and shameful) and will also prescreen with the FNS prescreening tool. Kyleton County FIA will share its caseworker training program with ACES. The project coordinator will train new outreach workers to ensure their sensitivity to the various barriers faced by individuals and to work with the clientele in a manner that mitigates each individual's stigma or embarrassment.

> A summary of the project plan includes a brief description of how the organization will work with people who have language or cultural differences.

Management Structure: The current part-time food-stamp outreach worker will become the project coordinator for the expanded project. She will be directly responsible for recruiting, training, and scheduling all new staff. She will be supported in her position and responsibilities by ACES' program director, executive director, food program (pantry) director, and its CARES coordinator, who provides training programs for the congregations, including poverty simulation workshops, budgeting, volunteering, and church leadership. A support staff will be hired to assist the Outreach Team with office services and with weekly, monthly, and quarterly data reporting to ensure that the Team is on track for achieving the project outcomes.

> Each of the primary sections of the proposal have been summarized in the executive summary.

Environmental Organizations

Environmental protection agencies exist to protect natural lands, animal and plant species, water resources, air quality, or all of the above through advocacy, research, education, and preservation programs.

Strategies

Foundations may focus their environmental program funding on preserving or improving one aspect of the environment and/or on one programmatic strategy. It is, therefore, critical that grantwriters for environmental organizations carefully read grantmakers' guidelines to ensure that goals for programs are a good match and involve the same aspect of environmental protection. Local and national foundations often have environmental protection program areas, and grants are available from both state and federal programs.

Sample: Environmental Grant Proposal

> This is a project being undertaken by a collaborative of organizations in a geographic region.

1. Need

Great Lakes Environmental Awareness Network (GLEAN) is an environmental information communication project proposed by Green Valley Metropolitan Council (GVMC) for the Metropolitan Statistical Area bounded by Green River, Mount Very, and Hope, Midwest.

The objectives of GLEAN are to:

> While the writer refers to the following as "objectives" of GLEAN, they are not objectives because they are not measurable. This list should not be included in the Need section of the proposal.

1) Identify key community environmental indicators;

2) Using appropriate technology and techniques, track and measure data relative to the key community environmental indicators; and

3) Communicate data and information in a way that is accessible, timely, and meaningful and that empowers community members to make informed decisions about environmental matters.

> This statement identifies the value of the region as a location for the project's focus.

The Great Lakes ecosystem, which includes sixty-five species of flora and fauna indigenous only to this region, is currently threatened by water and air pollution, watershed disturbance, introduced species, and habitat loss. Midwest State specifically faces a unique air toxins transport concern in that a relatively high percentage of its air pollutants, all of which have negative effects on human and other species' health and the quality of our air and water, are imported from other parts of the United States.

In 1970 and 1994, the Center for Environmental Studies, one of the project partners, surveyed residents of Midwest state to determine the environmental issues of greatest concern. Both surveys returned identical results, determining that, in order of importance, residents are most concerned about water quality, air quality, and habitat loss/urban sprawl.

> This statement identifies the need in the specific community.

The greatest need among residents of Midwest state is education and awareness. No person wants to destroy or damage the natural resources that make the state unique—from the Great Lakes to farmlands, creeks, trees, animals, air, and plants. Too often, however, people do not make the connection between another housing development and its effects on the watershed, between an inadequate public transportation system and the quality of air, between sprawl and inner city poverty and segregation. Because they lack the data and larger picture on which to base decisions, residents too often allow individual, immediate desires to take precedence over the long-term health of the environment and the community.

In addition to providing education and a record of immediate and longer-range changes in the environment, GLEAN will provide timely information to enable Midwest state residents to make daily decisions about their own health and welfare. Knowing the air quality index will enable those with asthma, for instance, to make decisions about their activities each day. Up-to-the-minute data on the safety and health conditions of Great Lake waters will enable those with plans for sports or recreational activities to modify their plans accordingly.

2. Approach

"Approach" is another term for "project description."

To respond to the primary needs in Midwest State, GLEAN plans both educational and communication/awareness components. Each partner to the effort has specific responsibilities, based on the organization's strengths and mission, to fulfill the objectives of the project. Each partner will participate in the governance structure, which will be overseen by Green Valley Metropolitan Council.

1) Approach to identifying key community environmental indicators: A local process—The Convenor—has developed a means for establishing community indicators on quality-of-life issues and is in the process of developing an Office of Community Research to house the indicators and assess data for periodic reports to the community. The Convenor will aid GLEAN in developing the linkages between environmental indicators and other quality-of-life indicators and by providing a repository at the Office of Community Research for outdated data and possible longitudinal studies of the data.

The Convenor process may also be called on to assist in identifying existing sources of data and indicators, including those already identified as follows:

This list identifies data resources.

- The Midwest Department of Environmental Quality (MDEQ) measures the prime parameter of air quality, ozone, and maintains an Ozone Action website. The information contained in this website is valuable to individuals with asthma or lung disease and will be linked to the GLEAN database and communications network.

- Green Valley State University Water Resources Institute (WRI), a project partner, which gathers and monitors data on water quality. WRI maintains research vessels on Great Lake, which capture timely data on water temperature, dissolved oxygen, turbidity, conductivity, and Secchi readings, and provides analysis of aquatic organisms.

  WRI also provides digital data and maps on land use and land cover in three Counties. This data includes educational information on storm water runoff and prime/unique farmland.

- National Oceanic and Atmospheric Administration (NOAA), the prime source for real-time environmental data on Great Lake, which is the source of municipal drinking water for urbanized areas of west Midwest.

- United States Geological Survey (USGS).

- Midwest State Department of Natural Resources (MDNR).

The environmental indicators require collection and connection. Bringing the data together in one place will aid residents in seeing that land use affects water quality, for example, or that they can draw correlation between ozone measures and water quality on a particular day.

2) Approach to tracking and measuring data relative to the key community environmental indicators and linking information through technology: Only MDEQ currently operates a website and provides data on air quality in a form that is accessible by computer. GREAT, the

community's public-access network and website, will aid the data providers in interpreting their data for electronic transfer and display. Although NOAA has real-time data on Great Lake, it is not generally accessible by the public. WRI data on water quality and land use are currently stored in programs such as ArcView, ArcInfo, D-base, C-map, Excel, and Access, as part of a Geographic Information System (GIS).

The writer provides more detail here and makes the project objectives measurable.

3) Approach to communicating data and information in a way that is accessible, timely, and meaningful and that empowers community members to make informed decisions about environmental matters. The Center for Environmental Study (CES), a project partner, will provide an educational program and a media outreach program. Using its established linkages to all K-12 schools in Green River, Mount Very, and Hope, CES will market the GLEAN website to Intermediate school districts and the individual schools and provide workshops for educators on ways to incorporate environmental data into curriculum subjects such as science, social studies, liberal arts, and mathematics. In addition, CES will link with other educational providers such as World Resource Institute, Environmental Working Group, Project WILD, and Project Learning Tree, to make the best use of existing educational materials. These resources for teachers will also be provided as an ancillary to the GLEAN website.

In response to the need of Midwest state residents to understand the relationships between environmental factors, CES will work with City Media Center and other project partners to develop a series of positive, "this is what you can do" one-minute media spots on the challenges facing the Great Lakes called "What's it to Midwest State?" This portion of the project is designed to reach an audience that might normally be unaware of or uninformed about the problems facing the Great Lakes ecosystem. They are the people whose lives are affected by these problems, whose tax money goes to correct them, and whose votes may decide the policies that are established to control them. The radio spots will run during peak commuter hours to capture as many listeners as possible.

This passage proposes a plan to inform citizens, a priority goal of the project and a primary need of the community. Project plans should always link back to the needs or problem statement.

Data and indicators captured by the GLEAN website will be translated into usable, easy-to-understand language with captions, icons, photos, and straightforward text. Accompanying text will be written at or below an 8th-grade reading level. In the event that technical terms are used, they will be accompanied with readable explanations from CES's environmental dictionary.

All imported data will be interpreted and displayed in a way that reveals the links between land use, water quality, air quality, personal decisions, and public health.

Finally, through the Convenor process, the project partners will convene community members in forums and other meetings to discuss environmental issues and impacts. GVMC has ongoing meetings of township and city officials throughout the region; these groups will have access to the data to inform their decision making. The community's public-access network, GREAT, also hosts an annual cyberspace community meeting, which includes a forum for those who wish to discuss or learn more about environmental issues. This forum will be used to further inform the public about the GLEAN website and to enable participants (projected 1,000 per year) to familiarize themselves with the interactive environmental website.

3. Expected Results/Benefits

Besides the obvious benefit of enabling time-sensitive relay of information that protects individuals' health and welfare, Midwest State can further current efforts by GVMC, WRI, CES, and others to inform the public about the importance of crossing political boundaries to plan land uses.

> This is bordering on alphabet soup. The grantwriter should have written out all the names again here.

The public will be more informed about land use and its impacts on air and water quality and more committed to supporting elected and appointed leaders who are committed to preserving farmlands and reducing urban sprawl. New leaders will likely emerge as they grow more knowledgeable about the interrelation between the environmental issues.

The constituency in Midwest State will be better educated on environmental issues, and thus, better able to make informed decisions on how to reduce negative environmental impacts. They will increase their positive involvement in their daily activities such as reducing energy or water consumption, using natural lawn and garden fertilizers, and purchasing products made from post-consumer recycled materials.

Economic Development

Economic development organizations offer job training and seeking programs, job retention and business location initiatives, regional planning and initiatives, business development, and more.

Strategies

Economic development efforts are often a result of collaborations rather than programs offered by just one organization. As such, they often appeal to local foundations, particularly corporate foundations and corporate giving programs, and to city and state government funders.

The sample that follows is a concept paper. This is similar to a preproposal or letter of inquiry, but is less formal. Generally, use a concept paper to capture results of collaborator discussions. After all the organizations agree to the outline of the project, you can reframe the concept paper as a preproposal or letter of inquiry for a foundation.

Sample: Economic Development Concept Paper

Work To Work Green River

A New Cycle

Communities and governments have long talked about breaking the cycle of welfare dependence and unemployment. But no program, no matter what organization or governmental entity founded it, has entirely broken the cycle. Cycles are sturdy things. Difficult to break; perhaps not as difficult to replace.

> Because this is a concept paper, it can attempt to capture the reader's interest with an arresting opening paragraph.

More than a dozen organizations and businesses in Green River, Midwest, propose a new cycle: Work-To-Work, a cycle of success and employment, a cycle individualized for each participant, a cycle that will become as difficult to break—or break from—as the one of dependence.

Work-To-Work is a first of its kind; a new cycle that:
- provides company-to-company career movement;
- is founded in a collaboration between business and nonprofit organizations;
- builds on current local and state initiatives to reduce welfare rolls;
- creates for participants an environment for success; and
- disallows failure by providing participants unlimited opportunities to find, maintain and grow in employment.

Target Population

> This acknowledges that there can be many reasons why a person is not earning enough to support a family. Acknowledging a problem is the first step to solving it.

This new cycle moves individuals from unemployment to entry-level employment then to career employment and advancement. Potential participants include those who have never been employed, are currently underemployed, and those who are unprepared for work. Participants will include those who, for any number or combination of reasons—including physical, emotional or mental handicap; past discrimination; language barriers; addiction; homelessness; incarceration, or seemingly insurmountable barriers—have become chronically unemployed.

Individualized Support Services

> The writer is able to create his or her own subheadings because a concept paper need not follow a prescribed outline.

In many cases, these individuals have tried and failed to secure or excel in full-time employment that provides a hopeful future with opportunity for advancement and personal growth. They require a unique set of services to overcome real and perceived barriers and support their efforts to try again. These services may include in full or in part: job training, counseling, on-the-job mentoring, transportation, child care, interview training, and asset identification. Above all, support must be individualized to overcome fears and to assure the participant that he or she has numerous opportunities to become successful in work.

Process Plan

> This is not a "one size fits all" solution and will appeal to funders who like to invest in innovative, sometimes risky, new initiatives.

As illustrated on the attached flow chart, the model uses a case management approach to removing barriers and developing skills. The case manager assesses potential participants, creates development plans, makes referrals, prepares participants for the workplace, counsels on personal and professional issues, keeps records of progress, and coordinates seamless support efforts with participating trainers, job coaches, employer representatives, and service providers.

> The project will use existing resources through a referral system provided at a central intake site.

Some participants may be referred directly to employment at Major Engineering, a plastics manufacturer. Other participants who are immediately employable, but require development and/or additional training, will be referred to Hamburger Joint for entry-level service employment. This employment will enable project staff to work on personal issues such as timeliness, accessing necessary transportation and child care, working well with others, etc. The majority of participants will be referred to training, either within the collaborative or from another source, or to counseling to address personal issues that inhibit employability.

Stand-alone training modules will allow participants to take only those training sessions that are necessary to employability, thus speeding the process and encouraging progress among participants. Modules will include:

- test-taking (for employers who use screening tests to ascertain skill levels)
- interviewing skills and practice
- planning and preparing for the workplace (life skills)
- employer expectations

In addition, participants will receive support services as needed (transportation, child care referral and/or subsidies, and others), and will be encouraged to "job shadow" those already employed. So participants will not lose essential income or services during training, they will be paid for training and, if they qualify, may receive some free services such as transportation or child care. ◄

> The project may be costly; the grantwriter should point out the cost of continued welfare in comparison to the cost of the project.

Once in the Work-To-Work employment cycle, several opportunities encourage new employees' commitment and self-sustainment. If an employee chooses to remain with Hamburger Joint, he or she can move into store management or a support function and increase his or her pay rate from the $6-$6.50/hour starting wage. Alternately, the employee may wish to move from the service sector at Hamburger Joint to the manufacturing sector at Major Engineering. In these cases, employees earn $7 per hour to start and may increase their wages incrementally to as much as $12.50 per hour in as short a time as two years. Both employers provide tuition reimbursement, which encourages participants to continue their advancement throughout their adult lives. ◄

> The project has identified at least two employers interested in participating.

Uniqueness

Several things make this model unique. First, the model is founded in a growing collaboration between service sector and manufacturing employers and provides company-to-company career movement.

Second, this is a collaborative approach to assisting individuals regardless of the depth or specialness of their need. The collaboration includes social service organizations that provide case management services and referrals and joins services such as employment agencies, child care providers, and transportation providers to provide seamless support for participants. Brief biographies of current collaborating organizations are attached.

The model builds on several current local and state initiatives, including School-to-Work, an effort to encourage development of employability skills among the average 24 percent of youth who do not target college after graduation. Two state initiatives that are part of the project include Project Zero, the Midwest State governor's mandate to reduce welfare rolls to zero; and

Work First, the innovative Midwest State program that requires employment simultaneously with training for those dependent on government aid.

Fourth, the Work-To-Work cycle affords participants numerous chances to be successful and provides built-in elements to minimize failure. Once assigned a case manager, each participant has continuous follow up that includes at least one social-service agency, a job coach at his or her place of employment, assistance with child care and transportation, and skill-building training modules. Support continues throughout pre-employment and through the sixth month of service sector employment. When and if a participant moves from the service sector to the manufacturing sector, support continues throughout the transition and for the first six months of employment.

> This describes the network of services that will be established to ensure participant success.

Finally, the model creates an environment for success among employers by providing cultural diversity training for employer personnel, as needed, orientation for coaches; advice on ADA compliance and accommodation; and coordination with job supervisors to ensure success of Work-To-Work participants while on the job. Once established, the process will become a model for other area employers that are willing to provide trained job coaches and on-site supervision of Work-to-Work participants.

> Americans with Disabilities Act should be spelled out.

Benefits

The Work-to-Work Initiative anticipates several benefits for participants, employers, and the community at large:

Employers: Because Kyleton County has a very low unemployment rate (2.6 percent in the first quarter of 1998) and is reliant on the manufacturing and service industries (which provide 23 percent and 27 percent of area jobs respectively), employers require new, innovative processes for recruiting qualified employees and for tapping new populations of workers. It is, therefore, in the employers' best interests to work with the Work-To-Work collaborative to ensure that their workplaces are desirable and accessible, that wages are competitive, and that they provide ample opportunity for future advancement.

> This may not remain true if unemployment rises.

The Work-to-Work project is launching its pilot with one service and one manufacturing business (Hamburger Joint and Major Engineering); however, the collaborating organizations will be working with other area businesses to encourage their participation. In addition to having a new source for skilled employees, area industries will realize reduced time to fill job openings, reduced turnover, and increased employee satisfaction as measured in an annual survey.

Participants: Participants will derive the following benefits: an identifiable, achievable set of steps to move from unemployment or underemployment to a good job; incremental pay increases; increased job satisfaction as measured in an annual survey; a balanced lifestyle that values both work and family, and ample opportunity for continued advancement via employment and education.

Community: Since one of the area's primary attractions to new businesses is a strong, committed workforce, the community will benefit with a continued influx of new manufacturing and service businesses. Existing businesses will remain in the community, participate in Work-To-Work, and continue to contribute to the health of the economy in Midwest State.

The writer identifies all the beneficiaries from the proposed project.

The Work-to-Work collaborators anticipate similar benefits to employers and new employees in communities around the nation. They, too, can provide an alternative to the cycle of dependence that cripples our communities and wastes talents and lives—a new cycle that encourages growth, advancement, and self-sufficiency for life.

CHAPTER 11
While You Wait

Contrary to the old saying, from a grantwriting perspective, waiting is not the hardest part. Writing is. From the potential grantee's perspective, perhaps it's true that waiting is difficult, particularly if you do not have a date for review of proposals or decision making. At the absolute earliest, you can expect a decision one month after application, but generally it takes from two to six months to learn of the outcome of your pending proposals. In the interim, there's work to do for both the grantseeker and the grantmaker. Maybe a look at the work of a grantmaker will make the time pass more quickly.

Due Diligence

Due diligence is a term commonly used by grantmakers to describe the process of investigating the applicant organization, and its capacity for delivering its objectives, prior to recommending its proposal for funding. The government performs due diligence when a staff person checks to be sure your organization is eligible under the enabling legislation, that it has honorable financial standing (Dun & Bradstreet report), and that it does not otherwise have outstanding issues with the grantmaker (e.g., has defaulted on a previous grant or has not submitted final reports for a previous grant).

Foundation grants officers are responsible for performing due diligence on all proposals they are potentially bringing forward to their board of trustees for determination. Foundation due diligence often involves face-to-face meetings with the potential grantee in the foundation office or at the applicant's site (a site visit), requests for additional information, and a number of background checks on financial or IRS reports. In addition, a grants officer may seek information from collaborators and from others in the community.

Grants officers play a dual, and sometimes conflicting role, as both sentries and stewards of the foundation assets. On the sentry side, the grants officer performs an investigation similar to those performed prior to investments in real estate or other tangibles in the business world. Grants officers use the investigative process to ensure that the organization is legitimate and to analyze the risk of the potential foundation investment. The grants officer takes on the steward role once he or she brings forward a proposal to his or her board of trustees with a recommendation for funding; he or she becomes an advocate for the grant proposal and applicant organization. Remember, the questions a program officer asks during the due diligence process are not intended to put you on the spot; rather, they are intended to provide the officer all the ammunition he or she needs to make a case for funding your proposal.

It is important for grantwriters and executive directors to prepare for the due diligence process. During the process, the grants officer must clarify the proposal and find answers to a number of questions about the applicant, many of which were not asked in the grant proposal. Such questions may include the following:

Organizational Stability and Sustainability
- Does the organization have the capacity to do as it promises?
- Are there red flags in the organization's financials that indicate potentially serious problems?
- Is the organization's governance strong and appropriately involved?
- Is there a long-range strategic plan that incorporates the proposed activities?

Track Record
- Has the organization been successful in achieving prior objectives?
- Is the organization respected both in its community and among its peers?
- Can the organization provide documentation of outcomes from prior projects?

Partners
- Does the organization have documented support from partners critical to the project?
- Does the organization have a reputation for collaborating with others?

Program
- What is the organization's capacity to identify and respond to community needs?
- Is service delivery appropriate and respectful?
- Do programs align with the mission of the organization?

Site Visits

The government does not perform site visits. Foundation grants officers, especially those that are not headquartered in your community, often do. A site visit is a meeting at the applicant's office and/or program site during which the foundation grants officer asks questions and, ideally, sees first-hand the activities or need for programs you have described in your proposal.

Preparing for Site Visits
A good grants officer will have read your proposal ahead of time, let you know if there is anyone in particular other than the primary contact with whom he or she wants to meet, let you know how long he/she can stay, and come in with a list (often mental) of points to discuss in relation to your proposal.

Make sure that you plan your site visit activities so that there is time for the grants officer not only to get his or her questions answered, but to meet with the people (e.g., finance officer) who can best answer the questions. It is generally a good idea to have the CEO of the applicant at the meeting and, when appropriate, the organization's board chair. Plan your activities strategically. While the babies at the facility might be compelling and cute, if your project is about the adult care portion of your program, spend your site visit time there.

It is critical that the CEO, board chair, financial officer, and any other staff present at the site visit have read and understand the grant proposal. They should read it again within the days prior to the site visit, and, to the extent possible, anticipate questions the grants officer will ask. If they have questions or issues with the proposal, they should have a meeting before the site visit so they are speaking with one voice. If the grantwriter is not a staff member of the applicant organization, it is not appropriate for that person to attend a site visit meeting. Instead, the grantwriter should attend a premeeting to help prepare the staff of the organization for the visit.

Tips for Site Visits

· Reread your proposal in the days prior to the site visit.

· Have a premeeting with all attendees other than the grants officer to address any outstanding questions.

· Provide simple refreshments. Grants officers are not swayed by lavish meals and cannot accept gifts; in fact, such things may make them suspicious.

· If possible, schedule the site visit at a time that your program site is active with program participants.

· Keep the tour of your facilities brief.

· Prepare requested documentation in advance.

· Answer questions candidly.

· Relax. A nervous host makes guests uncomfortable.

· Follow up within days of the meeting with a simple thank you note and/or with additional information if requested.

Following Up

Sometimes a grants officer will ask a question that requires further research or additional information that is not immediately available. Send replies to those questions or additional documentation as soon as possible after the site visit, preferably within forty-eight hours. Even if the grants officer indicates that he or she will not be back in the office for a week, the postmark will indicate that your response was timely. Enclose a thank you note with the information and a brief reminder of the questions to which you are responding.

If the grants officer did not request additional information, follow up with a simple written thank you note.

Reporting Interim Progress or Setbacks

In the interim between submitting a proposal and learning of the funding decision, share your good news and don't try to hide the bad. For example, if you are raising funds from multiple sources and during your proposal review you are notified of an award by another funder, share this success with your grants officer. Also notify the grants officer of any major negative events that have occurred during the review process. If, for instance, your financial officer has been arrested for embezzlement from his or her church or your organization, you must inform your grants officer immediately. While the grants officer may decide to delay bringing your proposal forward for decision making, this delay is far preferable to the alternative. Going before trustees without all the information needed can make both you and your grants officer look bad in front of the trustees. This will result not only in a denial of funding for the current proposal, but likely in a denial of future proposals.

Why Does It Take So Darn Long to Get an Answer?

While every foundation is different, there are a number of common activities that dictate a longer timeline than anyone would like. Most foundations have studied their process in an effort to streamline their systems and get to yes (or no) more quickly, but a four- to six-month decision timeline is common.

If trustees are the final decision makers, timelines revolve around their meetings. If the board meets only twice a year, that means there are six months between decisions. Grants officers, in between meetings, must prepare their board packets and have them printed, proofread, and submitted to the board a few weeks prior to the meeting, a process that often takes at least one month.

Add to that the time involved in the due diligence process, site visits, and writing up often complex recommendation documents. Further, grants officers may be working on several proposals at once and simultaneously performing other functions essential to their jobs, such as ongoing grant follow-up and reporting, research, internal projects and meetings, and community-related meetings often requiring travel. You can see that it can easily take several months, if not longer, to shape and write the recommendation for your proposal.

Recycling Grant Proposals

Remember, few funders want to be the only ones investing grant dollars in your project. Even the federal government likes to see that the applicant organization is committed to raising local dollars to launch or continue an important project. Thus, until the project and/or nonprofit organization is financially stable and sustainable, the grantseeker's work is not finished.

You should be doing two things: revising your project proposal to meet the requirements of other funders and looking beyond the obvious sources for some more creative match-ups.

As you have seen from the sample grant proposals in this book, there are many similar sections in the proposal: there's always a need or problem statement, a project description, evaluation, budget, and abstract. There are often similar additional questions such as the constituent involvement in the project design and/or evaluation, the history of the organization, management structure, and key personnel. So, why not just print out and send the same proposal to numerous funders?

Not a good idea.

Even if you are sending a proposal to funders that all use a common grant application from their regional association of grantmakers (RA), you will want to modify each proposal to appeal to each different audience of grant reviewers. Think about it this way—when you get a generic piece of mail that's also sent to your neighbors, what do you call it? Junk mail. If you have not taken the time and effort to learn about the individual funders, it will show, and your proposal will appear to be little more than junk mail to its recipient.

Every good project has numerous aspects that make it a good project: for example, you may represent a youth center with a mission to reduce delinquency in an urban neighborhood. In addition to offering recreation, you have an after-school tutoring program, a fitness center operating during the day for stay-at-home mothers, a book club, and an after-school cooking class just for boys. Emphasize each aspect of the organization with its appropriate funder. One might have a goal to improve educational outcomes for urban youth—tell them about the tutoring club. Another is concerned with wellness—tell them about your fitness program, and so on. Don't keep information from your foundation audience. Simply focus on what you know will interest a specific foundation.

Sections such as the organizational history are reusable with minor modifications, but sections such as the program description with its goals, objectives, outcomes, and timelines must be rewritten for every audience so that it matches the foundation's own goals.

While you will not adjust a budget total depending on whom you ask, you might carve out a special niche in a larger project that you think will interest a specific funder. If you have a chance, discuss this with a grants officer beforehand. If they agree, ask one to fund the educational component of your youth center and another to underwrite the cost of equipment and a coach for your fitness classes. If you cannot ask beforehand, be sure to include the components as line items in the budget so the foundation can choose for itself what activities it would prefer to fund.

Finally—and critically—be sure that you check to ensure that all mentions of any previous funder audiences are expunged from your proposal!

Expanding Your Search

If your nonprofit still needs funding once you've exhausted your search for appropriate funders and sent individualized proposals to them, begin looking at less obvious potential matches. If you have signed up to receive notices from the federal department of education at your school district, sign up for some other departments too. Perhaps the department of commerce will offer a program that funds creative internships for high school students, the department of health and human services is looking to establish school-based counseling centers, and the department of agriculture is offering schools the opportunity to write a curriculum for a comprehensive educational program on farming and food.

The same is true for foundations. If you are writing for a school, don't overlook foundations that fund land or water conservation efforts; instead, see if your school program curriculum focusing on water resources matches the interests of one of the foundations.

One caveat that can't be said often enough: do not twist your programs into pretzel shapes to fit a grantmaker's guidelines. If it's a quality project from a quality organization, there's a funder out there waiting for it.

Ten Mistakes Grantseekers Make

1. Sending a "Dear Friend" letter to corporations and foundations. Take the time to get the name of the contact, spell it correctly, and know the gender of the addressee.
2. Sending the same form proposal to numerous corporations and foundations. Instead, take the time to find out what the foundation will fund and what its areas of emphasis are. Make contact before applying and ask for guidelines or application procedures.
3. Not following the application procedure, not paying attention to guidelines, and not supplying all the information requested. Not including requested forms such as your 501(c)(3) letter or board roster. If you simply cannot get the information requested, you must write an explanation.
4. Calling once a week to find out the status of your request. When your grants officer knows, you'll know.
5. Submitting vague requests. Be specific about what you want: money, manpower, equipment?
6. Not being qualified to receive funds from the foundation. If you're not a 501(c)(3) organization, and that's what a grantmaker requires, don't waste your time and the foundation's.
7. Asking for what the foundation cannot contribute. For instance, some people will request free phone service from SBC's Foundation. They cannot, by law, provide that.
8. Assuming the foundations knows all about your program, who it benefits, and how valuable it is to the community. Tell how you are involved in your community, why the community needs this project, who will benefit, and what your capacity is in staff and financial resources.
9. Not telling the foundation your long-term plans. What happens when funding runs out? Do you plan to carry out the project by other means?
10. Giving the foundation the silent treatment. It's not enough to say thank you when you get the check. Show your gratitude by letting the funder know what you did with the money and what you achieved with their funds. Ask the funder if you may recognize their gift in brochures or newsletters. Keep your relationships strong by keeping your promises.

From The Institute for Conservation Leadership, Bozeman, Montana.

Continue Your Research

Besides continuing your grant source search while you wait for a decision on your last proposal, you should also spend your time identifying new trends in grantmaking. In the past decade or less, funders have changed their focuses. Once government and most foundations focused almost entirely on funding projects where they were needed most. Today, while need still drives funding allocations, many funders are looking for projects that propose creative solutions to community problems.

If you sign up to receive grant notices (www.grants.gov and www.fdncenter.org), you will begin to notice similarities, or movements, in criteria and programs across governmental departments and among foundations. For instance, the federal government began offering bonus points for faith-based organization applicants in 2002, a practice that held true across most departmental offerings. They stopped around 2004 and began a different approach to improving faith-based organizations' competitiveness on federal grants. Foundations began, almost collectively, to emphasize outcomes rather than objectives about a decade ago. And collaboration has been an emphasis of many grantmakers for many years.

Try to spot these trends and prepare your organization to respond to them. For instance, if you see two RFPs or guidelines that both ask for your plan for professional development programs for staff, you should begin considering professional development plans for your staff or build that component into the design of new projects.

When Government Administrations Change

Each presidential and congressional administration brings with it a platform of ideas for improving life in the U.S. Grant programs offered by the federal departments generally follow suit (when Congress endorses the president), so within a year of an administrative change, you can see grant programs changing. If the president is elected to a second term, the grant programs change dramatically to support the ideas he proposed in his campaign or the initiatives and crises to which he must direct financial resources. Programs funded by state government also transform with changes in administration. There is nothing a nonprofit can do to create an environment more receptive to its proposals, nor anything it can do to prevent an environment that is not. The best thing a grantwriter can do during a change is to anticipate these shifts and help the nonprofit position itself so that it is ready to respond to new grant opportunities.

Often throughout an administration a particular program is offered year after year, so if your proposal fails once, it can be revised and submitted again. However, you must be aware that changes in administration and the composition of Congress can cause the end of a grant opportunity. Endeavor to get it right the first time and no later than the second.

When Foundation Staffing, Structures, or Programs Change

Nothing in grantwriting is more disappointing than learning that your favorite grants officer is resigning from his or her position. Some are years-long relationships and, though projects are not funded based on this, the relationship has deepened the understanding of the nuances of your organization and its situation, making your job as grantseeker easier. That aside, many grants officers are caring, compassionate, intelligent people, the sort of people that grantwriters—who are generally also caring, compassionate, and intelligent people—enjoy meeting and getting to know.

If you lose your grants officer, be sure to meet his or her replacement, particularly if you have a grant from the foundation at the time of the changeover. You may simply have a meeting to update them on the progress toward your objectives or, in some cases, your former grants officer will introduce the two of you to facilitate the transfer of responsibilities.

When a grantmaker's program focus or grantseeking processes change, you may or may not be notified. If a program focus changes, your existing grant will not be in jeopardy; however, you will not likely receive funding again from that source unless you also meet the new program criteria. When processes change in community foundations, the foundation often has a series of meetings that grantseekers can attend to hear about the changes; when they change in private foundations, you are often left to your own devices to approach the foundation in the correct way. Never use old guidelines to submit a grant to a funder. Always double check the foundation's website or request a new set of guidelines and applications for each grant.

CHAPTER 12
Yes or No

You Got the Grant!

Congratulations! Your hard work has paid off and your organization has been awarded a grant. If you are a staff member of your organization, you've just begun the real work; if you've written the grant, the applicant likely has a few more writing jobs for you.

If it wasn't determined before you applied for a grant, decide immediately how you can use the announcement of your award to the grantmaker's and your organization's best advantage. Receipt of the grant means that you have an organization worth talking about.

Sometimes announcement of a successful grant award is a part of your grant contract. On occasion, particularly with corporate giving programs, the grant proposal often contains a section on how you will acknowledge the grantmaker's gift. Perhaps they want you to put up a permanent sign, announce the grant award to the media, or use their name in your organizational literature. Be sure to acknowledge all gifts in the way the donor prefers.

If you still have money to raise, use a grant award as an inducement to attract other funders. Announce that the gift has brought you to the half-way point of a $2 million capital campaign or that it has enabled you to purchase a van and you're looking to local funders to help you underwrite other program components.

If your grant is for operations, the press may not find it newsworthy, but you know how precious these unrestricted funds can be. Share the news with your board and have a brief celebration with staff. In other words, take the good news and share it!

Is Your Organization Media Ready?
You will not send out a media release for every grant you get. But you will for some, so you want to have a strategy. Plan ahead of time how your organization will work with local media and build your relationships with reporters and department leaders.

Develop a media list with fax numbers, addresses, and email addresses. When your grant award is newsworthy, for example, if you have a project or initiative that you'll be launching soon and this grant is a milestone in its launch, take the grant award as your cue to announce the project to the world.

Consider a media conference and invite the grantmaker (or federal representatives if you received a federal grant) and plan a demonstration of your new project, if possible. Write a media release that states the facts and creates excitement about the project. If you also plan a media conference, include an announcement of the event in your release. Send a draft of your media release to the grantmaker so they can approve it before you send it to media.

On page 209 is a sample news release about a grant award. Like a grant proposal, it has a format that you can follow.

Sample: Media Release

FOR IMMEDIATE RELEASE

CONTACT: Ed Director

June 12, 2005

Green Valley Metro Council

555.555.5555

> Indicate the person the media can contact if they have questions while writing your story.

> The date of release is given to media. Sometimes the media release is sent before-hand and is designated "for release on..." rather than for immediate release.

TECHNOLOGY INFRASTRUCTURE GAPS UNDER REVIEW

> Provide a headline.

GREEN VALLEY, MIDWEST, June 12, 2005. The Green Valley Metropolitan Council today announced that its Electronic Technology Infrastructure Planning (e-TIP) Commission will launch a full-scale investigation into the existing technology infrastructure and identify potential or existing gaps in service needed to access electronic information, thanks to a grant from Meridian's "Digital Inclusion Award Program."

> The dateline includes the city, state, and date of release.

> The first paragraph states the news item.

The e-TIP Commission, which was empaneled by The Green Valley Metropolitan Council in fall 2004, consists of representatives from County and City government, the City Media Center, The Convenor, Green River Area Chamber of Commerce, The Right Place, Service Network, and Hospital Health. U.S. Representative Robert Prader, a Washington D.C. advocate for equitable access to technology, endorsed the Commission and has promised to attend future meetings when he is in Green River.

> Media releases typically are double spaced.

Commission member Barbara Keller, President of the Right Place, which promotes Green River as a place for business relocation, said, "The work that the Commission will take on is critical to our current economic health and our future growth. Businesses need to know that, if they decide to come to the Green River area, we're prepared to offer state-of-the-art electronic connections to the Internet and e-business."

The third and fourth paragraphs usually contain quotes by leaders of the organizations. The grantmaker might also provide a quote for you to include in the release.

David Crane, executive director of the City Media Center, said, "Closing the Digital Divide is another way to build unity and equity in our community. That makes the Commission's work critical to the social fabric of greater Green River."

The e-TIP Commission will build on lessons learned in Austin, Texas, and other communities that have launched similar projects. Members will spend a year identifying the existing technology infrastructure and gaps between that and the ideal. Early in year two, they will produce maps and write a report outlining their recommendations for ensuring that all residents have access to information technology. Before disbanding in year three, members will work with area businesses and organizations to promote implementation of their recommendations.

The release includes the amount of the award.

Ed Director, executive director of the Green Valley Metropolitan Council, said, "We're very pleased that Meridian recognized the importance of planning for technology and provided this $42,500 grant. Coupled with matching funds from the Commission members and local Foundations, the Meridian grant will allow us to hire a project coordinator and move the initiative forward."

John Bear, mayor of Suburb and chair of the Metro Council, said, "Cooperative efforts like the e-Tip Commission, which bring together the private, public and nonprofit sectors are very

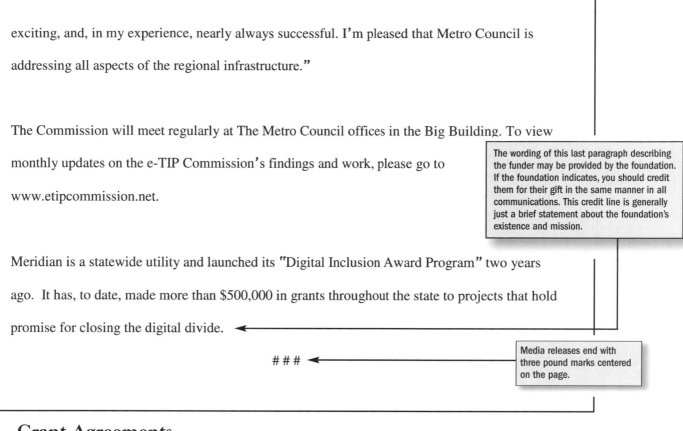

exciting, and, in my experience, nearly always successful. I'm pleased that Metro Council is addressing all aspects of the regional infrastructure."

The Commission will meet regularly at The Metro Council offices in the Big Building. To view monthly updates on the e-TIP Commission's findings and work, please go to www.etipcommission.net.

> The wording of this last paragraph describing the funder may be provided by the foundation. If the foundation indicates, you should credit them for their gift in the same manner in all communications. This credit line is generally just a brief statement about the foundation's existence and mission.

Meridian is a statewide utility and launched its "Digital Inclusion Award Program" two years ago. It has, to date, made more than $500,000 in grants throughout the state to projects that hold promise for closing the digital divide.

#

> Media releases end with three pound marks centered on the page.

Grant Agreements

A grant agreement is a contract between the grantmaker and grantee that outlines the terms of the work to be performed, payment information, and, often, reporting requirements. The agreement can be very technical and involved, or it can be quite straightforward and understandable. Unless both you and the grants officer have negotiated different terms than those presented in your proposal, you will often see the goals and objectives you set forth in your proposal reiterated in the agreement. The method and timeline for the evaluation is also restated in the grant agreement.

When you receive a grant agreement, have a meeting with your executive director, finance officer, and board chair, if appropriate. If you agree to the grant terms, both the executive director and sometimes the board chair will sign the agreement and return it to the foundation with their thank you letter. It is considered bad form to cash a check for an enclosed payment before returning the signed grant agreement.

If the grant is large and complex, a good grants officer will set a time to talk with you about the foundation's expectations. If you don't hear from the officer, call him or her and schedule a meeting. In the meeting make sure that you are absolutely clear about conditions and reporting requirements.

In the sample below from a corporate foundation, the funder expects that within a year the organization will have completed its challenge, made capital improvements, and progressed in its service goals. That may still be true and you will be on track to deliver on the promises made in your proposal. But, as likely, some circumstances may have changed in the months since you wrote the proposal; for example, a key employee has taken a maternity leave that could delay the project. If you think you'll need more time, ask now for that six-month extension.

Sample: Grant Agreement

October 7, 2005

Name
Address
City, state, zip

Dear _____:

At their October 3, 2005 meeting, the trustees of the Large Corporate (LC) Foundation awarded your organization a $160,000 grant ($125,000 outright and a $35,000 1:1 challenge grant in year two for business and individual donors) to support the Helping Hands capital campaign. A check for $125,000 is enclosed.

> In year two, the organization must raise $35,000 from businesses and individuals to request the final payment on the grant.

After you have raised the challenge ($35,000) portion of the grant, you will need to submit a list of donors/businesses and their contribution amounts before the Foundation will release its payment. Money that will be eligible for the challenge includes all cash, pledges, and/or grants raised specifically for your program between October 2, 2005 and November 15, 2006. Please discuss the terms of the challenge grant with your board to determine whether you feel you can successfully meet the challenge.

> The foundation will not accept funds raised before that date as meeting the challenge.

> If the staff and board agree that they cannot meet the challenge, they should politely decline the entire grant, including the first payment that was enclosed.

On October 2, 2006, you will need to submit a brief yet complete report outlining the previous year's activities in order to receive the challenge portion of your grant. In this report, you should include the following information:

> This is information that was probably not promised in the proposal, but it is generally requested in progress reports to the foundation.

- Outlook for future funding
- Success you have experienced in raising additional funds
- Actual project revenues and expenditures
- Copy of your most recent audit
- Change, if any, in service population
- Roadblocks and/or successes you have experienced with the project
- Actual number of people served in each service in comparison to previous five years
- Modifications to the original project design

> Provide photos of the changes to the site after the capital campaign.

- Before and after photos
- Status of your rental agreements
- Impact of the new building on services
- Actual outcomes in comparison to planned outcomes as follows:

> The following list was taken from the objectives contained in the grant proposal.

  - 90 percent of clients reported that the food and clothing pantry resolved their immediate crises
  - 83 percent of returning clients reported that they had received a referral at their first visit
  - 25 percent of returning clients reported that the previous referral helped them meet their needs
  - 80 percent of returning clients reported that because of your help, they were better able to meet their needs than the last time they had visited
  - 100 percent of teen moms scored between 80 and 100 percent on the parenting attitude score

- 40 percent of teen moms scored between 80 and 100 percent on the communications skill assessment
- 100 percent of teen moms reported that they practiced abstinence or use effective contraception and were not pregnant. One hundred percent did not appear to be pregnant.
- 80 percent of teen moms said they felt confident they will finish school
- Actual success in moving capital campaign donors to annual donors

Also provide any other information you feel would be helpful as we evaluate the effectiveness of our grant to your organization. The report is due in the Foundation office by October 2, 2006. ◄————

> Immediately add the reporting date to your calendar.

Congratulations on the award. Please feel free to contact me if you have questions.

Sincerely,

Grants Officer

You Got the Grant, But...

Sometimes you get a grant, but it's not what you asked for. Sometimes, you didn't ask for a challenge grant, but that's what you got. Sometimes, you ask for a certain amount of money, and you are awarded less.

First thing to do? Be gracious. Thank the grants officer or other staff person that informs you of the award. You can ask questions about the terms of the award (duration, conditions, etc.), but be careful that you do not sound defensive or angry. There is no way to ask "why didn't we get what we asked for?" without sounding angry. Say thank you. Hold off making an announcement. Wait for the grant agreement.

When the grant agreement arrives, read it carefully. In many cases, a foundation will have reduced the level of service they are asking for under the grant terms, or they will have established a challenge requiring you to raise the additional funding before you can receive payment on their grant. Accept the grant graciously unless you are fairly certain that you cannot meet the challenge.

In rare circumstances, and primarily with government grants, you may be awarded a lesser amount than you requested, but you will be held in the grant contract to the same goals and objectives that you proposed. This is a difficult situation. Review the reporting requirements contained in the grant agreement. Government grants have increased their criteria for progress and close-out reports. So, you not only must perform on all your goals and objectives, but you must also carve out time to gather data and write comprehensive reports to the government. In these situations, if the grant award is substantially less and you are relatively sure you cannot achieve the objectives outlined in your contract, you may have to decline the award.

Progress Reports

Progress reports are reports made by the grantee to the grantor at various prescribed intervals during the grant period. A final report is written at the end of the grant period. Whoever coordinates or oversees the project implementation and day-to-day activities is the best person to write the progress report. Schedule these reports right away so you don't forget.

If you have not already established benchmarks, you should consider breaking annual goals into quarterly goals using the timeline and objectives from your grant. Benchmarks will help you report progress as often as quarterly. The following is a sample benchmark grid for a capital campaign:

Campaign benchmarks

2006/07	1st Q	2nd Q	3rd Q	4th Q
Project Coordinator in place	X			
Marketing Coordinator in place	X			
Developing/Implementing Marketing Plan		X	X	X
Project generated income	$5,000	$10,000	$15,000	$20,000
Events	15	30	45	60
Volunteers hours	50	75	100	120
Lease income	0	$2,000	$3,000	$3,000
Program income	$5,000	$10,000	$10,000	$10,000
Number of program participants	25	50	50	50
Number of Membership services rendered	0	50	75	100
Campaign Cabinet in Place	X			
25 Solicitations for funds accomplished		X		
$250,000 raised since Jan. 1			X	
Public portion of campaign launched – "Buy a Seat"				X

When you then write a progress report, you can see at a glance what you have promised to accomplish each quarter and report whether or not you are on track to achieve your objectives.

Be sure to deliver complete progress reports on time. If terms must be renegotiated (e.g., you have rethought your objective to hire a marketing coordinator as in the example above), you should call your grants officer to see if the contract can be revised.

Sample: Progress Report

Green River Youth Center, Inc.
Camp Orleans Improvement Project
Progress Report 1: January 2006

Progress Toward Stated Outcomes: ◄
The overall goal of this project was to strengthen and broaden programming by hiring a Camp Director and developing and implementing related activities at Camp Orleans. ◄

> An outline of the progress report is provided by the grantor, often in the grant agreement, but sometimes separately.

The Executive Director of Youth Center hired a Camp Director on September 9, 2005. The camp director holds a Bachelor of Arts degree in education and has established a home in the Director's cabin at Camp Orleans. ◄

> Restate your goal and objectives from the grant proposal or grant agreement.

Other objectives for the project and progress toward each follow:
- Camp enrollment for summer 2005 was 328, up 10 percent from previous year.
- Private rental use of camp in 2005 included ten groups and more than seven hundred participants. The types of groups expanded to include Toys for Tots, Major manufacturer, suburban School District, Boy Scouts of America, Girl Scouts of America, Green River Police Department, Indigent Health Services, and Core City Ministries.
- Camp Orleans sponsored a week-long youth soccer camp with Green Valley State University in July 2005 and plans another in summer 2006.

Status of final two objectives, slated for summer 2006 and the end of the grant period:
- Youth Center has not yet developed and implemented the week-long youth leadership camp that is scheduled to begin in summer 2006 but expects it will meet this objective by the scheduled target date. Currently, Director and the camp director are meeting with various community leaders and interested business leaders to develop a curriculum and outcomes for this project.
- Youth Center anticipates that, despite a minor delay (three months) in hiring the appropriate Camp Director, it will still be able to demonstrate by year four that the Camp Director position is sustainable through increased uses and fees.

Although not a specific goal of the project, the new Camp Director benefited from his participation in a four-session outcomes assessment seminar held by United Way. His new skills will be applied to further collaboration with other camp directors and to all programs at Camp Orleans.

1. Special Terms and Conditions
The Foundation grant award of $35,000 had no special terms.

2. Use of Funds ◄
Youth Center has expended $20,139 of the $35,000 grant award toward camp/program improvements. Expenses include a minor soccer field, thirty-two bunk beds built to prototype, and renovations to two cabins. The remainder of the grant award has gone to pay a portion of improvements to the Camp Director's year-round home at camp.

> Describe grant fund expenditures in detail.

It's a good practice to save media stories about grant-funded programs and attach copies to your progress reports.

3. Unanticipated Benefits or Problems

Finding the right person with the appropriate skills, desire, and "calling" for the Camp Director position was Youth Center's primary hindrance toward completing objectives. It has been the Executive Director's experience that waiting for the right person is the most cost-effective and appropriate course of action, and he is pleased with his final choice. Camp Director has already garnered positive attention from the local media (see attached news article).

Youth Center has received throughout 2005 other positive media attention and coverage, which was quite unanticipated. Much of the attention has focused on community involvement with the organization and/or with Camp Orleans. Press clippings were attached to the May 2005 progress report. Although there is no tangible measure for the effects of the publicity, staff surmise that this will assist in several objectives, including increasing the number of campers each summer and increasing rental opportunities.

4. Continuation Funding

Youth Center is basically on schedule with supplementing the Camp Director's salary through increased camp rental and fees, and still projects that by year four, the salary for the position will be sustained entirely by camp income. New programs are self-sustaining after the initial cost of improvements, which are paid for with grant funds.

This section should address ways the organization used the grant to raise other funds.

5. Assistance with Additional Funding

The Foundation grant has enabled three significant projects to upgrade camp facilities for expanded and year-round use:

- Construction of a competition-quality minor soccer field at Camp Orleans at a cost of $12,595.
- Manufacturer employees donated materials and time to design and build a prototype bunk bed. As a part of the "Adopt A Cabin" program, these employees donated five crafted bunk beds to completely refurnish "their" cabin. They also provided Youth Center the prototype so that we were able to have another thirty-two bunks constructed at a cost of $142 each ($4,544 total).
- Renovations to two cabins included installation of running water and showers at a cost of $3,000.
- Renovations to the Camp Director's cabin ($5,000) to provide year-round accommodations.

6. Lessons Learned

The proposal to hire a year-round camp director and open the camp for year-round use by businesses and organizations was based in sound research on other successful programs. All new programs, including football and soccer camp, have been well received and Youth Center plans a youth leadership camp in summer 2006. Youth Center would not do anything differently but is open to lessons it may receive as this project unfolds.

Sorry, Your Proposal Was Not Funded

Statistics indicate that you will write more proposals that fail than succeed. All grantmakers receive far more proposals than they can fund.

Whose Fault Is It?

Even a proposal targeted to the right audience that exactly fits a grantmaker's guidelines and describes clearly and concisely an innovative response to an urgent community problem can fail to be funded. There are reasons outside your control.

Funders may have spent their allocation to a program area for the year, or they may have just attempted something similar to your project elsewhere. Foundations may have made a number of long-term grants and, as a result, have less money to grant overall in one year than another. The federal government may have an unstated goal to distribute grant money in each of the fifty states before funding additional projects, and your state has already gotten a grant.

Sometimes your proposal can look very promising. The staff of a foundation might think it exactly fits their guidelines; you've armed them with all the information they need to be advocates for your proposal and the foundation has the money. Yet, the grants officer calls after the trustee meeting to tell you your proposal has been denied. This is difficult for the program officer. It takes only one trustee to point out a flaw or to question an approach, and the trustee could have more influence than the grants officer over the board's final decision. Often, the grants officer will try to explain what happened to turn the decision, especially if the information will help you in other fund-raising or with later proposals to that foundation.

> **A Balancing Act: Encouragement Versus Promise**
>
> Program officers walk a fine line: they must encourage you through the grantwriting process but not imply that your proposal will be funded. A grants officer never knows how his or her board will vote. They will *never* tell you your funding is a guarantee; in fact, they will remind you throughout the process that they cannot predict an outcome. Despite that, many applicants take a grant officer's encouragement as promise. They hear what they want to hear. Be clear in your own mind during your pre-grant meetings with program officers that nothing is sure until the grant check is in hand.

Requesting Reviewer Notes

When you go through a competitive grants process such as those offered through government RFPs, you can request reviewer score sheets for review. These score sheets indicate the number of points each reviewer assigned to each section of your proposal and provides his or her comments on the section and on the proposal as a whole.

If you can, request reviewer comments (they will be offered in the decline letter), particularly if you intend to try again for a grant during the next cycle.

The following is a summary of grant reviewer scores and comments from a failed Department of Education grant for gifted and talented students:

Sample: Reviewer Comments

Section	*Maximum score*	Reviewer 1	Reviewer 2	Reviewer 3
Need for project	*20*	15	15	18
Project design	*25*	18	15	22
Project personnel	*10*	5	5	8
Management plan	*20*	10	12	15
Evaluation	*25*	18	25	20
Total	**100**	**66**	**72**	**83**

Strengths
R1: Project seeks to expand differentiated instruction that has been utilized and proven effective in gifted and talented (G/T) programs to all classrooms of the district. The plan would allow for unidentified G/T students' access to instructional methods that will increase the academic performance.

R2. The use of differentiated instruction in all classrooms will link G/T strategies for all students and may lead to significant gains in teacher knowledge, student achievement, or both. There exists a specific gap in services for G/T students.

R3. School district has serious commitment to G/T programs for K-6 students.

Weaknesses
R1. Although the project broadens the use of gifted and talented strategies for additional students, the whole school approach diminishes the value of the funding for the very population it aims to serve.

R2. The proposal does not add significantly to the research in the field of G/T students.

R3. The differentiation model assists all students. Consequently, it will require extensive efforts to meet the needs of G/T students.

Note that the reviewers had a wide range of scores, but they seemed to agree that the approach—expanding a gifted and talented teaching methodology called "differentiation" district wide—was not the primary purpose of this grant opportunity. In addition, the information provided by the federal government indicated that it received 140 applications for funding, and they funded fourteen projects from the competition. Even if the proposal had scored in the nineties, it likely would not have been funded with such stiff competition.

If the applicant intends to try again for a G/T grant, school administrators will need to agree to try a different program approach. However, if their commitment is truly to expanding G/T methodology throughout the district, they should stay committed to the approach rather than change it to chase grant dollars.

If, however, the approach were not in question, the grantwriter should take the review criteria and the comments on each section and use it to strengthen a proposal to submit in an upcoming grant cycle. As illustrated in the review comments, the two weakest sections overall on the grant application were project personnel and the management plan. While the need will likely not change before another grant cycle, the two weakest sections can easily be strengthened with more detail or a clearer articulation of the management plan.

Government grant competitions may come around again year after year and, thus, create new opportunities to learn from your earlier mistakes. However, if your proposal is not funded by a foundation, you should not resubmit, especially for the same project, unless asked specifically to do so by your program officer.

> If you have a grants officer who is specific in discussing flaws in your proposal as background to explaining why it was declined, do not take this as an invitation to fix the problem and reapply. Some grants officers hesitate to provide specific information because it creates unrealistic expectations that your grant will be successful next time.

CHAPTER 13
Professional Grantwriting

Is This the Life for You?

Sometimes freelance writers develop a specialty in grantwriting to tap into the nonprofit market and expand their clientele, sometimes fundraisers become great grantwriters while on the job, and sometimes nonprofit leaders develop grantwriting skills to make themselves more attractive to potential employers. Many of these people move quite naturally into full-time careers as grantwriters—spending their days (and nights) searching for the most appropriate funding matches, nurturing relationships with community partners and local funders, designing projects for reactive grantseeking, developing strategies for proactive grantseeking, and writing grant proposals and letters of inquiry.

Is it the right career for you?

Fundraisers and Grantwriters

People who do not work with the nonprofit sector often confuse the jobs of fundraisers and grantwriters; however, they are very different jobs for very different types of personalities. Which are you? Take this short quiz to determine which is right for you: fundraiser or grantwriter.

Select one of the following choices:

Column One	Column Two
I like meeting new people.	I prefer to work alone.
I love going out in the evening.	I prefer quiet evenings at home.
I'm not at all shy.	I'm generally introspective and quiet though I can rise to the occasion in meetings with small groups.
I dress well; grooming is important to me.	I love casual Fridays when I can be myself.
I have the gift of gab.	I have the gift of prose.

Fundraisers, or "development directors," are generally far more social than are grantwriters, and they need to be. Though fundraisers often write proposals as a part of their work, their larger job is to cultivate relationships with individual donors and to ensure continued support for the organization's operations. If you selected more from column one than column two, you may want to look into developing your grantwriting skills to become the best development director you can be. If, on the other hand, you are really a writer trying to develop a specialized skill, you should be clear that you are seeking employment as a grantwriter.

Freelancers and Employees

The bad news is that while there is a market for grantwriting skills, there is also great difficulty getting a position when grantwriting is your only skill.

If a nonprofit organization is large enough to have a full-time fundraiser on staff, that person usually writes grants, coordinates fund-raising events, builds relationships with community donors, and handles public and media relations for the organization. Generally, very few nonprofit organizations hire a full-time grantwriter. Only some of the largest nonprofits can afford both a fundraiser and a grantwriter. If you are looking for a full-time grantwriter position, you should look for employment opportunities in larger school districts, universities, hospitals, national-scope nonprofit organizations, or research centers.

Freelance grantwriters, on the other hand, can find work in any community that has nonprofit organizations—in other words, in any community. Nonprofit organizations always need someone knowledgeable and skilled to search for opportunities, to discuss proactive grantseeking strategies, and to write proposals on their behalf. Freelance work requires flexibility to work through peaks and valleys of your workload—the ability to go without sleep in the former case, and a savings account in the latter.

Specialists and Generalists

Every segment of the nonprofit sector has its own specialized vocabulary, and it is important that the grantwriter learn that vocabulary both as a means to express the organization's mission and goals and as a way to communicate with the audience, particularly if the proposal judges are peers and experts in the field. Remember, though, to explain all insider language when you are writing to an audience of generalists in the subject.

Some grantwriters specialize in a particular segment of the nonprofit sector, such as writing proposals for medical research or for health services. These individuals generally have special education or a background in the field and have learned the vocabulary and concepts necessary to develop knowledgeable, strong proposals.

Most grantwriters, however, are generalists who work with nonprofits that do not require extensive and specialized skills and knowledge in addition to those required to be a good writer and grantseeker.

Earning Potential

Different regions of the country have different costs of living and earning potential, so it is impossible to say what you should charge for grantwriting. In general, a full-time employed grantwriter should earn a salary commensurate with that of other midlevel managers in the nonprofit organization. A grantwriter may not earn the same wage as midlevel managers in regional businesses because work in the nonprofit sector often pays less than similar work or positions in the for-profit sector.

Freelance writers can establish their own hourly or project rates, though many have two rates—one for business and one for nonprofit, with the nonprofit rate being slightly lower. This is one of the few instances in which the value the market holds for a service or product does not necessarily dictate what it will pay. Everyone in the nonprofit sector must be careful stewards of the organization's money, ensuring that the always scarce funds are spent on services to the target population. A survey of grantwriters nationally indicates that fees range from $20 to $100 per hour, with $60 per hour being the most common rate. If you are just starting out, set a rate toward the low end and work up as you prove your worth.

If you intend to write grants as a freelancer for several nonprofit organizations, you should be sensitive to their budget issues. Try to establish a flat rate for projects so the organization can budget for your services. Once you become experienced, you can look at an RFP and judge the amount of time it will take to complete the project. Add about ten hours to the project budget if you are working with a new client and need to plan time for extra meetings or reading and research. Provide the potential client with a budget that says, "project rate will not exceed $——." It's also a good idea to show the potential client how they can save money by saving you time. Is there someone on the client's staff willing to call to gather data you need? Is the executive director willing to take on completing the forms and can the finance director complete the budgets so that you are not drafting them for the clients' review? When clients receive a final invoice below your ceiling estimate, they are pleased with both themselves and you—and they are more likely to call you again the next time they apply for grants.

On rare occasions, after you have built a clientele, one or more clients may put you on retainer. That is, they offer a monthly fee in return for a minimum number of hours. The terms are negotiable, but you might consider reducing your hourly rate, for instance, from $60 to $50 in return for a guaranteed $1,000 monthly income and twenty hours of work. These situations help stabilize a freelancer's finances and assures the nonprofit of your ongoing interest and effort.

Building Your Grantwriting Business

Breaking into the Field

Many grantwriters break in to the field of grantwriting on the job; for example, a fundraiser or executive director who writes a grant out of necessity. If you are considering grantwriting as a consultant to nonprofits, you should probably volunteer to write a few proposals to build your skills. Your first foray into grantwriting should be a reactive proposal in which you follow the directions and help the organization shape a program that responds to the RFP and the needs of the target service population.

Meanwhile, explore the philanthropic landscape in your community. If you have a community foundation, ask for a meeting with a program officer. Review the foundation's guidelines and develop a list of relevant questions regarding the programming of the foundation. Ask general questions such as:

- What makes a strong proposal for this foundation?
- What are your red flag topics or strategies, the things you don't want to see?
- How does the grant review process work? Who performs due diligence? What kind of questions do you ask?
- How can I provide the best grantwriting service to my future clients?

You should never have this interview with the trustee of a staffed foundation. Trustees hire staff to field meetings from grantseekers of all kinds.

Explore publications and websites by funders, philanthropy-focused service agencies such as regional associations of grantmakers, the Council on Foundations, and Philanthropy News Digest. Learn more about the resources available to strengthen nonprofit organizations by accessing search engines and using key words such as "NPO good practices."

If your local foundations do not have a staff, do your exploration on websites and ask questions of other grantwriters through Internet forums. One such forum is available at Philanthropy News Digest: http://members4.boardhost.com/PNDtalk. Join a local association of fundraisers or take college or university classes in grantwriting, nonprofit management, and/or professional writing.

Marketing Your Skills

Word of mouth is your best sales tool. One satisfied client will refer you to his or her peers in the nonprofit sector. For a freelance writer, every job you do should generate another—either from the same organization or from a referral from that organization. Remember, however, that the organization will only refer you if you have done a good job for them. They will judge your performance and attitude regardless of the outcome of your proposals (though, of course, successful funding is always better). So treat every client like they are your only client. Keep your promises. Meet your deadlines. Be respectful of others' ideas and leave your ego at home on editing days.

Advertising in the newspaper or telephone yellow pages does not generally yield good results. Grantwriting is a specialty not sought by the general public that uses these shopping tools. Instead, if one is available, sign up with a consultant referral network established for nonprofit organizations, establish a website of your own, and develop a brochure and business cards that you can mail to nonprofit organizations in your community. If you have a specialty, such as educational grants, contact your local or intermediate school district and pay for an advertisement in an upcoming newsletter.

Finally, explore websites offering jobs in fund-raising or grantwriting. Some have separate listings of organizations looking for consultants that may be of interest to grantwriters.

Transferable Skills

While your grantwriting skills will be in demand by the local nonprofit sector, you may also want to market the skills you developed writing grants in the business or public sector. Often grantwriters become very aware of the intricacies and systemic nature of social issues and can write compelling reports for government or funders on those issues. Businesses submit bid proposals frequently. These formats are similar to grant proposals, so your skills could be in demand in the business sector as well. You have developed skills in analytical reading, clear and concise writing, following directions, and meeting deadlines, among other things, each of which is in demand in the workplace. A good grantwriter will never want for a job. It's more likely that, if you have freelanced for a number of years, you won't want a "real" job.

You may also lead workshops on grantwriting for segments of the nonprofit sector, such as grantwriting for educators, grantwriting for healthcare workers, or grantwriting for the arts.

Client Benefits

A good business of any kind is one that provides a necessary and high-quality product or service for its customers. Nonprofit organizations value grantwriters. A good grantwriter saves the executive director (ED) time; he or she comes with a deep expertise that the ED does not have to replicate, and the grantwriter offers a service that is essential to the nonprofit's continued success.

Staff grantwriters provide their employers with several benefits. The staff grantwriter:

- Constantly scans the horizon for appropriate funding sources or RFPs
- Knows the organization and its target population well and can describe it easily
- Can advocate for the organization in contract negotiations or during the development of collaboratives
- Has good relationships with and access to the finance officer, ED, and other organization personnel and can get reviews, work, and approvals quickly
- Can provide a funder perspective during the project design process

Freelance grantwriters offer their own set of benefits to nonprofit clients. They:

- Often are very aware of other resources in the community (possibly their other clients) and can make suggestions for creative and workable collaborations
- Can be less expensive in that they require only per project fees and not ongoing salary or benefits
- Are more realistic (perhaps because they are less personally invested) about a proposal's chances of success

Funder Benefits

Some funders strongly discourage the use of professional grantwriters. They believe that no one but the leader of a nonprofit organization can better explain what a project's goals and objectives are and how the work plan will be carried out. They balance this view against another reality: some good ideas get lost in poor communication.

A good grantwriter, however, can be an asset to funders. Grantwriters can write clearly and concisely, communicating good ideas so they don't get lost in a mass of alphabet soup and institutional jargon. More importantly, they can remind the leaders of organizations to hear what's actually being said in meetings, rather than simply hearing what they want to hear. They can break the bad news to a grantseeker when it's clear in a meeting that the grants officer is trying nicely to dissuade them from proposing.

Grantwriting with Integrity

Relationships with Funders

Your relationships with funders and nonprofit executive directors are professional; your behavior should be professional at all times.

While it is important for you to learn as much as you can about your reading audience, you must keep some distance from local funders. At no time should you contact the trustee of a foundation or speak with a trustee about a foundation grantmaking decision, even if you encounter the person outside the foundation environment and even if the trustee is your own father or mother.

Unless you are writing as a staff member, it is inappropriate to contact a program officer regarding a grantmaking decision. If you are on staff, approach this carefully and, when you are told the reason for a "no," accept it with grace. If the door is still open to future proposals, ask questions about how you can best approach the foundation with a different proposal next time.

The biggest mistake that grantees (and grantwriters if they are one and the same) make in their interactions with funders is to be ungrateful. It's surprising, but program officers will tell you that they most often hear bitter complaints, not when a grant is not made at all, but when a proposal receives a smaller grant award than requested. The proper response is not "well, why'd they do that?" or "how am I supposed to raise a match for that?" or "I can't possibly complete the project with that." The proper response is "thank you." If the grant agreement then arrives and holds you to the original goals and objectives but does not provide enough money to support those efforts, you may have to turn down the award, but again, you can do so politely and rationally.

Chasing Dollars Versus Making Matches

Just because there's an RFP out there and your organization qualifies does not mean you have to write a proposal. Be sure that the project is one that you planned to do anyway or that something you have in mind fits with only minor changes to the objectives of the funder.

> Nationally there are a few for-profit businesses that offer to write federal grants for organizations that they never meet. The grantseeker sends a fee and receives a federal grant proposal that lays out a responsive program. The grantseeker has only to add a few minor details and fill in the blanks with its name. This approach invariably fails and would call any grantwriter's ethics into question. A grant proposal should describe a local problem and a unique and individualized approach to solving it. The grantwriter and grantseeking organization should have a close relationship and open communications.

Also, do not try to use grants to shore up budget shortages year after year. Deficit funding is a bad business practice. Remember, if you are not able to sustain a successful program after a launch grant ends, you probably should not have proposed it in the first place.

Fees as a Portion of Grant Funds

There are several reasons why an ethical, professional grantwriter does not work for a portion of grant funds or does not work for a fee contingent on the success of the application.

First, writers generally do not work "on spec." Grantwriters are no exception and for good cause: the success of a proposal is 100 percent dependent on the quality of the program that is being proposed. The grantwriter may give the proposal an edge by making the subject clearer and by following directions, but grantmakers confirm that the quality of writing is rarely the reason a grant is made or not made.

Second, grant budgets should contain only those line items necessary to carry out the project. Few funders pay for grantwriting services and none would pay to reimburse the organization for program expenses incurred prior to the grant award. Plus, most funders require, at minimum, financial reporting of grant expenditures. If they find out that the nonprofit took a percentage off the top to pay for grantwriting services, the organization is unlikely to ever get another award.

Third, the grantwriter spends his or her time writing the grant, and that time is worthy of compensation whether or not the product (a grant proposal) is funded.

Fourth, and most importantly, if the grantwriter has a financial interest in the outcome of an application, he or she is more likely to write a proposal that answers the need and interests of the funder over the needs and interests and mission of the organization.

Grantwriting services fall under most organizations' administrative budgets, where they have allocated money for fund-raising, technical assistance, or consultants. A community foundation, United Way, or a technical assistance fund of some kind may support fees to write a federal grant in rare instances, such as the preparation of a grant proposal for a collaborative approach to problem solving. On even more rare occasions, a local funder may ask and pay a grantwriter to assist a key potential grantee in framing its proposal more clearly.

> Nonprofit organization board members cannot benefit financially from their positions on the board. If a grantwriter is asked to serve on a nonprofit board of directors, he or she may be asked to write grants as a way of performing one of the primary duties of a board member: raising funds. In most of these cases, the grantwriter may not invoice for his or her work.

The Grantwriter's Scope of Involvement

If you are on staff or ED of the organization, of course, you will be involved in the implementation and reporting for all grant-funded projects. If you are a freelance grantwriter, your scope of involvement could include writing the grant, the thank you letters, media releases, and perhaps drafts of progress reports with the project coordinator. The grantwriter who is not part of the organization, however, should not be involved in project implementation or service delivery.

A freelance grantwriter should not write his or her services into a grant proposal. Do not create a line item in the budget for reports you intend to write. Do not perform an evaluation of the project even if you are qualified to evaluate. By the time the proposal is written, the writer is far too close to provide an objective view of the organization's achievement of goals and outcomes. Do not renegotiate terms among the collaborators, even if several of them are also clients. Do not become involved in the implementation of a project, even if the nonprofit organization does not follow the timeline for work. This is between the nonprofit and the grant funder.

In other words, write proposals. Do your best work on every project. Care about the role you play in improving your community and the lives of its residents. And be emotionally and financially satisfied with providing an important and valued service to all segments of your community. You are not only grantwriting like a professional, you have become a professional grantwriter.

GLOSSARY

501(c)(3)

Section of the Internal Revenue Code that designates an organization as charitable and tax-exempt. Organizations qualifying under this section include religious, educational, charitable, amateur athletic, scientific or literary groups, foundations, organizations testing for public safety, or organizations involved in prevention of cruelty to children or animals.

Advocacy

The act or process of defending or maintaining a cause or proposal. An organization may have advocacy as its mission (or part of its mission) to increase public awareness of a particular issue or set of issues.

Allocation Grant

Funding set aside for a specific purpose, such as a line item in the grant budget.

Annual Report

Reports issued each year by charities to provide donors and prospective donors with information about their income, expenditures, programs, and progress.

Anthropological Evaluation

An evaluation that uses quantifiable data sparingly. Instead, it relies on extensive stakeholder interviews to capture important information.

Applicant

Organization that has submitted a grant request to a foundation.

Application Package

Cover sheets, forms, and directions that are included with guidelines or RFPs.

Assets

Holdings in the form of cash, stock, bonds, real estate, etc. In the case of a foundation, assets are generally invested and the income is used to make grants.

Assurances

Forms that must be signed and submitted to the federal government stating that the organization practices equal opportunity, has an environmental policy, or agrees to some other requirement of the granting department.

Audit

An independent examination of the accounting records and other evidence relating to a business to support the expression of an impartial expert opinion about the reliability of the financial statements.

Benchmark
(1) A standard of reference used for comparison. The performance of a learner is measured against a benchmark, such as the performance of an expert.(2) A company's use of information about other firms in the same industry used for comparisons and to set standards and goals.

Bequest
A gift of assets made at death by an individual through a will or trust. Charities accept bequests in several forms including specific sums or assets, a percentage of the revenue of the estate, and contingent bequests.

Block Grants
A type of grant in which the donor government may structure and design an intergovernmental program for a variety of purposes.

Board Member
A member of an organization's governing board. Also called Trustee.

Board of Directors
The group of volunteers with the responsibility for governance and supervision of the policies and affairs of the organization, its committees, and its officers. It carries out the purpose of the organization.

Board of Trustees
The group of volunteers with the responsibility for governance and supervision of the policies and affairs of the organization, its committees, and its officers. It carries out the purpose of the organization.

Bricks and Mortar
An informal term indicating grants for buildings or construction projects.

Budget
A detailed breakdown of estimated income and expenses that can be used as a tool for projecting revenue and expenditures for the ensuing fiscal year.

Budget Forms
Line item list of items to be funded, including personnel, wages and fringe benefits, projected travel expenses, training, etc. Form usually provided by grantor.

Budget Narrative
Details pertaining to the budget. Explanations and justifications of proposed expenditures, including calculations, other sources of funding, distribution of funding, estimated or actual costs.

Bylaws
Rules that govern how an organization operates.

Capacity
The ability to perform or produce a desired output.

Capacity Building

(1) The development of an organization's core skills and capabilities, such as leadership, management, finance and fund-raising, programs and evaluation, in order to build the organization's effectiveness and sustainability. (2) The process of assisting an individual or group to identify and address issues and gain the insights, knowledge, and experience needed to solve problems and implement change.

Capital

Funding sought to support construction or renovation of a building or its infrastructure, or equipment.

Capital Campaign

Drive to raise and collect money/funds that will finance an organization's building or renovation project.

Case Statement

Statement of need or problem.

Catalog of Federal Domestic Assistance (CFDA)

List of government grant programs from all departments..

Certifications

See "assurances."

CFDA Number

Identification number assigned by the federal government to its grant programs.

Challenge Grant

Money that is donated to a nonprofit if other donors contribute a predetermined or matching amount.

Charity

Nonprofit organization that operates for the purpose of helping /benefiting a certain segment of society.

Checklist

Often provided by the funder, this is a list of the components that must be included in the grant proposal. Sometimes the checklist is submitted and sometimes it isn't. Check instructions.

Chief Executive Officer (CEO)

Hires, supervises, and evaluates staff and serves as a liaison between staff and board. The chief executive officer and the board serve as checks and balances for the organization. Also called Executive Director.

Cluster Evaluation

A means of determining how well a collection of projects or programs fulfills an objective.

Collaboration

A mutually beneficial and well-defined relationship entered into by two or more organizations to achieve common goals. The relationship includes a commitment to mutual relationships and goals, a jointly developed structure and shared responsibility, mutual authority and accountability for success, and sharing of resources and rewards.

Collaborative Funding

A cooperative effort among funders to address a particular need or project more effectively. Collaboration can involve information exchange, program or project review, and/or shared funding responsibility.

Community Foundation

A tax-exempt, nonprofit, autonomous, publicly supported, nonsectarian philanthropic institution with a long-term goal of building permanent, named component funds established by many separate donors for the broad-based charitable benefit of the residents of a defined geographic area, typically no larger than a state.

Company-sponsored Foundation

A private foundation whose assets are derived primarily from the contributions of a for-profit business. While a company-sponsored foundation may maintain close ties with its parent company, it is an independent organization with its own endowment and, as such, is subject to the same rules and regulations as other private foundations.

Conditional Grant

A grant in which the funding will not be released until specific conditions set by the grantmaker are met.

Conflict of Interest

A situation in which the private interests of someone involved with an organization could cause him or her to make decisions that are not in the best interest of the organization.

Constituency

In the case of grants, most often the beneficiaries of a project or the target population.

Consultant

A professional employed on a contractual basis who has expertise in a specific field. Usually employed for a special project such as planning or evaluating.

Corporate Foundation

This type of private foundation receives its funding from the for-profit company whose name it bears, but is legally an independent entity. Corporations may establish foundations with initial endowments, then make periodic contributions—generally based on a percentage of the company's profit—to the foundation, or combine both methods to provide the foundation's resources.

Corporate Giving Program

A grantmaking program established and administered within a for-profit corporation. Corporate giving programs do not have a separate endowment; their expense is planned as part of the company's annual budgeting process and usually is funded with pretax income. Corporate giving programs are not subject to the same reporting requirements as corporate foundations.

Corpus

The original gift and ongoing principal that forms the asset base from which a foundation or endowment operates.

Council on Foundations (COF)

A membership support organization that serves foundations.

Data Universal Numbering System (DUNS)

A unique nine-character identification number provided by the commercial company Dun & Bradstreet (D&B). Required information for federal grant applications.

Decline

Often call a "declination," the refusal or rejection of a grant request. Some declination letters explain why the grant was not made, but many do not.

Declining Grant

A multiyear grant that becomes smaller each year in the expectation that the recipient organization will increase its fund-raising or income from other sources.

Deficit Funding

Funding to cover debt or an unexpected shortfall in the budget. Most foundations do not provide this kind of funding.

Demonstration Grant

A grant made to establish an innovative project or program that will serve as a model, if successful, and may be replicated by others.

Determination Letters

The letters provided by the IRS stating that the organization has been determined to be a tax-exempt charitable organization under section 501(c)(3) and ruling on its public support status under section 509(a). Many foundations require copies of both letters to be submitted with grant proposals.

Development

A term used to define the total process of organizational or institutional fund-raising, frequently inclusive of public relations and (in educational institutions) alumni affairs.

Direct Costs

Actual cost to operate a proposed project.

Diversity

Full participation by members of many different groups.

Donor

Individual or organization that makes a grant or contribution. Also called a Grantor or Benefactor.

Due Diligence

Investigation process done prior to certain activities, such as recommending a grant, to verify disclosures and analyze risk.

DUNS Number

See Data Universal Numbering System.

Earned Income

Money received by an organization in return for the sale of a product or rendered service.

Effectiveness

The extent to which a program has made desired changes or met its goals and objectives through the delivery of services. Effectiveness can be judged in terms of both input and output.

Endowment

A permanently restricted net asset, the principal of which is protected and the income from which may be spent. It is controlled by either donor restriction or the organization's governing board.

Ethics

(1) The moral considerations of the activities of an organization. (2) A system or code of conduct that is based on universal moral duties and obligations that indicate how one should behave. It deals with the ability to distinguish good from evil, right from wrong, and propriety from impropriety.

Evaluation

Assesses the effectiveness of an ongoing program in achieving its objectives. Relies on the standards of project design to distinguish a program's effects from those of other forces, and aims at program improvement through a modification of current operations.

Evaluation Plan

A written document describing the overall approach or design that will be used to guide an evaluation. It includes what will be done, how it will be done, who will do it, when it will be done, and why the evaluation is being conducted.

Executive Director

Hires, supervises, and evaluates staff and serves as a liaison between staff and board. The executive director and the board serve as checks and balances for the organization. Also called Chief Executive Officer (CEO).

Expenditure Responsibility

When a private foundation makes a grant to an organization that is not classified by the IRS as tax-exempt under Section 501(c)(3), it is required by law to ensure that the funds are spent for charitable purposes and not for private gain or political activities. Special reports on the status of the grant must be filed with the IRS.

Experimental Evaluation

This type of evaluation design uses a control group, double-blind studies, and often, longitudinal work over a period of many years. It is related to the scientific evaluation approach but is even more rigorous.

Faith-based Organization

Nonprofit organizations affiliated with a particular church or faith, but established as a separate entity.

Family Foundation

"Family foundation" is not a legal term, and therefore, has no precise definition. Approximately two-thirds of the private foundations in the U.S. are believed to be family managed. The Council on Foundations defines a family foundation as a private foundation whose funds are derived from members of a single family. At least one family member must continue to serve as an officer or board member of the foundation, and as the donor, they or their relatives play a significant role in governing and/or managing the foundation throughout its life. Members decide if they wish to categorize their private foundation as a family or independent foundation. In many cases, second- and third-generation descendants of the original donors manage the foundation. Most family foundations concentrate their giving locally.

Federal Register
See Catalog of Federal Domestic Assistance

Fiduciary
An individual or entity responsible to manage assets for the benefit of others.

Financial Statements
Presentation of financial data including balance sheets, income statements, and statements of cash flow, or any supporting statement that is intended to communicate an entity's financial position at a point in time and its results of operations for a period then ended. Also called financial reports.

Financial Sustainability
The ability of an organization to develop a strategy of growth and development that continues to function indefinitely.

Fiscal Agent
A nonprofit, tax-exempt organization that acts as a sponsor for a project or group that does not have its own tax-exempt status. Grants are made to the fiscal agent, which manages the funds and is responsible for reporting back to the grantor on the progress of the project.

Fiscal Management
Includes basic compliance with IRS regulations and the myriad of federal, state, and local requirements for staff and programs. This also includes the unenforceable, but equally important, ethical practices and stewardship of resources carried out on behalf of the public.

Form 990
The IRS form filed annually by public charities. The IRS uses this form to assess compliance with the Internal Revenue Code. The form lists organization assets, receipts, expenditures and compensation of officers.

Form 990-PF
The IRS form filed annually by private foundations. The IRS uses this form to assess compliance with the Internal Revenue Code. The form lists organization assets, receipts, expenditures, compensation of directors and officers, and a list of grants awarded during the previous year.

Formative Evaluation
A type of process evaluation of new programs or services that focuses on collecting data on program operations so that needed changes or modifications can be made to the program in the early stages. Formative evaluations are used to provide feedback to staff about the program components that are working and those that need to be changed. Also called process evaluation.

Foundation
An entity that is established as a nonprofit corporation or a charitable trust, with a principal purpose of making grants to unrelated organizations or institutions or to individuals for scientific, educational, cultural, religious, or other charitable purposes. This broad definition encompasses two foundation types: private foundations and public foundations.

Fund
(1) Used variously to denote the vehicle for securing contributions, the goal of a capital campaign, goals of a special program or project, or a philanthropic foundation. (2) As a verb: To give value to a trust, as to fund with securities or cash.

Funding Cycle
In most foundations, the period when applications are sought, accepted, and decided upon. Some donor organizations make grants at set intervals (quarterly, semiannually, etc.), while others operate under an annual cycle.

Funding Opportunity Announcement
A publicly available document by which a federal agency makes known its intentions to award discretionary grants or cooperative agreements, usually as a result of competition for funds. Funding opportunity announcements may be known as program announcements, notices of funding availability, solicitations, requests for proposals, or other names depending on the agency and type of program. Funding opportunity announcements can be found at www.Grants.gov and on the Internet at the funding agency's or program's website.

Funding Opportunity Number
The number that a federal agency assigns to its grant announcement. See CFDA number.

Funding Priorities
The defining of types of activities a foundation is interested in funding. These are generally set by an assessment of community needs and a selection of goals that can reasonably be accomplished with a foundation's resources.

Funding Round
A chronological pattern of making grants, reviewing proposals, and grantee notification. Some foundations make grants at set intervals (quarterly, semiannually, etc.) while others operate under a continuous cycle.

Fund-raising
Overall effort by an organization to raise funding, including but not limited to grant seeking, special events, year-end requests for support, bequests, and building relationships with major donors.

General Support Grant
A grant made to further the general purpose or work of an organization, rather than for a specific purpose or project.

Gift In-kind
A donation of goods or services rather than cash or appreciated property.

Goal
A focus of accomplishment supported by a series of objectives needed to realize it or a broadly stated subsidiary result.

Government Grants
Tax dollars that the government (usually federal or state) redistributed to communities through programs.

Grant
An award of funds to an organization or individual to undertake charitable activities.

Grants.gov

A storefront web portal for use in electronic collection of data (forms and reports) for federal grant-making agencies through the grants.gov site (www.grants.gov).

Grants.gov Tracking Number

A number that is used by grants.gov to identify each application it receives.

Grant Agreement

A legally binding written understanding between the grantor and grantee specifying terms for a grant's expenditure and reporting. Foundations may include boilerplate language that prohibits grantees from engaging in lobbying or other advocacy activities.

Grant Application

Form that is filled out by one requesting a grant.

Grant Cycle

The schedule of when grant applications are reviewed, awards are announced, and evaluations are due.

Grant Guidelines

A statement of a foundation's goals, priorities, criteria, and procedures for applying for a grant.

Grant Proposal

Documents (forms and narrative) written and used to apply for funding for a specific project or purpose.

Grants Officer

See Program Officer

Grantee

Organization that receives a grant.

Grantee Financial Report

A report detailing how grant funds were used by an organization. Many corporate grantmakers require this kind of report from grantees. A financial report generally includes a listing of all expenditures from grant funds as well as an overall organizational financial report covering revenue and expenses, assets, and liabilities.

Grantor

Organization that awards a grant.

Grantmaker

Individual or organization that makes a grant.

Grantmaking Priorities

The defining of types of activities a foundation is interested in funding. These are generally set by an assessment of community needs and a selection of goals that can reasonably be accomplished with a foundation's resources.

Grant Seeker

A grant applicant, or a responder to a request for proposals.

Grantseeker Workshop

Workshops targeted to specific RFPs and sponsored by funding agencies to provide additional information about the proposal process.

Grantseeking

The process of reviewing possible funding sources, narrowing the field of likely prospects, and applying for grants.

Grants to Individuals

These awards are given directly to individuals, not through other nonprofit organizations. Many foundations specifically exclude grantmaking to individuals. In order to make grants to individuals, a private foundation must have a program that has received formal IRS approval.

Grantwriters Workshop

Workshop held by an independent business to provide expert assistance in developing your grantwriting skills.

Grantwriting

The preparation of narrative, budget, and applications for funding.

Guidelines

A statement of a foundation's goals, priorities, criteria, and procedures for applying for a grant.

Identity Numbers

Tax identification or other identity number made to an organization by the federal or state government.

Impact

The fundamental intended or unintended change occurring in organizations, communities, or systems as a result of program activities. The extent to which the program has made a long-term change in the program participants or in broader social conditions.

Impact Evaluation

A type of outcome evaluation that focuses on the broad, long-term impacts or results of program activities.

Impressionistic Evaluation

A simple method of evaluation that primarily consists of an informed opinion by a knowledgeable observer; rarely includes quantifiable data.

Independent Foundation

A nongovernmental, nonprofit organization with funds (usually from a single source, such as an individual, family, or corporation), managed by its own trustees or directors, that was established to maintain or aid charitable activities serving the common welfare, primarily through grantmaking.

Independent Sector

(1) Collectively, nonprofit or tax-exempt organizations that are specifically not associated with any government, government agency, or commercial enterprise. Also referred to as third sector, nonprofit sector, social sector, and civil society sector. (2) A coalition of foundations, corporations, and national nonprofit organizations that promotes the values of philanthropy, volunteerism, and nonprofit initiative.

Indirect Costs

Costs that have been incurred for common or joint objectives of a university or nonprofit organization and the sponsored program, and which, therefore, cannot be identified specifically in reference to a particular project, such as building operations and maintenance, laboratory space, library service, utilities, and administrative services.

In-kind Contribution

Support, offered by an agency and partners, to a project in the form of such things as staff time, office or other space, utilities, volunteer hours, and products. A donation of goods or services rather than cash or appreciated property.

Input

The resources used in a program.

Interagency Agreement

A written document outlining roles and responsibilities for collaborating agencies and signed by representatives of each agency.

Intermediaries

(1) Firms that act as a link between producers and consumers in a channel of distribution. (2) Firms that make subgrants or regrants with grant funds.

Internal Revenue Service (IRS)

The federal agency with responsibility for regulating foundations and nonprofit organizations and their financial activities.

Learning Organization

An organization that looks for meaningful solutions, then internalizes those solutions so that it continues to grow, develop, and remain successful. Learning organizations incorporate ideas from many sources and involve a variety of people in problem solving, information sharing, and celebrating success.

Lessons Learned

The process of discovering what happened and why through evaluation, then applying what is learned to improve future performance.

Letter of Inquiry

A brief letter outlining a program and its funding needs sent to a foundation to determine if it would be interested in the project and would like to receive a full proposal.

Letter of Intent

(1) A grantor's letter or brief statement indicating an intention to make a specific gift. (2) A letter required by some foundations or government agencies to state the intent of a nonprofit organization to apply for a specific grant, usually in response to a request for proposals.

Letter of Support

Written by a collaborating organization, community leaders, program collaborators, and grantseeking organizations in support of the proposed project.

Leverage
A method of grantmaking practiced by some foundations. Leverage occurs when a small amount of money is given with the express purpose of attracting funding from other sources or of providing the organization with the tools it needs to raise other kinds of funds.

Leveraging Funds
Use of a foundation grant as a means of attracting grants from other sources and other types of financial support.

Lobbying
Efforts to influence legislation by influencing the opinion of legislators, legislative staff, and government administrators directly involved in drafting legislative proposals. The Internal Revenue Code sets limits on lobbying by organizations that are exempt from tax under Section 501(c)(3). Public charities may lobby as long as lobbying does not become a substantial part of their activities. Private foundations may neither lobby nor fund lobbying activities.

Local Government
A local unit of government, including specifically a county, municipality, city, town, township, local public authority, school district, special district, intrastate district, council of governments (whether or not incorporated as a nonprofit corporation under state law), any other regional or interstate entity, or any agency or instrumentality of local government.

Logic Model
A systemic, visual way to present a planned program with its underlying assumptions and theoretical framework. It is a flow chart that traces how inputs and activities interact to produce outcomes and impacts.

Longitudinal Study
An investigation or study in which a particular individual or group of individuals is followed over a substantial period of time to discover changes that may be attributable to the influence of the treatment, or to maturation, or the environment.

Management Plan
Narrative supporting plans for managing a project.
Matching Grant
(1) A grant or gift made with the specification that the amount donated must be matched on a one-for-one basis or according to some other prescribed formula. (2) A grant made in response to a challenge grant.

Matching Support
Grants made to match funds provided by another donor and paid only if the donee is able to raise additional funds from another source.

Media
A means of communication, such as newspapers, magazines, film, telephone, radio, television, and the Internet.

Mission Statement
(1) The major criterion used by states and the IRS to determine if the organization qualifies as a nonprofit. (2) The evaluative measure by which a nonprofit organization measures its success. (3) The goal of a nonprofit organization and its programs and services.

Multi-year Grant

A commitment by a foundation to provide support for more than one year (typically two to five years) contingent upon satisfactory grantee performance.

Need Statement

Sets the stage for a proposal by describing your community, the target population, grantseeking organization and what it does, and other relevant data that supports the need for the project.

Nongovernmental Organization (NGO)

The United Nation's term for a nonprofit organization that is not fully funded or controlled by government and that is promoting human well-being on a not-for-profit basis. When it exists in only one country, it will be considered a national NGO, and when it exists in a number of countries in a region, it will be considered a regional NGO. The organization should have a legally established constitution, a clear purpose, and visible activities with a governing body that has the authority to speak for its members. It may or may not be affiliated with an international organization.

Nonprofit

Organizations that have tax-exempt status under Internal Revenue Code Section 501(c)(3), but are not private foundations under Internal Revenue Code Section 509 or are among those rare operating private foundations (private foundations that implement programs similar to public charities). These organizations are tax-exempt, and contributions to them are tax deductible under such Internal Revenue Code Sections as 170, 642, 2055, and 2522.

Nonprofit Infrastructure

A collection of nonprofit organizations deemed critical to the healthy social functioning of a specified geographic area.

Nonprofit Organization (NPO)

Organizations that have tax-exempt status under Internal Revenue Code Section 501(c)(3), but are not private foundations under Internal Revenue Code Section 509. These organizations are tax–exempt, and contributions to them are tax deductible under such Internal Revenue Code Sections as 170, 642, 2055, and 2522. A nonprofit is governed by a volunteer board of directors, operated for public benefit, and its business is not conducted for profit. Organizations of this type are said to belong to the nonprofit or third sector. They are neither government (public sector) nor business (private sector).

Nonprofit Sector

Organizations that are private, nongovernmental, and seek to serve the public good without the motivation of profit.

Nonsupplanting Funds

Funds that may not take the place of operating costs. For instance, if the organization is paying for a staff position, it may not, if it is prohibited from supplanting, make the position a grant-funded one.

Not-for-profit Organization

Organizations that have tax-exempt status under Internal Revenue Code Section 501(c)(3), but are not private foundations under Internal Revenue Code Section 509. These organizations are tax-exempt and contributions to them are tax deductible under such Internal Revenue Code Sections as 170, 642, 2055, and 2522. A nonprofit is governed by a volunteer board of directors, operated for public benefit, and its business is not conducted for profit. Organizations of this type are said to belong to the nonprofit or third sector. They are neither government (public sector) nor business (private sector).

Objective

A significant step toward a goal, or a precise, measurable, time-phased result.

Operating Budgets

Budgets associated with the income-producing activities of an organization. The overall allocation of a nonprofit's annual resources.

Operating Foundation

Private foundations that use the bulk of their income to provide charitable services or to run charitable programs of their own. They make few, if any, grants to outside organizations. To qualify as an operating foundation, the organization must follow specific rules in addition to the applicable rules for private foundations. The Carnegie Endowment for International Peace and the Getty Trust are examples of operating foundations.

Operating Funds

Funds to cover the regular personnel, administrative, and other expenses for an existing program or project.

Organizational Capacity

An organization's capability and competence as measured by its ability to fulfill its mission and programmatic objectives through responsible stewardship of organizational plans and resources.

Outcome Evaluation

An evaluation used to identify the results of a program's effort. This type of evaluation provides knowledge about the extent to which the problems and needs that gave rise to the program still exist, ways to ameliorate adverse impacts and enhance desirable impacts, and program design adjustments that may be indicated for the future.

Outcomes

The measurable results of a project. The positive or negative changes that occur in conditions, people, and policies as a result of an organization's or program's inputs, activities, and outputs.

Output

The tangible products of a project or program activities.

Output Indicator

A measure showing the product or accomplishment of the activities of an organization or individual employee over a specific period of time.

Partnership

Individuals or organizations working together in a side-by-side effort to accomplish a common goal with a shared sense of purpose and responsibility for the outcome.

Pass-through Foundation

Foundations that receive monies and make distributions to donees with little or no principal remaining with the foundation.

Passive Grantmaking Approach

An approach taken by a foundation that does not have a strategic plan or designated areas of grantmaking interest, but rather accepts and funds unsolicited proposals and never dictates results to grantees.

Payout Requirement

The minimum amount that a private foundation is required to expend for charitable purposes (includes grants and necessary and reasonable administrative expenses). In general, a private foundation must pay out annually 5 percent of the average market value of its assets.

Performance Measures

Ways to measure objectively the degree of success a program or employee has had in achieving stated objectives, goals, and planned activities.

Philanthropy

(1) Voluntary action for the public good. (2) Love of humankind, usually expressed by an effort to enhance the well-being of humanity through personal acts of practical kindness or by financial support of a cause or causes. (3) Any effort to relieve human misery or suffering, improve the quality of life, encourage aid or assistance, or foster preservation of values through gifts, service, or other voluntary activity.

Pilot Funding

A grant given to a project for the purpose of carrying out a trial. This will enable the outcomes to be evaluated before any further funding or expansion of the project. Pilot projects are often for a duration of one year.

Positioning

Placement of a company, its products, or services in a market category or in relation to its competition.

Preemptory Grantmaking Approach

An approach taken by a foundation that has a rigid strategic plan and designated areas of grantmaking interest, that never accepts or funds unsolicited proposals, and always dictates desired results to grantees.

Preliminary Proposal

A brief draft of a grant proposal used to learn if there is sufficient interest to warrant submitting a proposal.

Prescriptive Grantmaking Approach

An approach taken by a foundation that has a rigid strategic plan and designated areas of grantmaking interest, that never accepts or funds unsolicited proposals, and always dictates desired results to grantees.

Private Foundation

Also known as private charitable foundation, it engages in giving money that comes from a wealthy person, family, or corporation to community agencies.

Private Sector

Also known as the for-profit sector. Organizations and businesses that provide services and products based on market demands for a fee with the intention of producing a profit for owners and shareholders.

Proactive Grantseeking

In this book, used to describe the process of identifying appropriate matches between programs of funders and non-profits and applying for grants.

Pro Bono

Provision of products or services at low or no cost. Also termed "pro bono publico."

Program (or Project) Grants

Funds to support specific projects or programs as opposed to general support grants.

Program Activities

The process, tools, events, technology, and actions that are an intentional part of the program implementation. These interventions are used to bring about intended changes or results.

Program Budgeting

Budgeting based on individual program needs as opposed to organizational needs.

Program Capacity

The degree of ability of a program to accomplish its intended purpose.

Program Evaluation

The measurement of the effectiveness of a specific project or program by a research institute and other program evaluator.

Program Officer

A staff member of a foundation or corporate giving program who may do some or all of the following: review and analyze grant requests and process applications for the board of directors or contributions committee and develop and manage program strategies.

Program Related Investment (PRI)

A loan or other investment (as distinguished from a grant) made by a foundation to another organization for a project related to the foundation's philanthropic purposes and interests.

Programs

Services, opportunities, or projects usually designed to meet a social need.

Proposal

A written application, often accompanied by supporting documents, submitted to a foundation, corporate giving program, or government agency in requesting a grant.

Proposal Writing

The process of creating a written request or application for a grant, gift, or service.

Public Charity

A nonprofit organization that qualifies for tax-exempt status under section 501(c)(3) of the IRS code and that receives its financial support from a broad segment of the general public. Organizations exempt under Section 501(c)(3) must pass a public support test to be considered public charities, or they must be formed to benefit an organization that is a public charity. Charitable organizations that are not public charities are private foundations and are subject to more stringent regulatory and reporting requirements.

Public Foundation

Public foundations, along with community foundations, are recognized as public charities by the IRS. Although they may provide direct charitable services to the public as other nonprofits do, their primary focus is on grantmaking.

Public Support Test

There are two public support tests, both of which are designed to ensure that a charitable organization is responsive to the general public rather than to a limited number of people. One test, sometimes referred to as 509(a)(1) or 170(b)(1)(A)(vi) for the sections of the Internal Revenue Code where it is found, is for charities such as community foundations that mainly rely on gifts, grants, and contributions. To be automatically classed as a public charity under this test, organizations must show that they normally receive at least one-third of their support from the general public (including government agencies and foundations). However, an organization that fails the automatic test still may qualify as a public charity if its public support equals at least 10 percent of all support and it also has a variety of other characteristics—such as a broad-based board—that make it sufficiently public. The second test, sometimes referred to as the section 509(a)(2) test, applies to charities, such as symphony orchestras or theater groups, that get a substantial part of their income from the sale of services that further their mission, such as the sale of tickets to performances. These charities must pass a one-third/one-third test. That is, they must demonstrate that their sales and contributions normally add up to at least one-third of their financial support, but their income from investments and unrelated business activities does not exceed one-third of support.

Qualified Report

The auditors' report, qualified or unqualified, is based on reporting standards established by the American Institute of Certified Public Accountants (AICPA). It should state whether, in the auditors' opinion, the financial statements and notes fairly represent the financial position of the organization in accordance with generally accepted accounting principles. In certain circumstances, the auditor may be unable to render an unqualified opinion on the financial statements, in which case either a qualified or adverse opinion would be issued or the auditor may disclaim an opinion. In a qualified report, a separate explanatory paragraph should be included as to the reasons for the qualification. The SEC will generally not accept an auditors' report, which is qualified as to either audit scope or the accounting principles used. An audit opinion may also be modified due to going uncertainties.

Qualitative Evaluation

Mainly concerned with the properties, the state, and the character (i.e., the nature) of phenomena. It implies an emphasis on processes and meanings that are rigorously examined, but not measured in terms of quantity, amount, or frequency.

Quantitative Evaluation

Involves the use of numerical measurement and data analysis based on statistical methods. It is an assessment process that answers the question, "How much did we do?"

Query Letter
A brief letter outlining an organization's activities and its request for funding. Such letters are sent to a potential funding agency to determine if it would be appropriate to submit a full grant proposal or application. Many funding agencies prefer to be contacted initially in this way prior to receiving a complete proposal. See also: letter of inquiry.

Reactive Grantseeking
In this book, used to describe the process of responding to a request for proposals.

Regional Associations
Intermediary organizations that provide services to a common type of organization in a defined region. Regional associations generally provide services such as technical assistance, professional development opportunities, and networking.

Regional Associations of Grantmakers
Membership organizations for foundations that provide their members with education, networking, and services, and represent the interests and concerns of foundations with policymakers.

Request for Proposals (RFP)
A document outlining the types of project the funder is interested in funding, the criteria a potential applicant must meet in order to qualify for the grant, and the directions for submitting your proposal.

Religious Organizations
According to the IRS, organizations that are not churches, but are typically entities whose principal purpose is the study or advancement of religion.

Research Grants
Grants awarded to institutions to cover costs of investigation and clinical trials. Research grants for individuals are usually referred to as fellowships.

Review Criteria/Evaluation Criteria
Guidelines or the rubric used by judges to judge the strength and value of a proposal and how that proposal will meet the grantor's objectives.

Review of Literature
Review of research on a topic or issue, cited, and stated to support the case for a grant application and the reason that model of service was selected; required by federal departments and some medical funders.

RFP
See Request for Proposals.

Scholarship
Any activity of critical, systematic investigation in one or more fields and the submission of one's findings for criticism by professional peers and the public through published writings, lectures, or other modes of presentation.

Scholarship Fund

A fund established by donors specifically interested in promoting education. Scholarships may support any level of education and can be directed toward students attending a particular school, studying a particular field, or coming from a geographical area.

Scientific Evaluation

An evaluation approach that relies mainly on quantifiable data with rigorous and replicable analytical methods.

Sector

A distinct part or division of the economy. We commonly divide the economy into three sectors: private (business), public (government), and nonprofit (or voluntary) sector.

Seed Funding

Funding that assists with the establishment phase of a project. This is generally given to a small project at an early stage of its development before the total concept has been formulated.

Seed Grant

A grant or contribution used to start a new project or organization. Seed grants may cover salaries and other operating expenses of a new project.

Self Assessment

The process of evaluating one's own organizational or personal effectiveness. The term is sometimes recommended for restriction to processes that are focused on quantitative and/or testing approaches.

Site Visit

A grantmaker's visit to the physical location of an applicant or grantee to meet with the grantee's staff, board members, and/or clients. With current grantees, it may be used as an informal evaluation.

Staff

The personnel who carry out a specific enterprise.

Standard Form 424 (SF424) Series Forms

Standard government-wide grant application forms including: SF424 (Application for Federal Assistance cover page); SF424A (Budget Information Non-construction Programs); SF424B (Assurances Non-construction Programs) ;SF424C (Budget Information Construction Programs); and SF424D (Assurances Construction Programs), plus named attachments including Project Narrative and Budget Narrative.

State

Any of the several states of the United States, the District of Columbia, the Commonwealth of Puerto Rico, any territory or possession of the United States, or any agency or instrumentality of a state exclusive of local governments.

State Single Point of Contact (SSPC)

Person or office in your state that catalogs who has applied for what grants and assists grantwriters by responding to questions during the application process.

Start-up

Organizations or programs in the formative stage.

Start-up Funding

Funding that assists with the establishment phase of a project or organization. This is generally given to a small project at an early stage of its development before the total concept has been formulated or any plan for future expansion is made. The idea is to nurture a project's beginning.

Stewardship

The guiding principle in philanthropic fund-raising is stewardship. It is defined as the philosophy and means by which an institution exercises ethical accountability in the use of contributed resources and the philosophy and means by which a donor exercises responsibility in the voluntary use of resources.

Summative Evaluation

An evaluation of the outcomes of the project. It is designed to present conclusions about the merit or worth of an intervention and recommendations about whether it should be retained, altered, or eliminated.

Support Letters

Letters indicating contributions or support for grant applications.

Supplies

(1) All personal property excluding equipment, intangible property, and debt instruments. (2) Inventions of a contractor conceived or first actually reduced to practice in the performance of work under a funding agreement.

Sustainability

The ability of an organization to develop a strategy of growth and development that enables it to continue to function indefinitely.

Sustainability Plan

Applicant's plan for raising money that will continue a program after the original grant expires.

Tax-exempt

Refers to organizations that do not have to pay taxes such as federal or state corporate tax or state sales tax. Individuals who make donations to such organizations may be able to deduct these contributions from their income tax.

Tax-exempt Organizations

Organizations that do not have to pay state and/or federal income taxes. Organizations other than churches seeking recognition of their status as exempt under Section 501(c)(3) of the Internal Revenue Code must apply to the Internal Revenue Service. Charities may also be exempt from state income, sales, and local property tax.

Technical Assistance Grant

A grant or in-kind contribution for management assistance to help a nonprofit organization operate more effectively. Accounting, consulting, financial planning, fund-raising, and legal support are some common types of technical assistance.

Theory of Change

Highlights the underlying assumptions, beliefs, and theories about creating change.

Third Sector

A modern substitute for voluntary or nonprofit sector. It usually refers to all organizations that are not part of the business or government sectors. It could include unions, churches, clubs, associations, fund-raising charities, self-help groups, grant-making trusts and foundations, community organizations, pressure groups, etc.

Tipping

When a grant is made that is large enough to significantly alter the grantee's funding base and cause it to fail the public support test, it "tips" out of nonprofit status. This would result in the grantee's conversion to a private foundation and would be detrimental to both grantor and grantee. It would also require expenditure responsibility on the part of the grantor.

Trustee

A member of an organization's governing board.

Unqualified Report

The standard unqualified financial report is regarded as a clean bill of health. The auditor made no exceptions and inserts no qualifications in the report. An unqualified opinion can only be expressed when the independent auditor has formed the opinion on the basis of an examination made in accordance with generally accepted accounting principles, applied in a consistent basis, and including all informative disclosures necessary to make the statements not misleading.

Unsolicited Proposal

A proposal sent to a foundation without invitation or prior knowledge on the part of the foundation. Some foundations will not accept unsolicited proposals or applications.

Vision Statement

The ideal future the organization is striving to achieve.

ONLINE RESOURCES

Primary Grant Opportunity Search Sources

- www.grants.gov (federal grants)
- www.fdncenter.org (foundation grants)

Nonprofit Support Organizations (National)

- The Alliance for Nonprofit Management   www.allianceonline.org
- Center for Excellence in Nonprofits   www.cen.org/site/cen
- Council on Foundations   www.cof.org
- Executive Service Corps   www.escus.org
- Independent Sector   www.indepsec.org
- National Council of Nonprofit Organizations   www.ncna.org
- Society for Nonprofit Organizations   www.snpo.org

Support for Grantwriters

- Association of Fund-raising Professionals   www.nsfre.org
- The Foundation Center   www.fdncenter.org
- The Grantsmanship Center   www.tgci.com
- Message Board (Philanthropy News Digest)   http://members4.boardhost.com/PNDtalk

INDEX

INDEX—SAMPLE DOCUMENTS

About the Authors

Since 1987, Nancy Burke Smith has been a freelance writer specializing in grant proposals and other communications for nonprofit organizations, including philanthropic organizations such as the Council of Michigan Foundations, Council on Foundations, W.K. Kellogg Foundation, C.S. Mott Foundation, St. Mary's Doran Foundation, Steelcase Foundation, Frey Foundation, Nokomis Foundation, and Grand Rapids Community Foundation. She served for more than a year as interim program officer at the Frey Foundation where she reviewed grants and made recommendations for funding to the board of trustees.

Besides grant proposals, Smith has researched and written numerous monographs and feature articles and essays on such topics as CEO-led civic leadership groups in the U.S., race relations, economic development, philanthropic training for children/young adults, historically Black colleges and universities, the digital divide, and urban sprawl. In 1999, she researched and wrote a full-length biography of a former physician and community leader in Grand Rapids, and in 2002 she cowrote *The Everything Grantwriting Book*.

As principal of Works Associates, E. Gabriel Works provides consulting services that focus on enhancing the practice of philanthropy. Since 2001, Works has leveraged her distinctive knowledge of private, community, and corporate philanthropy into a special niche focused on developing and delivering national training programs for foundation professionals and supporting professional development initiatives. To date, she has been responsible for the development and ongoing performance of six intensive training courses offered nationally.

Works is senior consultant to The Grantmaking School at the Dorothy Johnson Center for Philanthropy and Nonprofit Leadership. She has served in the program departments of both the Charles Stewart Mott and Frey Foundations, and in 1991 authored *Effective Corporate Philanthropy: Building a Giving Program with Impact for* Issue Network Group. She has extensive experience in the nonprofit sector, including service as community relations/fund development director for a community health center and as leader of a major community revitalization project. Additionally, she has experience in the private sector having headed an accounting practice on Beaver Island, Michigan, and later providing business writing and computer training services.

Works holds a BA in liberal arts from Denison University, a certificate in language and art history studies from the Université de Besançon, France, and was accredited as an Enrolled Agent with the U.S. Treasury.